FLAVIUS
JOSEPHUS

FLAVIUS JOSEPHUS

Eyewitness to Rome's
First-Century Conquest of Judea

MIREILLE HADAS-LEBEL
translated by Richard Miller

Macmillan Publishing Company
New York

Maxwell Macmillan Canada
Toronto

Maxwell Macmillan International
New York   Oxford   Singapore   Sydney

Macmillan Publishing Company
866 Third Avenue
New York, NY 10022

Maxwell Macmillan Canada, Inc.
1200 Eglinton Avenue East
Suite 200
Don Mills, Ontario M3C 3N1

Macmillan Publishing Company is part of the Maxwell Communiction Group of Companies.

Library of Congress Cataloging-in-Publication Data

Hadas-Lebel, Mireille.
  [Flavius Josèphe. English]
  Flavius Josephus: eyewitness to Rome's first-century conquest of Judea/by Mireille Hadas-Lebel: translated by Richard Miller.
      p.   cm.
  Includes index.
  ISBN 0-02-547161-9
  1. Josephus, Flavius. 2. Jewish historians—Biography. 3. Jews—History—Rebellion, 66–73.
I. Title.
DS115.9.J6H3413   1993   92–11296   CIP
933'.05'092—dc20
[B]

Macmillan books are available at special discounts for bulk purchases for sales promotions, premiums, fund-raising, or eductional use. For details, contact:
              Special Sales Director
          Macmillan Publishing Company
              866 Third Avenue
              New York, NY 10022

10 9 8 7 6 5 4 3 2 1
Printed in the United States of America

To my husband Raphaël
To my children Anne, Jean, Hélène,
Emmanuelle, and Laure

CONTENTS

I would like to thank Richard Miller, who has translated my book so faithfully and sensitively, and Melissa Thau, the editor who has supervised its journey in English.

—*Mireille Hadas-Lebel*

Résumé

TITUS FLAVIUS JOSEPHUS

NAME: Joseph

FATHER'S NAME: Matthias (Mattitiahu in Hebrew)

TRIBE: Levi (first priestly class)

CITIZENSHIP: Roman

DATE AND PLACE
OF BIRTH: Jerusalem, Year 3797 of the World's Creation, corresponding to Year One of the reign of Caligula and 37 C.E.

POSITIONS: Successively governor general of Galilee, Roman prisoner (67 to 69), interpreter in the Roman army, historian (imperial pensioner)

FAMILY STATUS: Married four times: 57?, 67, 69, 76; three children (Hyrcanus b. 73, Justus b. 77, Simonides-Agrippa b. 79)

EDUCATION:
Jewish studies: 51-53: in Sadducean, Pharisee, and Essene circles
53-56: with the hermit Bannus

Greek studies: Elementary level

LANGUAGES: Fluent in Hebrew and Aramaic, spoke but could barely write Greek and Latin

MILITARY SERVICE: General in Galilee in the Judean army from year 12 to year 13 of Nero's reign (66-67 C.E.)

DOMICILE: House of Vespasian, Rome

PUBLICATIONS: *The Jewish War* (*JW*) published in 75?, *Jewish Antiquities* (*JA*) published in 93?, *Against Apion* (*AA*) publication date unknown, *The Life* (*L*) published in 95?

DRAMATIS PERSONAE

Agrippa I
Great grandson of King Herod and of Mariamne, daughter of the Hasmonean Hyrcanus II, friend of the Roman emperor Caligula. Reigned over Judea from 41 to 44 C.E.

Agrippa II
Son of Agrippa I, protégé of Claudius, did not reign over Judea itself, but controlled some of the northeastern territories (including Tiberius and the Golan Heights) which once belonged to Herod's realm.

Anan (Hanan)
Very common name at the time. A Hanan son of Hanan was high priest at the outbreak of the Judean revolt. He was later assassinated by the Idumaeans in Jerusalem, who viewed him as too moderate and too ready to come to terms with the Romans.

Berenice
Daughter of King Agrippa I and sister of King Agrippa II. She was married three times, first to Marcus Julius Alexander (nephew of Philo of Alexandria and brother of Tiberius Julius Alexander), next to her uncle, King Herod of Chalcis, and, lastly, to Polemon, king of Cilicia. She is best known, however, for her liaison with Titus, the conqueror of Jerusalem.

Eleazar son of Ananias (Hananiah)
One of the young priests who launched the revolt against Rome by refusing to perform sacrifices to the emperor in 66 C.E.

Eleazar son of Simon
Head of one of the factions that waged civil war in Jerusalem just before the siege led by Titus.

Eleazar son of Yair
Descendant of Judah of Galilee, leader of the defenders of Masada.

Epaphroditus
Nero's freeman, who helped the emporer commit suicide. He might be the same who protected Josephus in Rome and encouraged him to write his *Jewish Antiquities*.

Flavius Silva
Roman general who led the seige at Masada.

Florus
The last of the Roman procurators prior to the Jewish revolt in 66. His greed, cruelty, and outrageous injustices prompted the Jewish people to rebel against Roman rule.

Gorion son of Joseph
One of the moderate leaders of the revolt; assassinated by the Zealots in Jerusalem.

Helena
Queen of Adiabene, converted to Judaism along with her sons, Izates and Monobazius. They abetted the Jewish revolt and were buried in Jerusalem in what is today known as the Tomb of the Kings.

Herod, king of Judea
Son of Antipater the Idumaean, who gained the favor of the Romans. He was appointed king of Judea by the Roman Senate at the urging of Mark Antony, but was detested by his Jewish subjects. He reigned from 37 to 4 B.C.E.

John of Gischala
Son of Levi. One of the leaders of the Judean revolt, first in Galilee, then in Jerusalem; accused Josephus of treason in Galilee. He was taken prisoner at the end of the siege of Jerusalem, but was spared by the Romans.

Jesus (Joshua) son of Saphias
Leader of the city of Tiberias (Archontes) and subsequently of its anti-Roman party.

Jesus (Joshua) son of Gamala
A much-respected priest to whom the Talmud attributes the organization of the Judean school system; he perished alongside other moderate leaders of the revolt prior to the siege of Jerusalem.

Johanan ben Zakkai
A famous Pharisee rabbi who purportedly predicted Vespasian's ascension (as did Josephus). According to rabbinic sources, Vespasian granted Johanan the right to found a school in Yavneh.

Judah the Galilean
In the year 6 he promulgated an ideology Josephus called the "fourth philosophy" and which he believed to have contributed to the unrest that eventually led to the revolt.

Justus son of Pistos
A native of Tiberias and leader of one of the three parties in that city; he often changed camps and later wrote a history (now lost) of the war, an act that infuriated Josephus and that inspired him to answer with his *Life.*

Menahem
One of the Sicarii leaders, a descendant of Judah the Galilean. An overly ambitious man, he was killed in Jerusalem at the beginning of the revolt.

Philo of Alexandria (20 B.C.E.?–45 C.E.?)
Famous Jewish philosopher and member of one of the noblest families in Alexandria; he defended the cause of Jewish civil rights before the emperor Caligula in the year 40.

Poppaea
Wife of Nero, a Jewish partisan and possibly a convert.

Simon bar Gioras ("Son of the Proselyte")
Extremist leader of the revolt and of one of the factions that waged civil war in Jerusalem, he was captured by the Romans after the siege and executed in Rome during the triumphal ceremony there.

Simon son of Gamaliel

A famous Pharisee rabbi, the son of Gamaliel, the teacher of the apostle Paul; he was one of the moderate leaders of the revolt.

Tiberius Julius Alexander

Nephew of Philo of Alexandria; he abandoned Jewish traditions and was appointed prefect of Egypt. He then went on to slaughter thousands of his compatriots while suppressing their rioting in 66 C.E.; he was the commanding Roman general during Titus' siege of Jerusalem.

Titus

Son of Vespasian; conqueror of Jerusalem in 70 C.E. and emperor from 79 to 81 C.E.

Vespasian

General dispatched by Nero to subdue the Jews; in 67 Josephus predicted his accession as emperor of Rome, and Vespasian was indeed acclaimed emperor by his troops in 69. He reigned until 79 and was succeeded by his son Titus.

FLAVIUS
JOSEPHUS

PROLOGUE

Flavius Josephus: the hybrid name by which he has become known to us is a reflection of his character in all its contradictions, of the fate of the man, of the posthumous reputation of the historian.

Joseph is the biblical name given him at birth by his father, Matthias. Only later, when the emperor Vespasian made him a Roman citizen, did his "barbaric" name became a cognomen linked with the name of the benefactor who had freed him after having taken him prisoner, a Flavian. Born in Jerusalem in 37 C.E. and raised in the best Judean tradition, Joseph son of Matthias was to end his days at Rome where, from the year 70 of our era to the end of the first century, he devoted himself to history and apologetics—a history of the national disaster that led to the disappearance of the Second Temple and depopulated Judea and, later, a monumental history of a nation conquered but proud in its antiquity and nobility, the apologia of a nation disparaged even by the Alexandrian rabble in Rome, but an apologia for himself as well, a man suspect both in the eyes of his coreligionists and in those of the Roman courtiers.

This vast *oeuvre,* which has come down to us in Greek and which includes *The Jewish War* (seven books) (*JW*); *Jewish Antiquities* (twenty books) (*JA*); *Against Apion* (two books) (*AA*); and an autobiography, *The Life (L),* had continued to be read in the Christian West from Renaissance times down through the nineteenth century.

Only in our own century, so neglectful of the humanities, has it been neglected. Yet there was a time when in France, Holland, and England every Christian family had its copy of *Flavius Josephus* just as it had its copy of the Bible, a copy of the *War* or *Antiquities* on whose flyleaf were inscribed the names of newborn members of the family as readily as in the Gospels. For the Christian world, he was not so much the "Greek Livy" Saint Jerome called him as he was the only Jewish historian to have mentioned (if not professed) Christ, albeit in only one very brief and much-disputed passage (see the Epilogue for specific details). He was also a wonderful narrator of Jewish religious history and a witness to what some Christians regarded as its culminating episode—the condemnation of an entire people to eternal tears and wanderings. Indeed, Flavius Josephus' work has owed its very survival to this last misapprehension.

In the eighteenth century a French Jesuit known as Père Hardouin, generally regarded as one of the odder personalities of his day, found himself unable to contain his irritation with an author whom he regarded as being far too popular in Protestant lands and, what was even worse, a writer who had been translated into French by a loathsome Jansenist,[1] Robert Arnauld d'Andilly (brother of the great Arnauld), and imposed the spelling "Josèphe" to distinguish the historian of antiquity from the various "valid" Christian saints who bore the same name. Indeed, this may well be the only legacy left us by this curious Jesuit figure, who also maintained that the Aeneid was actually a Christian allegory concocted by a thirteenth-century Benedictine and firmly believed that Jesus and the apostles had preached in Latin. In English, although not for the same reasons, the name Josephus has generally been reserved for the Jewish historian.

For Judaism, Joseph son of Matthias, although he never renounced his birth or his faith, is regarded as a lost sheep—lost for having been suspected of treason, lost for having gone to Rome to dwell in the palace of his conqueror, lost for having published (even if not to have written) his work in Greek, lost for having been taken up by the Christians from the very earliest days of the Church along with that other Jew, the philosopher Philo of Alexandria.

Appropriated by the theologians, Josephus was also to a large extent lost to the history of Rome, notwithstanding his important contribution to that field. When dealing with the period in which he had lived, Roman historians relied heavily on the Latin writers, particularly Tacitus and Suetonius, and relegated Josephus to the role of a mere chronicler of specifically Judean matters. Yet so closely had such matters been linked to events in Rome that two conquering generals in Judea, Vespasian and Titus, had gone on to head the Empire. On the circumstances surrounding their accession to the throne, their personalities, their entourages, their behavior in battle, the testimony of Josephus (who, unlike other writers, had been in daily contact with them) is irreplaceable. And while the Latin historians so exhaustively studied in the West furnished countless dramatic subjects for the theater to later generations of writers, playwrights have almost totally ignored Josephus' work, nearly every page of which is fraught with drama.

Indeed, the fate of the "Jew of Rome" on whose life Lion Feuchtwanger was to base a trilogy of novels in the years between the two World Wars has been a strange one from every point of view.

Why write a novel about the historian when a biography is a novel in itself? Has Josephus himself not provided us with the kind of personal data almost never found in the works of other writers of antiquity, writing as he did a partial autobiography and including himself as a character in his narrative of the *War*? Too, the interest of his own personality, complex as it is, is nothing compared to that of the times in which he lived. As a witness to and actor in Jerusalem's struggle against Rome, he was eyewitness to the end of an era and reported on it in words that are pregnant with a despair his detractors have always seen fit to denigrate. Without his testimony we would know nothing of the history of Judea between 100 B.C.E. and year 74 of our era apart from a few fragmentary words from the pens of Greek or Latin authors or the semilegendary tales of the Talmud, from which we would vainly have to attempt to reconstruct the final days of Jewish independence—the reign of Herod, the era of the procurators and especially the full-scale war between Jews and Romans that raged from 66 to 73 and culminated in the burning of the Temple in 70 and the ensuing fall of the Jewish fortresses, the last being Masada.

While narrating a terrible tragedy, Josephus also evokes for us Jewish society as it existed prior to that tragedy, and although he was not especially impressed by or even aware of the birth of Christianity, he does give us great insight into the milieu in which it occurred. Every modern writer who has dealt with the history of Palestine in Jesus' day or with the history of the Jews under the Roman Empire has borrowed from him shamelessly. Some have even denigrated their precious source the better to highlight their own purportedly original contributions.

The target of so much slander—or at the very least accused of rabid partiality—and what historian can escape the charge when reporting events he has personally witnessed?—Josephus deserves the place he claimed, with justified pride, for himself: "The historian deserving of praise," he wrote in the preface to his account of the war, "is the one who records events whose history has not hitherto been written and who creates a chronicle of his time for future generations."

So we turn to this historian so aware of his own worth and so miraculously spared from oblivion, a man who sought to understand a century that continues to determine our world today: one of glory for Rome and of crises, hopes, and tragedies for Judea, and one in which the Christian world was born. But this witness to his century also had an exceptional life of his own, and it too deserves our attention.

I

A YOUNG
JUDEAN
ARISTOCRAT

I, Joseph son of Matthias, priest of Jerusalem . . .
THE JEWISH WAR I, 3

A GREAT FAMILY OF JERUSALEM

The first lines of Josephus' autobiography (commonly known as *The Life* in English) reflect a pride of caste undiminished by exile: "My family is no ignoble one, tracing its pedigree far back to priestly ancestors. With us a connection to the priesthood is the hallmark of an illustrious line" (*L* 1).

Had Josephus been writing solely for the benefit of his coreligionists, he would needed only to have said that he was a *cohen*. Nowadays the family name "Cohen" is often of fairly recent adoption and no longer a sure guarantee of priestly lineage; twenty centuries ago, however, we can safely assume that the tradition of correct lineage was still maintained with a certain rigor.

The priests (or *Cohanim*) themselves belonged to the tribe of Levi. The tribe had been granted no territory in biblical times, for its mission was to be a higher one: the preservation of the Covenant. Among the tribe's notable members were Aaron and Moses, the sons of Amram, but only the progeny of Aaron, the eldest son, was to provide the high priests "anointed of the Lord," or allowed to boast the name and title of *cohen*.

The priestly caste itself had its own strict hierarchy. According to the biblical Book of Chronicles—which cannot be earlier than the fourth century B.C.E.—King David (early tenth century B.C.E.) in his old age had numbered and divided the whole of the tribe of Levi into classes. Within the tribe, Aaron's descendants were divided by lot into twenty-four classes, foremost of which was that of Yehoyarib. The distinction still held good in Josephus' day, and our author prided himself on belonging to the most illustrious family of the first class.

Alliances were strictly controlled within the priestly caste. Even today, according to rabbinical law a *cohen* cannot marry a divorcée. Josephus himself tells us that the Jewish aristocracy, which took on an essentially sacerdotal character following the disappearance of the royal House of David (following the Babylonian conquest in 586 B.C.E.), had its own matrimonial code like any other aristocracy: "A member of the priestly order must, to beget a family, marry a woman of his own race, without regard to her wealth or other distinctions; but he must investigate her pedigree, obtaining the genealogy from the archives and producing a number of witnesses. And this practice of ours is not confined to the home country of Judea, but wherever there is a Jewish colony, there too a strict account is kept by the priests of their marriages; I allude to the Jews in Egypt and Babylon and other parts of the world in which any of the priestly order are living in dispersion. A statement is drawn up by them and sent to Jerusalem showing the names of the bride and her father and more remote ancestors, together with the names of the witnesses" (*AA* 31–33).

Josephus adds that, owing to the strict care with which such archives were kept, the genealogy of the high priests could be traced back for two thousand years. In the case of his own lineage, he goes back only as far as a distant grandfather, Simon, known as "the Stutterer," who was still alive in the reign of John Hyrcanus (135 to 104 B.C.E.).

At that time Judea had just broken free from the yoke of the Seleucids, the Greek dynasty that had taken over Syria following the Alexandrian conquest. In the uprising against the Seleucids the sons of a priest named Matthias, from the city of Modin, had particularly distinguished themselves. (Matthias was a descendant of Hasmon, whence the name "Hasmonean" by which the family is known.) Three of his five sons (known as Maccabees) were later to attain supreme power: Judah, the leader of the nation, was recognized by Rome, which signed a treaty of friendship and alliance with him in 161 B.C.E.; Jonathan, who was given the title of high priest following a period of religious upheavals; Simon, who inherited the title upon the death of his elder brother along with additional privileges that reflected Syria's growing political autonomy. Hyrcanus succeeded his father, Simon. He accumulated temporal and spiritual powers, but bore only the title of high priest. The Jews were able to shake off the yoke of Syria without Roman help.

The year 104 B.C.E. marked the beginning of the brief reign of Aristobulus (104 to 103 B.C.E), son of the above, who was dubbed "Philhellenic," who shocked his subjects by taking the title of king. Everyone was well aware that the Bible held the two functions to be strictly separate: royalty was reserved to the tribe of Judah, while only Aaron's descendants could exercise the priesthood. However, the title of king remained an appanage of the Hasmonean dynasty and was borne, in turn, by Alexander Jannaeus (103 to 76 B.C.E.), his wife, Salome Alexandra (76 to 67 B.C.E.) and their younger son, Aristobulus II (67 to 63 B.C.E.), who had proved himself more avid for power than his elder brother, the ne'er-do-well Hyrcanus II.

Rome, which had only recently gained a foothold in Syria, took advantage of a war of succession between the two brothers fomented by an Idumaean intriguer named Antipater. Thus, in 63 B.C.E., Pompey, with the help of Hyrcanus' troops, laid siege to Jerusalem, which was defended by Aristobulus. The capture of the Holy City by the Romans (during the Yom Kippur fast) marked the *de facto* end of Judean independence. One of Aristobulus II's sons, Antigonus, managed to remain in power in the land for nearly four more years (40 to 37 B.C.E.), thanks to Parthian assistance, but Rome had already raised up a formidable rival to him in the person of Herod son of Antipater. A friend and creature of the Romans and the Eastern Greeks, whom he flattered by founding such Hellenistic cities as Caesarea, Herod soon became known to the Romans as "The Great." In the eyes of the people over whom he ruled, however, he was always known as "The Impious," despite his costly restoration of the Temple in Jerusalem.

THE HERODIAN DYNASTY

Josephus, who claimed to be "of royal race" through his mother,[1] had no connection with the usurper Herod, whose long reign (37 to 4 B.C.E.) had left such a somber memory; rather, he describes himself as a descendant of the legitimate Hasmonean dynasty, for according to him his great-great-grandfather on his father's side, a son of Simon the Stutterer named Matthias, had married the daughter of the high priest Jonathan. One of their sons, also named Matthias and nicknamed "The Hunchback," who was born "in the first year of the reign of Hyrcanus" (135 B.C.E.), had in turn had a son named Joseph, born "in the ninth year of the reign of Alexandra" (70 B.C.E.). Although the difference in age appears somewhat excessive, this is the Joseph our author introduces as his paternal grandfather, father of his father, Matthias, who in turn was born in the tenth (and last) year of the reign of Archelaus, son of Herod—that is, in year 6, which was also the year in which Judea was brought under the direct control of Rome, henceforth to be governed by a prefect of equestrian rank resident in Caesarea.

Following Jewish tradition, at his birth (in the year 37), Josephus was given the name of his paternal grandfather, as had been the case with his father, Matthias as well. Thus, his Jewish name is correctly Joseph son of Matthias, to which he was entitled to add the title *ha-cohen*, "the priest," to indicate his sacerdotal origins.

Josephus describes his father as a man noble both in character and by birth: "Distinguished as he was by his noble birth, my father Matthias was even more esteemed for his upright character, being among the most notable men in Jerusalem, our greatest city" (*L* 7). Eager to prove that this admired father had never disavowed him, he availed himself of his support at a delicate moment in his own life. In 67, Josephus, just thirty years of age and already entrusted with defending Galilee against the Romans, began to arouse the suspicions of the Jewish insurgents, hints of which soon reached the ears of important persons in Jerusalem. At the time, Matthias was residing in that city. Warned through his connections of what was being bruited about against his son, he managed to

send him a timely warning. In his lengthy letter he also asked to see
him once again before dying (*L* 204). Josephus, however, was not
eager to return to his birthplace, where there were many indications that he was not viewed with favor. His father himself was
arrested soon afterward by the extremist party in Jerusalem and
probably died in prison in 69 or 70 (*JW* V, 533). We will never
know whether Josephus' father believed his son to be a traitor
or hero.

It is likely that Josephus' last news of his mother arrived in
70, in tragic circumstances. At the time, he was in the service of
the Roman Titus, who was laying siege to a divided Jerusalem that
was starving and nearly exhausted. On two occasions Josephus
harangued the city's defenders, urging them to surrender. In reply a
stone was hurled at him; he was struck on the head and for a while
he was thought to have been killed. Later, he was to learn of his
mother's reaction to the false report of his demise. She too was in
prison at the time, although we do not know whether or not this
was because of an accusation of treason against her son. Addressing
her guards, she made a patriotic speech against Josephus. He, however, confident of his mother's affection, tells us that in private, in
the company of her own servants, she sorely lamented that the fruit
of her womb should perish before her (*JW* V, 545). It is likely that
Josephus learned of this from his brother Matthias and the handful
of friends fortunate enough to have escaped the massacre that followed the fall of the Holy City.

THE EDUCATION OF A
YOUNG PRIEST

Josephus tells us that in his youth he had been brought up along
with his brother, which implies that they were close to each other
in age. However, without undue modesty, he dwells on his own
successes: "I made great progress in my education, gaining a reputation for an excellent memory and understanding" (*L* 8).

We can be sure of the kind of education he received, for it
would have been a purely religious one based on the Torah.

Indeed, the Sacred Books were believed to contain all the knowledge a man needed to live in the world. In it, he would find a code for his cultural, moral, social, and political behavior, as well as an account of the world and the earlier generations of mankind, all of which he was taught to impute to one single and omnipresent God.

Although the apostle Paul distinguished between faith and the law the better to contrast them, Jews of his day, like Josephus, found both in the Torah: for them, the law was truly "the form of knowledge and of the truth" (Romans 2:20), and faith was the true piety that inspired the practice of the moral virtues taught by the law. For that reason the Jews regarded the profane sciences promulgated by the Greeks as mere frivolous pastimes compared to sacred knowledge. A second-century rabbi renowned for his mathematical and astronomical knowledge was to write that such sciences were mere "appetizers" or "condiments" to whet the appetite for the sacred sciences on which men should base their lives (*Sayings of the Fathers* III, 23).[2]

This virtual lack of interest in the exact and natural sciences was of course duly noted by certain Egyptian Greeks or hellenized Egyptians of the early first century, who began to evidence virulent antijudaism: they accused the Jews of being "the most witless of all barbarians" (by which they meant "non-Greeks") and of being the only people to "have contributed no useful invention to civilization" (*AA* II, 148). To which apologists of Judaism like Philo of Alexandria (and, later, Josephus himself) could reply that their religion was a philosophy in and of itself, one quite different from Greek philosophy, which was elitist by nature, for Judaism addressed itself to everyone, even the very young. "The result then, of our thorough grounding in the laws from the first dawn of intelligence is that we have them, as it were, engraven on our souls" (*AA,* II, 178).

We have little knowledge of the contemporary educational system in Judea. We do know that no separation was made between family, synagogue, and school. Education in the home afforded training in religious practice from early childhood on, even before such practice could be justified by study. "Again, the Law does not allow the birth of our children to be made occasions for festivity and an excuse for drinking to excess. It enjoins sobriety in their upbringing from the very first. It orders that they shall be taught to read, and shall learn both the laws and the deeds of their forefathers, in order that they may imitate the latter, and, being grounded in the former, may neither transgress nor have any excuse for being ignorant of them" (*AA* II, 204).

The father's role in his son's education was primordial: "What is a father's duty to his son?"[3] asked some rabbinical texts, which went on to answer: "To teach him the Torah." As soon as a child had been weaned he was expected to participate in feast days and in the various other religious rites that punctuate Jewish life. His studies began as soon as he learned to speak. First, his father was to teach him the *Sh'ma,* the statement of divine oneness set out in the Book of Deuteronomy, the same formula given by Christ as the first of the commandments:[4] "Hear, O Israel, the Lord is God, the Lord is one. Thou shalt love the Lord thy God with all thy heart, with all thy soul and with all thy strength." Next came the teaching of the Torah, combined with instruction in the sacred language, i.e., Hebrew.[5]

The father's role was even more crucial in that prior to the period in which we are interested the notion of primary school does not seem to have existed. According to the Talmud, the founder of the first school system for children was the same man to whom Josephus refers as his "intimate friend," Jesus (Joshua) son of Gamala, and the man who reported to Matthias the plot against his son when the latter was serving as a general in Galilee! The Talmud justifies Josephus' great esteem for him:

"Forsooth, this man's name, Joshua ben Gamala, is a blessed one! For without him the Torah would have been forgotten in Israel. Indeed, in earlier times when a child's father was living it was the father who taught him, and if he had no father he received no teaching. Then it was decreed that teachers be recruited in Jerusalem. Even then, however, when a child had a father, it was the father who brought him to Jerusalem to be taught, and if he had no father he received no teaching. Then it was decreed that teachers be recruited in each district and that boys were to attend school at the age of sixteen or seventeen. This was done, but if the teacher happened to punish them they would rebel and leave school. Finally, Joshua ben Gamala decreed that schoolteachers be appointed in each district and town and that children were to attend school from the age of six or seven."[6]

Joseph could not have followed this course of primary education initiated by his friend Joshua, for the latter was not to exercise the functions of high priest until shortly before the war; he was eventually assassinated by the Idumaeans, the allies of the Zealots (anti-Roman nationalists), just before the siege of Jerusalem (*JW* IV, 316). The child Josephus was probably taught by his father, with the help of a tutor.

Each stage of Jewish schooling relied heavily on memory. This faculty, which is the principal one upon which Josephus prided himself, was always highly developed in Eastern cultures, and even today it plays a highly important role in traditional Jewish teaching. Memory also played an important part in the transmission of a correct text of the Bible, since the documents of the time were written without vowels—which are, in fact, a fairly recent addition: the system prevalent today came into existence sometime after the eighth century C.E. A text consisting solely of consonants can often be open to plural readings unless backed by a well-established oral tradition. The child's first teacher would instruct him in the traditional readings by having him repeat the text aloud, a further aid to memorization. Thus, a student, particularly a gifted one, would fairly quickly learn by heart the five books of the Pentateuch (the Torah), which were the foundation of all his studies: "But should anyone of our nation be questioned about the laws, he would repeat them all more readily than his own name" (*AA* II, 178), Joseph proudly writes.

Sabbath and feast-day readings in the synagogue also played a part in etching the divine Word on the mind. As its Greek name (*synagogé*) implies (it corresponds to the Hebrew *bet-knesset*), the synagogue was primarily a meeting place. There, where men were often grouped by profession or corporation, public readings of the sacred text took place on the weekly day of rest. "Every week men would desert their other occupations and assemble to listen to the Law and to obtain a thorough and accurate knowledge of it" (*AA*

II, 175). No one was to be allowed to be ignorant of the religious
patrimony that was to govern his life. Philo of Alexandria gives the
following background for these sabbath readings: "The Lawgiver
[Moses] decreed that the Jews should be taught the ancestral laws;
he ordered them to come together on the seventh day and listen to
the reading of the laws so that no one would be ignorant of them"
(*Hypothetica* VII, 10 and 12).

Indeed, from this period on, Sabbath readings have combined a passage of the Pentateuch or Torah with a passage from the
Prophets: "And he came to Nazareth, where he had been brought
up and, as his custom was, he went into the synagogue on the sabbath day, and stood up for to read. And there was delivered unto
him the book of the Prophet Isaiah" (Luke 4:16-17).

In those days biblical Hebrew was not understood by everyone. Spoken Hebrew was strongly influenced by Aramaic, and Aramaic was gaining ground, even in Judea. Greek was the dominant
language in other Eastern Mediterranean communities—Alexandria, Antioch, and Ephesus, as well as in Corinth and the other
towns in which Paul preached. To ensure that all the faithful,
including women and children, would be able to understand what
was being read, each synagogue employed a *meturgeman* who could
recite the biblical text in a language accessible to the local population, making a kind of paraphrase sprinkled with exegesis. These
explanatory recitations would also be followed by a sermon that
relied heavily on a solid familiarity with the sacred texts, as can be
seen from those of the apostle Paul (Acts 13:15, *et seq.*).

According to Philo, the sermon based on scripture was
intended principally for moral edification: "On the seventh day,
thousands of schools were at work in each town for the teaching
of intelligence, moderation, courage, justice, and the other virtues.
Those attending them sat in orderly rows, calmly lending their
total attention to catch every delectable word, whilst one of the
teachers stood before them dispensing the noblest and most worthy lessons to assist them in confronting all the situations of life"
(*Special Laws* II, 62).

The synagogue to which the boy accompanied his father
supplemented the teaching he received during the week. From ear-

liest childhood on, everything was referred to the Torah. Thus was the verse of the *Sh'ma* put into practice: "Thou shalt talk of them when thou sittest in thy house . . ." It was a form of education that created an unbreakable bond with ancestral tradition: "There should be nothing astonishing in our facing death on behalf of our laws with a courage which no other nation can equal" (*AA* II, 234).

There is nothing to indicate that children who, like Josephus, were members of the priestly caste received any special instruction. Rather, it appears that a type of teaching originally intended for a social elite had been extended to include the people as a whole. This would explain why Leviticus was the first biblical book to which children were exposed.[7] The priests gave priority to the sacerdotal code from which they derived their powers. Study of the written law contained in the Torah was followed by study of the remainder of the Bible and the unwritten or oral law, which was in those days limited to the Mishnah. A second-century rabbi was to describe the earliest stages of life as follows: "At five years of age, the Bible, at ten the Mishnah, at thirteen the Commandments" (*Sayings of the Fathers* V, 24). The Mishnah is the underpinnings of the Talmud. Its present-day version was compiled around the year 200 by Rabbi Judah, known as the "Prince" and spiritual leader of the nation, on the basis of earlier traditions passed down orally from generation to generation. Although not yet codified in Josephus' time, he probably benefited from the teachings of this oral tradition, which entailed the use of reason as well as memory.

A CHILD PRODIGY

The age of thirteen is an important landmark in the life of a Jewish boy: childhood is behind him and he is entering puberty; he is therefore expected to respect the divine commandments and is admitted to adult society. If knowledgeable enough, he is treated as an equal. Joseph was treated like a master. "While still a mere boy, about fourteen years old, I won universal applause for my love of letters; insomuch that the chief priests and the leading men of the city used constantly to come to me for precise information on some particular in our ordinances" (*L* 9).

We cannot help being struck by the Gospel parallel: "And it came to pass, that after three days they found him in the Temple, sitting in the midst of the doctors, both hearing them, and asking them questions. And all that heard him were astonished at his understanding and answers" (Luke 2:46-47). However, Jesus was only twelve and was questioning the doctors; Joseph, at fourteen, had already become an adult and was being questioned *as* a doctor. Excessive vanity? Yet the two accounts have one point in common: in that ancient Eastern culture in which the respect owed to age was considered a religious duty, there was also room for admiring even the very young whose intelligence made them stand out. Far from being counseled to keep silent in the presence of their elders, they were encouraged to give older heads the benefit of their young minds and the freshness of their adolescent thinking.

Josephus' vanity appears much less flagrant if we consider the priesthood of his day. For the high priesthood was no longer synonymous with knowledge. During the Hasmonean era (104–76 B.C.E.) the two functions, royal and priestly, had for a time been linked. When he had assumed power, Herod had not claimed the title of high priest, for which his birth, indeed, disqualified him, but had entrusted the position to Aristobulus, the brother of his wife, Mariamne, the daughter of Hyrcanus II. Popular favor quickly shifted to the young, handsome Aristobulus, who was descended from the legitimate kings, and Herod soon fell prey to jealousy. One day the youth, who was barely eighteen, was found drowned in the palace pool in Jericho, and the people were quick to accuse the King of a murder that was to be but the first in a long series. Herod, having rid himself of a dangerous rival, now attempted to downgrade the high priesthood by conferring the honor on "common" priests with no hereditary legitimacy, selecting them more for their docility than for their learning or wisdom and removing them whenever it suited him. The same procedure was followed in the reign of his son Archelaus and later by the Roman authorities. During the short interlude of illusory independence (41 to 44 C.E.), when Agrippa I, a descendant of both Herod and the Hasmoneans (he was Mariamne's grandson), reigned over Judea, the king did not reclaim the priesthood for himself.

Upon Herod's death, his brother, Herod of Chalcis, was empowered by the emperor Claudius to select the high priests (*JA* XX, 15). On the eve of the war against the Romans (66 C.E.), this power was in the hands of Agrippa II, son of Agrippa I, who no longer reigned over all Judea, as had his father, but rather over a disparate group of territories located in the northern part of the country. Around the year 60 the high priesthood had become totally decadent: the four families from which the high priests had been recruited since 37 B.C.E were ranged against each other, familial factions engaged in stone-throwing battles, the clique in power controlled the tithe wrung from the other priests, and Roman support had to be paid for in silver. The high priesthood changed hands with increasing frequency: there were as many as twenty-eight high priests in 107 years, whereas there had been only ninety-three since the time of Aaron (thirteenth century B.C.E.) and under the Hasmoneans only eight in the course of 115 years.

Josephus' gloomy picture of the last years of the high priesthood is borne out by later rabbinical sources, which do not conceal their contempt for all these obviously illegitimate high priests. The Talmud preserves the memory of posts that were bought and paid for changing hands yearly (Babylonian Talmud, *Yoma* 18a, *Yebamot* 61a) and anathematizes the unworthy: "For they are high priests, their sons are treasurers, their sons-in-law administrators and their servants beat the people with rods" (*Pesahim* 57a). Only Joshua ben Gamala escapes condemnation. Josephus, who shared this opinion, also made an exception for the high priest Ananias, a victim of the Zealots during the siege.

Thus, increasingly corrupt, the priestly milieu also began to decline into ignorance. This probably explains why the Mishnah (*Horayot* III, 8) tells us that an educated bastard should be given precedence over an ignorant high priest. Consideration is even given to the case of a high priest's being unable to read or explicate scripture: should such an unfortunate event come to pass, another is to be authorized to do so in his stead (Mishnah, *Yoma* I, 6).

TROUBLED TIMES

Since the early part of the first century, the country had been expe-
riencing endemic unrest, the only period of calm having occurred
during the short reign of King Agrippa I. In 46—Josephus was not
yet ten years of age—Rome had sent as procurator of Judea an
apostate Alexandrian Jew, Tiberius Alexander, who had abjured the
faith of his fathers for the sake of his career. He was the son of an
eminent Jew, Alexander Lysimachus, a man wealthy enough to have
lent money to the mother of the emperor Claudius as well as to the
young and prodigal Agrippa I and noble enough to have married
one of his sons, Marcus, to the famous Berenice, daughter of the
king of Judea (she would marry two more times before her fateful
meeting with Titus). The family's piety had always been unquestioned: Alexander Lysimachus had paid for the decoration of the
Jerusalem Temple doors, and his brother was that celebrated Philo
of Alexandria who devoted his life to vindicating Judaism and who
in his old age had been a member of a delegation sent to Rome to
defend the rights of the Alexandrian Jews before the emperor
Caligula. Tiberius Alexander, however, was to prove himself a perfect agent of Roman power and deal with his former coreligionists
with an apostate's zeal. No sooner had he been appointed procurator of Judea than he had ordered the crucifixions of Jacob and
Simon, the sons of a certain Judah the Galilean, who, in reaction
against the population census ordered by Rome, had begun as early
as the year 6 to propagate subversive slogans proclaiming that the
only master was the Lord.

Josephus was an eyewitness to a terrible riot that occurred
during the procuratorship of Cumanus, Tiberius Alexander's successor, which resulted in a bloodbath in Jerusalem. The disturbance
broke out during Passover, a feast that always attracted thousands of
pilgrims to the Holy City. One of the Roman soldiers assigned to
maintain order in the Temple precincts made a provocative gesture.
The excited mob began to shout insults at the procurator. The
troops intervened. The terrified populace fled into the narrow
alleyways, where many—twenty thousand, according to Josephus—
were trampled to death. A short while later, Cumanus, a corrupt

taker of bribes, sided with the Samaritans in a conflict between them and the Jews. The governor of Syria, who was hearing the appeal, condemned to death four Jews accused of inciting an uprising against Rome and dispatched the high priest Ananias and his subordinate, Ananus, to the emperor Claudius in chains. Claudius ultimately found for the Jewish side, but never before had a high priest been subjected to such degrading treatment. Just as Josephus' childhood was drawing to an end, another high priest named Jonathan, who had been so bold as to remonstrate with the procurator Felix, was murdered by an agent of the latter, who managed to cover up his part in the affair. Because of the actions of those whom Josephus calls "brigands" or "hired assassins"—about whom more later—insecurity was rife throughout the land.

Such was the atmosphere in which Josephus lived in Jerusalem under the reign of Claudius, years in which his principal—indeed, only—goal was to gain knowledge.

II

SPIRITUAL
CHOICES

What man is wise? He who can learn from everyone.
SAYINGS OF THE FATHERS V, 1

As he entered adolescence, the young Josephus began to consider seriously the choice he would soon have to make among the three religious trends then prevalent in Judea: the Pharisee, the Sadducee, and the Essene. In referring to them he usually employs the Greek term *hairesis* (*L* 10), which is usually translated as "sect" (the word is at the root of our "heresy"), but to us today what he describes—with the exception of the Essenes—has little resemblance to what we mean by the word "sect" today.

For one thing, none of the three, including the Essene, appears to have been marginal. None was a truly isolated movement, self-contained or in any way arcane, for we find that Josephus was able to move from one to the other quite freely, even without the help of family influence. Indeed, *hairesis* would probably be more accurately translated by the word "choice," or "option." When referring to these movements Josephus sometimes uses the term "philosophies," but then, he was addressing a Greco-Roman audience accustomed to making choices among different philosophical schools—Stoics, Platonists, Pythagoreans, or Peripatetics—and trying to explain strange categories through the use of analogy.

THE PHARISEES

When he lists the three religious movements within Judaism, which he does in several instances,[1] Josephus always gives priority to the Pharisees. He does so for (at least) three reasons: the Pharisees were the largest of the groups, they had the widest following among the people . . . and Josephus was to conclude his own spiritual quest by joining them (*L* 12).

Nothing he writes about them corresponds to the cliché that has been handed down to us in the Christian Gospels; however, a careful reading of those books would reveal that they are always referring to the "bad" Pharisee, an example of the kind of caricature to which any religious practice can lead when second-rate individuals empty it of its original significance.

We know little about the era in which the movement began (third century B.C.E.?). Rather than drawing upon this or that scholarly study, however, let us examine the description Josephus has given us in the hope of discerning the reasons for his choice.

For a mind as interested in knowledge as was Josephus', the principal attraction was probably the Pharisees' great reputation for learning. In their company the brilliant student must have felt he had found his true teachers and that he was now being given access to more rarefied intellectual levels. In Pharisaic circles Josephus obviously reveled in that studious atmosphere he tells us had been created by two teachers in the days of King Herod who had incited their disciples against the impious king: "Their lectures on the Laws were all attended by a large youthful audience, and day after day they drew together quite an army of men in their prime" (*JW* I, 649).

The Pharisees' skills at exegesis had made them recognized authorities in *halakha,* which term includes anything concerned with how to obey the Holy Commandments prescribed in the Torah. They thus influenced not only the people, who preferred them, but also the Sadducees, who, although they professed different opinions, felt constrained to fall in with the majority when officiating in the Temple "since otherwise the masses would not tolerate them" (*JA* XVIII, 17).

Josephus may also have been drawn to certain of the Pharisaical beliefs that he later, after his brush with Hellenism, mentions as revealing a philosophy with affinities to Stoicism.

Although the Bible nowhere (with the exception of the late addition of the Book of Daniel) mentions the immortality of the soul, the Pharisees made it an essential tenet of their teachings. They related it to the principle of retribution: rewards and punishments were to be meted out after death, if not in life. The Pharisees thus held that man's choice is free—which did not, of course, put into question the fundamental principle of divine omniscience. They reconciled free will and providence: "Everything is foretold, but choice exists," to quote a rabbinical saying (*Sayings of the Fathers* III, 15) that sums up their position. We can see that Josephus might have felt they shared the position of the Stoics, who also believed strongly in implacable fate and held that there were actions that depended on us and others that did not. The emphasis on self-control and the suppression of the instincts also facilitated this parallel on the moral level.

The Pharisees had another quality that helps to explain their influence with the people: they had a reputation for being approachable and affable. This is the image that has come down to us from Hillel, the most famous Pharisee of the early first century. He taught to "seek peace, love all creatures and bring them closer to the Torah" (*Sayings of the Fathers* I, 12). A famous anecdote shows that his comportment was in line with his teachings. To a mocking unbeliever who jokingly asked him to teach him the entire Torah while standing on one leg, he is supposed to have replied calmly: "Do unto others as you would have them do unto you, that is the entire teaching of the Torah, the rest is nothing but commentary." He is often compared to his colleague Shammai, who in a fit of ill temper is supposed to have sent Hillel the impertinent skeptic in the aforementioned story who was made a proselyte by the latter's gentle reply.[2] However, the same Shammai also taught: "Speak little, act with decision, and be affable to all" (*Sayings of the Fathers* I, 15).

Over several generations of Pharisaic Judaism, therefore, we can discern two schools, that of Hillel and the more rigorous one of

Shammai. The former is generally considered the more important, for Hillel was the founder of a line of "patriarchs" who led the nation during centuries of trouble. Hillel's grandson, Gamaliel, is the doctor of law "had in reputation among all the people" (Acts 5:34), whose disciple the apostle Paul proudly claimed to be (Acts 22:3). Younger than Paul, Josephus actually knew Simon, Gamaliel's son: "This Simon was a native of Jerusalem, of a very illustrious family, and of the sect of the Pharisees, who have the reputation of being unrivaled experts in their country's laws. A man highly gifted with intelligence and judgment, he could by sheer genius retrieve an unfortunate situation in affairs of state" (*L* 191–192).

THE SADDUCEES

When at the age of nineteen (56 C.E.) Josephus finally chose the Pharisaic path, it was clearly Judaism's most vigorous branch. The Sadducees, by contrast, were losing strength. Fundamentally conservative on both the social and doctrinal levels, they recruited their followers from among the priestly aristocracy and rejected any belief not explicitly dictated by Holy Writ. Thus, the Sadducees denied the immortality of the soul and, perforce, resurrection. Their argument, quite obviously slanted to cast ridicule on Pharisaic belief, is reported in the Gospels: If, under Levirate law, a woman marry seven brothers in succession, of which will she be the wife on the Day of Resurrection?[3] When Saul of Tarsus, known as Paul, was summoned to appear before the Sanhedrin, he was easily able to create an uproar by stating: "Men and brethren, I am a Pharisee, the son of a Pharisee; of the hope and resurrection of the dead I am called in question" (Acts 23:6), thereby bringing all the Pharisees over to his side, who concluded: "We find no evil in this man" (*Ibid.*, verse 9).

At the same time, Josephus tells us, the Sadducees upheld man's total freedom, probably on the basis of this particularly explicit passage in Deuteronomy: "See, I have set before thee this day life and good, and death and evil" (Deuteronomy 30:15).

The principal reproach Josephus leveled against them would seem to have been their social comportment, which was obviously dictated by their caste prejudices; this would seem sufficient grounds for explaining their limited influence: "The Sadducees, on the contrary, are, even among themselves, rather boorish in their behavior, and in their intercourse with their peers are as rude as to aliens" (*JW* II, 166).

The Sadducees' severity was also evident, Josephus tells us, on the legal level: they obviously implemented biblical law in all its literal rigor. Josephus was twenty years old (57 C.E.) when Anan, the Sadducee high priest, profiting from the absence of the Roman procurator, ordered the stoning of James, brother of Jesus, for religious transgression. His narrative clearly takes the side of "the most moderate and most attached to the law" (most probably the Pharisees) who, through their protests to Agrippa II and Albinus, the procurator, caused Anan to be stripped of his office after only three months in his post (*JA* XX, 200-203).

Nor are rabbinical sources much gentler with regard to the Sadducees; we should not, however, lose sight of the fact that they reflect the Pharisaic trend, which was the only one to survive the war against Rome. In the last analysis, it is hard to arrive at an objective notion of the Sadducees, for whether we rely on Jewish or on New Testament sources, our only knowledge of them comes from their adversaries.

The caste consciousness so often evident in Josephus was not strong enough to bind him to the Sadducees—accepting the fact that his family may have adhered to their doctrine, which is not at all certain. Indeed, at this period Aaron's descendants did not feel themselves obliged to go along with Sadduceeism, and we find several Pharisaic priests.

THE ESSENES

Josephus' long dissertation on the Essenes gives ample evidence of his strong attraction to it. The abundant details he provides about their doctrine and way of life can be explained only by his having spent some time among them.

Of the three Jewish "philosophies," Essenism is the one that best corresponds to the notion of "sect." The Essenes were a very solid, homogeneous community, strictly organized, with firm rules governing initiation and exclusion. Groups of Essenes existed in every town in Judea. Whichever one Josephus frequented, he would first have had to come as a postulant. Anyone desirous of joining the sect was, he tells us, required to spend three years as a postulant. During the first year, the postulant had to do his best to imitate the Essene way of life, wearing a white robe and a linen pagne for ritual bathing. At the end of this first period, "he was brought into closer touch with the rule and allowed to share the purer kind of holy water" (*JW* II, 138), but was still required to undergo two more years of trial before being admitted into the community as a full-fledged member.

An ascetic community like that of the Essenes demanded rigorous conduct of its members and their solemn oath to respect the common rule. It was this that probably made Josephus draw back, in spite of his admiration for the Essenes. He tells us that the required oaths were "tremendous" (*JW* II, 139): the catechumen had to swear to practice piety toward God, to observe justice toward men, to wrong none whether of his own mind or under another's orders, to forever hate the unjust and fight the battle of the just, to forever keep faith with all men, especially those to whom God has entrusted power, to refrain from abusing power should he have it, to refrain, either in dress or by other outward marks of superiority, from trying to outshine other people, to be forever a lover of truth and to expose liars, to keep his hands from stealing and his soul pure from unholy gain, to conceal nothing from the members of the sect, and to report none of their secrets to others, even though tortured to death. He must also swear to transmit the rules of the sect exactly as he received them, and, "in like manner carefully to preserve the books of the sect and the names of the angels. Such are the oaths by which they secure their proselytes" (*JW* II, 139-142).

Of all the oaths, the most "tremendous" was the ceremony accompanying the final initiation into the sect. In the caves of Qumran, archeologists discovered manuscripts known as the Dead Sea Scrolls. These are divided into three categories: biblical books (already known), apocryphal books (almost all accounted for), and "Sectarian Books." Among the Sectarian Books, which most scholars attribute to the Essenes, is a scroll known as "The Rule," the internal rules of the community that had dwelt at Qumran in the past. It describes the ceremony of entrance into the "Alliance" down to the smallest detail. The priests blessed "the men chosen by God" and the Levites anathematized all who violated their oaths.[4]

The moral régime revealed in these sermons was accompanied by a very serious, even monastic, life-style, which is set forth in the "Scroll of the Rule" of the Qumran community (VI, 2-3): "They shall obey, from inferior to superior, with regard to labor and property. They shall eat together and together they shall pray and together they shall deliberate." Josephus is the best witness to the way the Essene day was spent: "Their piety toward the Deity takes a peculiar form. Before the sun is up they utter no word on mundane matters, but offer to him certain prayers, which have been handed down from their forefathers, as though entreating him to rise. They are then dismissed by their superiors to the various crafts in which they are severally proficient and are strenuously employed until the fifth hour, when they again assemble in one place and, after girding their loins with linen cloths, bathe their bodies in cold water. After this purification, they assemble in a private apartment which none of the uninitiated is permitted to enter; pure now themselves, they repair to the refectory, as to some sacred shrine. When they have taken their seats in silence, the baker serves out the loaves to them in order, and the cook sets before each one a plate with a single course. Before the meal the priest says a grace, and none may partake until after the prayer. When breakfast is ended, he pronounces a further grace; thus at the beginning and at the close they do homage to God as the bountiful giver of life. Then, laying aside their raiment as holy vestments, they again betake themselves to their labors until the evening. On their return they sup in like manner, and any guests who may have arrived sit down with them. No clamor or disturbance ever pollutes their dwelling; they speak in turn, each making way for his neighbor. To persons outside the silence of those within appears like some awful mystery; it is in fact due to their invariable sobriety and to the limitation of their allotted portions of meat and drink to the demands of nature" (*JW* II, 128–133).

The Scroll of the Rule gives us some idea of the penalties levied for infractions of the community laws: they range from a few days' banishment to total exclusion. The Essenes had a concern for physical purity that expressed their aspirations to moral purity, also reflected in their white raiment. They washed frequently and did not anoint their bodies with oil in the Greco-Roman way. "Oil they consider defiling, and anyone who accidently comes in contact with it scours his person" (*JW* II, 123).

This aspiration to purity also justified their misogyny. In their eyes a woman, a creature impure in essence, was unable to remain faithful to one man, and it was therefore better to protect oneself by renouncing marriage altogether (*JW* II, 121).

One branch of Essenism, however, awake to the serious threat such a doctrine posed to the future of mankind, favored marriage, but only on condition that it be made perfectly clear that its only purpose was procreation (*JW* II, 160–161). On this point the apostle Paul, although a declared Pharisee, would also appear to have been influenced by Essenism.

The Essene concept of virtue (which entailed both resistance to passion and self-mastery) eschewed pleasure as it did lust: "They do not change their garments or shoes until they are torn to shreds or worn threadbare with age" (*JW* II, 126). To demonstrate their contempt for riches and their desire for equality, new members had to turn over their property to the community. The community, which seems to have been wisely managed, would then provide for each according to his needs.

The same principle held good for the community in the larger sense. An Essene is at home wherever there are other Essenes: "On the arrival of any of the sect from elsewhere, all the resources of the community are put at their disposal, just as if they were their own, and they enter the houses of men whom they have never seen before as though they were their most intimate friends. Consequently, they carry nothing whatever with them on their journeys, except arms as a protection against brigands. In every city there is one of the order expressly appointed to attend to strangers, who provides them with raiment and other necessaries" (*JW* II, 124-126).

With regard to the Sabbath observance, the Essenes practiced a rigor Josephus clearly viewed as excessive: "Not only do they prepare their food on the day before, to avoid kindling a fire on that one, but they do not venture to remove any vessel or even to go to stool" (*JW* II, 147). He does not dwell upon it, however, and in particular he does not enlighten us about their response to two problems on which the Pharisees adopted a more relaxed position, namely, that of defensive war and that of healing the sick who, according to the Hebrew saying, "prevail over the Sabbath." The famous line in the Gospels, "The Sabbath is made for man, and not man for the Sabbath," is a perfect reflection of Pharisaic doctrine, but its context also demonstrates that that doctrine was beginning to meet with a certain amount of resistance.

The Essenes shared with the Pharisees a belief in the immortality of the soul. This enabled them to face unflinchingly the martyrdom to which the Romans were to subject them during the War: "Smiling in their agonies and mildly deriding their tormentors, they cheerfully resigned their souls, confident that they would receive them back again" (*JW* II, 153). They must have had explicit ideas about the rewards and punishments to be meted out after death: their Hell and their Paradise were very like those of the Greeks, according to Josephus, who, far from reproaching them, found their doctrine of the soul "an irresistible attraction."

Unlike the Pharisees, the Essenes do not seem to have made any special effort to reconcile man's freedom, tacit in the notion of retribution, with divine omniscience. Faithful to the notion of Fate, they had a reputation of being able to predict the future, an ability that Josephus did more than envy—as we shall see, he claimed the same power.

As for the remainder of their doctrine, the Essenes, as described by Josephus, seem in general to have taken to extreme limits certain aspects of the Pharisaic trends they shared. Thus, according to the Talmud (which has a similar basis), "the duty to do good knows no limits" (Mishnah, *Pea* I, 1). The Essenes, who had to ask permission from their superiors for almost everything, were absolved from doing so when practicing charity and assistance (*JW* II, 134); they readily took in the children of others (*JW* II, 120). However, their way of life reflected more than mere altruism: it attempted to give life to an ideal of absolute brotherhood.

Where the Law was concerned, both sects were extremely scrupulous. Whereas the Pharisees recognized three legal entities, according to the gravity of the offense—and their highest court had seventy-one members—the Essenes (still according to Josephus' testimony) never "passed sentence in a court of less than a hundred members; the decision thus reached is irrevocable" (*JW* II, 145).

Although Josephus avoids taking too personal a tone, his lengthy description of the Essenes contains sufficient information for us to understand that his eventual choice was otherwise, notwithstanding his attraction to the "sect." For a life of chastity, purity, and renunciation, the Essene discipline was a sublime ideal. Those who practiced it became models of virtue: "Holding righteous indignation in reserve, they are masters of their temper, champions of fidelity, very ministers of peace. Any word of theirs has more force than an oath" (*JW* II, 135).

But what happened to a person who, after having entered onto the Essene way, came to realize that he lacked the requisite firmness? Such a man was lost. Excluded from the group, he found himself bereft of means; bound as he was by oaths of purity, he was even unable "to partake of other men's food," and so was forced to eat grass, waste away, and perish of starvation. His only salvation lay in those who had cast him out, but they would agree to allow their erring brothers to rejoin them only when the latter found themselves in the final extremity, "deeming that torments which have brought them to the verge of death are a sufficient penalty for their misdoings" (*JW* I, 143-144).

For their part, the Pharisees, who also esteemed disinterested unselfishness, preached total self-reliance: "To say 'what's mine is yours, and what's yours is yours'—that is true piety, but to say

'what's mine is yours and what's yours is mine' is thoughtless obliv-
iousness" (*Sayings of the Fathers* V, 13). Josephus was far too prudent
to become an Essene.

THE CALL OF THE WILDERNESS

However, the Essene temptation is revelatory of the youthful desire
for purity felt by this man whose later career would be far more
pragmatic than idealistic.

    This impression is confirmed by the next step in Josephus'
spiritual journey. Having closely inspected the three religious tendencies we have mentioned, he then went into the wilderness to
join the hermit Bannus, whose teachings he was to follow from his
sixteenth to his nineteenth year. Essene asceticism paled before that
of this man whose life Josephus shared: "For raiment, Bannus had
only such clothing as trees provided, feeding on such things as grew
of themselves, and using frequent ablutions of cold water, by day
and night, for purity's sake" (*L* 11).

    We have no other knowledge of Bannus the Anchorite, but
we cannot help being reminded of John the Baptist, who also lived in
the wilderness, wore "raiment of camel's hair and a leathern girdle
about his loins," his meat locusts and wild honey.[5] All Bannus' ener-
gies were directed to purity, as symbolized by the frequent cleansings
in which he—like the Essenes—indulged. This too reminds us of
John the Baptist, whom Josephus mentions as a "good man" who
incited the Jews "to lead righteous lives, to practice justice toward
their fellows and piety toward God, and so doing, to join in baptism.
In his view this was a necessary preliminary if baptism was to be
acceptable to God. They must not employ it to gain pardon for whatever sins they committed, but as a consecration of the body implying
that the soul was already thoroughly cleansed by right behavior" (*JA*
XVIII, 117). By joining this Master whose harshly ascetic spiritual life
he was to share for three years, Josephus reveals a detachment from
the world that is surprising when we know the rest of his story.

    The theme of the wilderness in ancient Judaism has inspired
many erudite studies, all of which emphasize its essential ambiguity.

For the Hebrews who escaped from Egypt, the wilderness had been an unavoidable and redoubtable trial; the wilderness generation was condemned to end its forty years of wanderings without seeing the Promised Land. However, the wilderness is also a place of revelation, the place where Moses came face to face with God, where Elijah heard the "still small voice." For Hosea and Jeremiah it was a place of love, of God's nuptials with his people.

By selecting Qumran, in the depths of the Judean wilderness, as their settlement, the members of the Essene community were seeking to return to God by distancing themselves from populous cities, which, they believed, fostered an unhealthy way of life. It is written in the *Rule* (VIII, 12): "They absented themselves from the dwellings of perverted men to go into the wilderness, to follow in His path." In this reference to one of the most famous verses of Isaiah (usually mistranslated as "a voice crieth in the desert"): "The voice of him that crieth: In the wilderness, prepare ye the way of the Lord, make straight in the desert a highway for our God" (Isaiah 40:3) we can sense the appeal of the wilderness. The desert afforded a temporary haven, a purifying experience, a preparatory period of asceticism while one awaited the arrival of the Kingdom of God. The Qumran community withdrew into the wilderness to "prepare the way" for a new day.

It was not alone. On several occasions Josephus mentions (unsympathetically, we must add) the appearance in the years preceding the war of various *illuminati* who led their disciples off into the wilderness, like Theudas (*JA* XX, 97), who is also mentioned in the Acts of the Apostles as "boasting himself to be somebody." "Deceivers and impostors, under the pretence of divine inspiration fostering revolutionary changes, they persuaded the multitude to act like madmen and led them out into the desert under the belief that God would there give them tokens of deliverance" (*JW* II, 259).

The endemic unrest that began to develop in Judea under the Roman procurators during the reigns of Claudius (41–54 C.E.) and Nero (54–68 C.E.) sometimes took the peaceful form of wilderness pilgrimage and sometimes the violent shape of the Sicarii. Somewhere between these two extremes we have that false prophet from out of Egypt who led thirty thousand "dupes" to the Mount of Olives, from which he claimed he would make the walls of Jerusalem crumble through his words alone, force his way into the city, and make himself master of the Roman garrison there (*JW* II, 261–263). This episode, which is also mentioned in the Acts of the Apostles, suggests that the Jews of the Egyptian diaspora had fallen prey to a certain mystical exaltation mixed with anti-Roman feelings. It also demonstrates that in the eyes of impatient hotheads the advent of the Kingdom could occur only after the evil power holding sway in the land—namely, Rome—had been overthrown.

THE "FOURTH PHILOSOPHY"

We must also mention another current of Judaism, one that Josephus sometimes describes as a wholly discrete "fourth philosophy," sometimes as merely a pernicious offshoot of Pharisaism. Unlike the other three trends, we can date the first appearance of this one precisely.

In the year 6, Augustus, alarmed by all the unfavorable reports he was receiving, decided to remove Archelaus, Herod's heir, and sent him into exile in Gaul, in what is today the French city of Vienne. In so doing, the emperor was finally acceding, after considerable hesitation, to the request a Jewish delegation had submitted to him several years earlier beseeching him to rid Judea "of the royal line and any other government of the sort," and hand administration of the country over to the Roman legate in Syria—thus the dimensions of the hatred against Herod and his dynasty. This was done, but not until ten years after Archelaus had mounted the throne of Judea.

During that same year, the land thus came under the authority of Quirinius, the legate in Syria, who was assisted by Coponius, a knight. The first act of the Roman authorities was to decree a census of personal wealth. The Jewish population, unused to Roman administrative procedures, accepted this very badly, and it took the intervention of the high priest Joazar son of Boethos to restore calm—calm that was far from complete. A certain Judah, from the town of Gamala in the Golan (a region known to the Romans as Gaulanitidis) and a Pharisee named Saddok fomented considerable unrest, maintaining that such a census put the people in a servile position.

According to Josephus, their "philosophy" was notable for the almost unconquerable "passion for liberty" that distinguished them from the other Pharisees and that was based on their firm conviction that "God alone is their leader and master" (*JA* XVIII, 23). Far from arousing our author's admiration, he regarded this emphasis on liberty as nothing more nor less than the root cause of the country's downfall, "for Judah and Saddok started among us an intensive fourth school of philosophy; and when they had won an abundance of devotees, they filled the body politic immediately with tumult, also planting the seeds of those troubles which subsequently overtook it, all because of the novelty of this hitherto unknown philosophy" (*JA* XVIII,9).

At first glance the two founders of the movement would appear to be no more than nationalists highly jealous of national independence. Josephus gives only a cursory attention to the doctrine he so severely condemns. Yet the notion of "no other master but God" deserves closer examination, given the unrest to which it was to give rise in the years preceding the war. The disastrous memory of the reigns of the last kings left the disciples of Judah and Saddok totally uninterested in reestablishing a Jewish authority in the country to replace the Roman. In proclaiming that God was the sole master, they were in reality proclaiming the advent of the Kingdom; withdrawal into the wilderness was a transitional step toward that Kingdom, just as the wanderings of the Hebrews had been a transitional step between Egyptian exile and the Promised Land. But why were they so convinced that the Kingdom was at hand?

There were many contemporary so-called apocalyptic writings announcing the imminent Kingdom of God. Most of the Jewish apocalypses, which were probably written between the second century B.C.E. and the middle of the first century C.E. (*Enoch,* the third book of the *Sibylline Oracles,* the *Testament of the Twelve Patri-*

archs, the *Book of Jubilees*), included the notion of Judgment Day as foretold by the Prophets. That Day would be preceded by cosmic upheavals and an unprecedented series of evil deeds; a terrible war between Gog and Magog (referring to Chapters 38 and 39 of the prophet Ezekiel) would usher in the new era. The whole process forms what the "short synoptic apocalypse" of the Gospels (Mark 13, Matthew 24, Luke 21) calls "labor pains" preceding the Messiah's advent.

One biblical book, the Book of Daniel, stands out from all of this literature. Indeed, it was regarded as so authoritative that it became part of the canon. Generally believed to have been written in 167 B.C.E. in the aftermath of the shock created by the blasphemous setting up of the "abomination of desolation" (a statue of Zeus) by Antiochus IV Epiphanes in the Temple at Jerusalem, the Book of Daniel reflected a notion widely believed throughout human history and here probably adapted from a Persian tradition. The notion is set out in veiled but sufficiently clear terms in the famous visions to be found in Chapters 2 and 7.

In the first, the Babylonian king Nebuchadnezzar dreams a dream of an image or statue whose "head was of fine gold, and his breast and his arms of silver, his belly and his thighs of brass, his legs of iron, his feet part of iron and part of clay." The statue is smitten by a stone cut out without hands that became a great mountain and filled the whole earth; this "glorious" stone[6] represents the Kingdom that will pulverize the four preceding empires and exist for eternity. In the second episode Daniel himself dreams a dream during the reign of Belshazzar: Four great beasts emerged from the great sea: a lion with eagle's wings, a bear, a leopard with four wings, and a fourth creature, "dreadful and terrible." An "Ancient of Days" sits in judgment upon them; then appears one "like the Son of Man," and he is given dominion forever.

According to the interpretations of these two visions, the four metals and the four beasts represent the four successive empires that managed to establish quasi-universal domination, namely, Babylon, Media, Persia, and Greece. Greece is Alexander's empire (356–323 B.C.E.), which was split in two like the statue's feet into the kingdom of the Ptolemies in Egypt and the kingdom of the

Seleucids in Syria. It is also represented by a nameless beast with ten horns symbolizing the successive kings. While three of the beasts merely have their dominion withdrawn at the great judgment of the "Ancient of Days," the last is slain and its body cast into the flames, an expression of the hatred felt by the author of the Book of Daniel for the oppressor of his own day, the Greek kingdom of Syria.

Syria had become a Roman province in 63 B.C.E.; Judea came under direct Roman administration in the year 6, although it had formerly been a sort of Roman protectorate with a factitious independence. The Book of Daniel, which was still widely read, now had to be brought up to date. And indeed, in subsequent rabbinical tradition the theme of the four empires is maintained, but now it is Rome that assumes the role of the fourth empire. The revision may have been made as early as the year 6, when Rome assumed overt control over Judea, thus leading to the emergence of the "fourth philosophy."[7] The preaching of Judah (known as "The Galilean") and Saddok the Pharisee, which made use of the revision of the Book of Daniel, contained, in Joseph's words, "the roots of the evil that was later to spring up," for it fostered an apocalyptic unrest that, when directed against Rome, would inevitably lead to war.

Another example of this *aggiornamento* of sacred texts can be found in the Qumran sect, whose members, also caught up in the apocalyptic current, produced commentaries on the minor prophets Habakkuk and Nahum that made it clear that the enemies they had referred to as "Kittim"[8] were in fact the Romans. One of the sect's major scriptures describes a terrible eschatological war between the "Sons of Light" and the "Sons of Darkness."[9] Thus, reinterpreted in a spiritual context, the faults of the Roman administration led at least one growing fringe group of the population to view Rome as a kind of monster, with features that would later coalesce into those of the Beast of the Apocalypse depicted by Saint John.

A man consists of what he rejects as well as what he chooses. In Josephus' case, he expresses a visceral hatred of the "fourth philosophy" and the groups (Sicarii and, later, Zealots) inspired by it. That hatred can be explained in part by his belief that they were responsible for the national catastrophe that was to result in so many victims and in the burning and destruction of the Temple. Of course, this later reaction does not necessarily reflect the feelings of the young Josephus. In any event, when looking back upon his youth in his autobiography, Josephus does not mention the "fourth philosophy" at all, as though it were unthinkable that he could ever, even momentarily, have been drawn to it. Yet, when he deals with the theme of the four kingdoms, he does not reject the message of the Book of Daniel. Like his Pharisee contemporaries, he puts Kingdom Come sometime in the distant future, dependent, not on man, but on God alone (*JA* X, 210).

Thus, Josephus' experience in the wilderness was gained not as part of a large group led by the exhortations of a politico-religious leader with messianic pretensions but in austere and solitary withdrawal. His time in the desert is in no way incompatible with his ultimate choice, which was to be the doctrine of the Pharisees: "With him [Bannus] I lived for three years and, having accomplished my purpose, returned to the city. Being now in my nineteenth year I began to govern my life by the rules of the Pharisees" (*L* 12).

Pharisaism taught a dual doctrine of salvation. The fourth philosophy, which was an outgrowth or variant of Pharisaism, elected to emphasize collective salvation. It entailed a doctrine of individual salvation that held that the soul of the just would enjoy future life. In order to enter into the "world to come" so often mentioned in subsequent rabbinical sources (without any specifics about the contents of such a notion), one must take the path of virtue.

During his withdrawal into the wilderness, Josephus probably knew a period of spiritual uplift. Once the mystical flights of adolescence were over, however, his life seems to have been centered more on personal concerns in the here and now than on spiritual things in some far-off hereafter.

III

THE VOYAGE TO ROME

Like cormorants, they were borne on the waves in their black bark.

ODYSSEY XII, 418–419

In the great city of Rome there are 365 streets in each of which are 365 palaces, each of which has 365 floors, each of which contains enough to feed the entire universe.

THE BABYLONIAN TALMUD

We have no knowledge of the seven years between the end of Josephus' stay in the wilderness with the hermit Bannus and his mission to Rome in his twenty-seventh year.

THE RETURN TO JERUSALEM

In the year 56, Josephus, now nineteen years of age, returned from the desert to Jerusalem. Did he do so by choice or was he recalled by his family? Given our young eremite's age at the time and the customs prevalent in non-Essene Jewish circles at the time, it is possible his parents called him home to be married. "Eighteen years is the age of the nuptial canopy," says the rabbinical text on the stages of life (the same text quoted earlier on education). A young man who followed such counsel would thereby avoid debauchery and fulfill the biblical duty to procreate.

Our hypothesis is not totally without foundation. In a passage in the *War* (*JW* V, 419) Josephus makes passing reference to the fact that his "wife," along with his own family, was held prisoner in besieged Jerusalem. This cannot be the wife (a captive woman from Caesarea) given him by Vespasian in 69, a wife reported to have died a few months later, nor can it be one of the other women he was later to marry. Josephus must therefore have been married prior to the war to a girl of his own social milieu who had been chosen for him according to criteria of which he wholly approved: a high-born virgin whose lineage would have been spotless. Should we attribute his silence on the subject to the depth of his sorrow, his natural reticence? Might he have had children who had perished of hunger in the siege or were slain in the ensuing massacres while their father had been in safety with the besiegers?

Because of the blank years separating these two episodes in his autobiography—his reentry into Jerusalem from the wilderness and his journey to Rome—we do not know whether he ever practiced a profession. As a member of the priestly caste he would have been—at least theoretically—free from want, since under Biblical law all members of the priestly caste received the tithe. In these very same years, however, we know that certain poor priests did live in precarious circumstances: Josephus angrily reports that some even died of hunger (*JA* XX, 181) because they were deprived of their tithe, their only source of income, by other, reprehensible priests unworthy of the name. Josephus, however, was not among the poor. His family was not only noble, it was extremely wealthy. In the last lines of his autobiography he informs us that the family owned considerable land in the vicinity of Jerusalem (*L* 422). We deduce that they must have lived on their income.

THE MISSION TO ROME

In 64, "over twenty-six years of age," Josephus was sent on a mission to Rome. He writes that he was to accompany there certain priests with whom he was acquainted, "men of distinction." According to the spare account in the autobiography, Felix, Procurator of Judea (52–60), had "for reasons unknown" had the priests thrown in irons and sent off to Rome to "explain themselves" to Nero. Josephus proudly reports that he succeeded in his mission through the intercession of the empress Poppaea.

A more detailed account appears in the last book of the *Jewish Antiquities,* which deals with the period immediately preceding the war. We cannot, of course, be completely certain it is dealing with the same events. Briefly, however: King Agrippa II, whose lands were scattered in the northernmost part of the country, had managed to retain possession of his family's ancestral palace in Jerusalem. Raised in Rome and less respectful of ancestral traditions than his father, Agrippa I, of whom the Talmud has handed down a favorable image, he had had a belvedere built onto his Jerusalem palace from which he could observe everything that went on in the Temple without leaving his dining couch. The priestly aristocracy—both Sadducee and Pharisee—regarded this belvedere as an affront to the sanctity of the Temple and the rites practiced within its confines. They reacted by erecting a wall that cut off the view from the royal dining room but that also hindered the surveillance the Roman garrison maintained over the Temple, particularly on high feast days, when the crowds of people attending often gave rise to various problems. King Agrippa II and the procurator Festus (60–62) had then attempted to have the wall torn down, but in vain. According to the account in *Antiquities,* Festus gave permission for a Jewish delegation led by the high priest in person to appeal the case to Nero. The delegation succeeded thanks to the intercession of Poppaea, who pleaded with her husband in their favor, for "she was a worshipper of God." However, the empress detained "as hostages" in her house the high priest Ishmael, as well as Helcias, guardian of the Temple treasure (*JA* XX, 189-195).

According to his autobiography, Josephus interceded with Poppaea to free his friends the priests. Does this refer to the two hostages she had retained (it is unclear why)[1] or to other persons the procurator Felix had sent to Rome earlier?

GREEK STUDY

To be entrusted with such a mission Josephus had to have been more than a young man of good family and well versed in Holy Writ; he had to have been in possession of that other tool indispensable to a good ambassador: a linguistic ability that would have enabled him to plead his case; he would have had to speak, if not Latin, then Greek.

In those days Greek was the language of all cultivated Roman elite. We recall Horace's well-known line, "Greece vanquished has conquered her rough conqueror." At a time when the whole world, including the pagan East, was profoundly hellenized, Rome made no attempt to impose Latin on its Eastern provinces, for it too was deeply under the influence of that universally admired culture. Thus, Greek remained the language of the Roman administration in the East even after the arrival of the Romans.

In the large cities of the East such as Alexandria in Egypt or Antioch in Syria (today it is located in Turkey), both of which had large Jewish populations, we can be sure that the inhabitants were thoroughly hellenized. Judea, however, was a special case, for although a trend toward hellenization had been in evidence as early as *circa* 168 B.C.E, in the days of Antiochus IV Epiphanes, the Greek king of Syria, the Maccabean uprising had brought it to an abrupt end. The Hasmonean kings and, after them, Herod and his descendants, had probably been more open to Hellenism, but, at the same time, the Pharisees, who exercised the preponderant influence in the land, took care that the population continued to be well imbued with the Judaic spirit. Indeed, at times they even incited the people to open revolt when the kings encroached on what Josephus refers to as "ancestral customs."

The language spoken in Judea in the first century continues to be a subject of scholarly discussion today.[2] Some sources maintain that the language was Aramaic, a tongue related to Hebrew, which, from being a language spoken only by nomadic tribes in Syria and Chaldaea and later the administrative language of the Babylonian Empire, had gradually spread into the Mediterranean area. The movements of population following the Assyrian and Babylonian conquests had contributed to its dissemination: thus, the Cutheans from the East had introduced Aramaic into Samaria when they took over the lands of the ten "lost tribes" of Israel in the seventh century; Judeans deported to Babylon in 586 B.C.E. returned two generations later with an Aramaic script that replaced the old Hebraic-Phoenician writing . . . and probably with a better knowledge of Aramaic than of Hebrew. For two centuries (528–333 B.C.E.) the Persian Empire imposed its own administrative language—so-called Imperial Aramaic—throughout the Fertile Crescent as far as Egypt—in the fifth century B.C.E. we find Jewish soldiers in the Persian garrison at Elephantine (today Aswan, Egypt) writing in Aramaic to their coreligionists back in Jerusalem. Although, beginning with Alexander's conquests (333 B.C.E), Greek became the official language, as well as the language of educated persons, it did not succeed in supplanting Aramaic, which had conquered solid blocs of the population throughout the region.[3]

Notwithstanding the strong competition from Aramaic, Hebrew remained current until sometime around the second century of our era. Parts of the Bible (most of the minor prophets and the Hagiographa) are even pre-exilic. At Qumran the sect's literature would appear to be an attempt to imitate pre-Exile Hebrew. However, there is no doubt that at the time the Qumran texts were written, Hebrew had become quite different from what it was prior to the Exile. The extent of its modification can be gauged by comparison with what in the last century was called "neo-Hebrew," that is, the language in which the Mishnah, the basis of the Talmud, has come down to us (and dated from *circa* the year 200 C.E.). Its syntax differs considerably from that of biblical Hebrew, its morphology is highly aramaicized, and its vocabulary is replete with foreign terms in Aramaic, Greek, and even Latin. "Neo-Hebrew" has a popular flavor that makes it quite different from a "scholarly" language—Sorbonne Latin, for example. The Mishnah was written in this language because it was then still current, at least in the region. Galilee, which had been rejoined to the Hasmonean kingdom and rejudaicized around 100 B.C.E., was totally Aramaic-speaking, but parts of Judea *per se* must have preserved Hebrew at least until as late as Simon Bar Kokhba's revolt against Rome (132–135 C.E.), for a part of his war correspondence miraculously uncovered by archeologists in 1960 attests to the fact that he wrote with equal facility in all three languages: Hebrew, Aramaic, and Greek.

We can therefore surmise that Josephus must have known a "Levantine" linguistic situation in which a religious and national language (Hebrew) coexisted with both a regional and popular language (Aramaic) and a language of general culture that was also the language of the Roman administration in the East, i.e., Greek.

In Josephus' account of his education, which he provides at the outset of his autobiography, he makes no mention of any training other than Judaic. When and how, then, did Josephus acquire the knowledge of Greek indispensable for his Roman mission? He gives no information, but he does leave a clear impression that Greek had not been an important priority in his education.

"For my compatriots admit that in our Jewish learning I far excel them. I have also labored strenuously to partake of the realm of Greek prose and poetry, after having gained a knowledge of Greek grammar, although the habitual use of my native tongue has prevented my attaining precision in the pronunciation. For our people do not favor those persons who have mastered the speech of many nations, or who adorn their style with smoothness of diction, because they consider that not only is such skill common to ordinary freemen but that even slaves who so choose may acquire it. But they give credit for wisdom to those alone who have an exact knowledge of the Law and who are capable of interpreting the meaning of the Holy Scriptures" (*JA* XX, 263-264).

Thus, Josephus spoke Greek with an accent that made him immediately identifiable as an Easterner. As for writing it, he was loath to do so without assistance, as we shall see later. In fact, he had no more than a rudimentary knowledge of Greek culture, namely, its "grammar." Of course, the first stage of the study of Greek grammar included reading, writing, and recitation. In the second stage the study of Greek would have become more problematic for a Jew because it would have included a consideration of literary works that were tarred with the brush of paganism, prominent among them the Homeric epics. Christians of pagan origin were later to get around the obstacle of the mythology that so tainted Greek poetry by counseling their children to avoid ingesting the poison with which they might come in contact. Jews like Josephus, who learned Greek late in life and outside the scholarly framework pagans were able to enjoy, had to cleave to fabulists like Aesop or Babrius, traces of whom can in fact be found in some of the Talmudic apologues.

Because of the hierarchy Josephus himself established between sacred and profane culture, it is clear that a well-born

Jerusalem Jew, and member of the priestly caste to boot, would not have had his son taught Greek at an early age before having armed him against pagan culture. Once he had acquired an adequate religious protection, paganism would hold no threats for him, and were he to be destined for some responsible post he could then learn Greek without danger, as part of the preparation for that position. Thus, the Talmud notes that Greek was taught in the house of the patriarchs descended from Hillel "because they had relations with the authorities."[4]

Greek was banished from the education of young Jewish aristocrats only when the situation with Rome became particularly tense, and even then only theoretically. A well-known Talmudic anecdote relates that the nephew of a famous wise man of the early second century C.E. one day asked his maternal uncle: "Does someone like me, who has studied the whole Torah, have the right to study Greek?" In reply his uncle quoted a verse of Joshua: "Thou shalt meditate therein [the Torah] day and night" (1:8) and, not devoid of humor, added: "Go find an hour that is neither day nor night and then you can study Greek."[5] The anecdote confirms what Josephus implies: Only after he had thoroughly studied the wisdom of Israel did a young Jewish aristocrat come into contact with the wisdom of nations. For Josephus, therefore, his Greek studies must have occurred sometime around his twentieth year.

THE PERILS OF TRAVEL

Very few travelers took the land route when going from Judea or Syria to Rome. One did so only when some pressing business made it necessary to make the trip in the winter, when no ship would set sail. The route across the mountainous regions of Cappadocia and Phrygia, and then the Balkans and the Alps, was arduous, and the journey could take as many as a hundred days.

Thus, when going to Rome it was preferable to wait for those months when the travel time could be considerably shorted by traveling by sea. Sailors avoided the rainy season, from October to February, and most crossings were made from March to September. From a reading of the Acts of the Apostles (27:9-11) it would appear that the Jews had a rule not to travel in the autumn after the fast of Yom Kippur, which occurs around the end of September—early October, according to the year. The apostle Paul warns his traveling companions against undertaking a voyage after that date. His captain, however, who had probably given himself a few days' leeway, decided to set sail nevertheless, with the result that the boat was caught in a storm, just as Paul had feared.

Paul's voyage to Rome, where his case was to be heard before the Emperor, took place in 60 or 61, a mere three or four years prior to that of Josephus. Sailing from Caesarea, Paul's ship followed the coast to the north. Its original destination was probably the port of Brindisi, in the southern part of the Italian boot. According to the geographer Strabo (VI,3,7), travelers who had embarked from Asia or Greece usually arrived in Brindisi, whence they would continue for the rest of the way by land.

The journey was long and tiring, even in good weather. Philo tells us that Caligula advised his friend Agrippa I, who was on the way back to his kingdom, against making the crossing in the opposite direction, from Brindisi to Syria. In the Emperor's opinion the best maritime route was the one to Alexandria. One could set sail from Pozzuoli (Latin Puteoli, Greek Dicearchea) south of Rome, on one of the Alexandrian vessels, whose reputation was beyond reproach: "For the transports from that place are swift and their pilots of vast experience: like the drivers of racing chariots, they unswervingly keep to the most direct route."[6]

The most favorable period for the crossing from the Italian coast to Alexandria was in July-August, when the summer winds blew north-northwest. Pliny the Elder[7] reports that two Egyptian prefects who had left from Sicily made the crossing in seven and six days, respectively, and that fifteen years later a senator who had sailed from Pozzuoli, which lies farther to the north, had made it in barely nine days. Those were the record maritime speeds reported in the first century of the Christian era, the average being from eighteen to nineteen days.

We have no knowledge of the record times for voyages leaving from Alexandria. In spite of the apparent detour when traveling from Judea to Rome, the stopover at Alexandria would seem to have been preferable to any other itinerary. Vespasian, the commanding general in the Judean war, would pick Alexandria as his port of embarkation when he returned to Rome to claim the Empire after Nero's death; it was also Titus' port of choice when he returned home after the siege of Jerusalem in the year 70.

To gain time, military leaders or governors often took the same commercial boats used by private persons. Trade between Rome and Alexandria, which included all the products of the Far East in addition to grain and Egyptian papyrus, was extremely active. Thus, the traveler arriving in Alexandria could be sure of quickly finding a boat to take him to Italy. Josephus, whose narrative of his crossing is far less precise than that of the apostle Paul, does not tell us what route he took. From Jerusalem, he could also have gone to one of the country's ports, Caesarea or Acre, and continued by sea either to the north, like Paul, or to the south, had he opted for the Alexandrian layover. He could also of course have reached Alexandria by land, following the coast road, as Vespasian and Titus were to do later. In any event, we do know that Josephus' first long voyage was not without its excitements. As a matter of fact, his ship, with six hundred passengers on board, sank in the middle of the Adriatic. Eighty of its survivors were forced to swim all night before being picked up at dawn by a boat coming from Cyrenaica. Josephus' narrative thus indirectly informs us that he was a good swimmer (later, the Talmud was to lay on every Jewish father the obligation to teach his son to swim).

JEWS AND JUDAISTS IN FIRST-CENTURY ROME

Prior to setting out for Rome, Josephus must have been given the names of some influential people there who might be helpful to him in his mission. A quarter of a century earlier, when dispatched on an equally complicated mission to Caligula, Philo of Alexandria and the four emissaries accompanying him had been given a list of senators friendly to the Jews; however, alert to imperial disfavor, the senators had refused to open their doors to them when they arrived, saying they were not at home.

Philo's task had been made more difficult by a certain Helicon, a freed Egyptian slave in Caligula's entourage,[8] who had constantly whispered aspersions against the Jews into his master's ear. Josephus was to be more fortunate. Upon his arrival at Pozzuoli he met a Jewish actor named Aliturus, by chance a favorite of Nero, who had a country residence near the city. The "mime" theater in which Aliturus appeared was probably of the kind that specialized in the most vulgar and decadent type of comedy.

As a general rule, rabbis advised against Jews' attending any Roman performances, the arena games because of their cruelty and theatrical presentations because of their triviality.[9] Nevertheless, the example of Aliturus shows that some Jews practiced the profession; perhaps the communities in the Diaspora were less restrictive. It is also possible that Aliturus was a freed slave who had not been given any choice in the matter.[10]

Beginning in the early years of the first century, the Jews of Rome had inhabited a large district on the right bank of the Tiber. Far from being an elegant residential area, like the Delta Quarter (once a part of old Alexandria, Egypt, but no longer extant), where most Alexandrian Jews lived, this area was one of the typical slums that were to be found in all large metropolitan centers, inhabited for the most part by recent immigrants—a warren of narrow streets lined with tall and badly maintained buildings and with a teeming and motley population of small tradesmen, echoing with noises and reeking with smells—salted fish, sausages, and hot peas—mingled, of course, with the nauseating stench of the Tiber.[11]

Philo tells us that most of the Roman Jews were recently freed slaves.[12] Many of them were descendants of the prisoners of war brought back by Pompey after the taking of Jerusalem in 63 B.C.E. However, a Jew rarely remained a slave for long, for the Jewish communities and wealthy individuals considered it a religious duty to purchase the freedom of any coreligionist who had been taken in slavery. This is how the Roman Jewish community had begun, barely a century prior to Josephus' voyage. We get a glimpse of it as early as 59 B.C.E., when Cicero spoke out in defense of

Lucius Valerius Flaccus, a governor who had confiscated funds sent by the Jews of his province to the Temple in Jerusalem. In the crowd assembled to hear Cicero's oration in the Forum were a number of Jews who gave vocal expression to their hostility.[13]

Caesar was to decree a number of privileges designed to enable the Jews to practice their religion freely across the breadth of what was already almost an empire: the right to assemble, dispensation from military service and from any courtroom appearance on the seventh day, and permission for the collection of funds for the Temple. As a result, after Caesar's assassination on the Ides of March no group evidenced as much sorrow as the Jews of Rome, who stood vigil for several nights beside his funeral pyre.[14] Augustus continued the policy enacted by his adoptive father. Philo tells us that he never prevented the Roman Jews from meeting in their synagogues (there appear to have been four in his day) nor from sending money to the Temple in Jerusalem. Careful to see that the Jews were not overlooked when the monthly distributions of corn or money fell on a Sabbath, Augustus took pains to have their share set aside for them until the following day.[15]

Of course the Roman Jews were not all poor, downtrodden creatures, for had that been the case they could not have attracted so many proselytes from among upper-class Roman society, as Horace accuses them of doing in his *Satires*. The Roman community must have had its leading citizens, and from time to time it welcomed visiting Judean notables, not to mention princes who had been exiled or who had come to Rome to complete their education in the world's capital. When in the year 4 a Judean delegation arrived to petition Augustus to depose Archelaus, Herod's successor, eight thousand Roman Jews thronged the audience the Emperor granted them in the Temple of Apollo (*JA*, XXII, 301). If that number is exact—and how can we know?—the Jewish population of Rome in the early first century must have been in the neighborhood of forty thousand, a considerable number.

Even if we reduce that estimate by half or by a fourth, it appears certain that the Jews formed an important community within the city. Tiberius, on the advice of Sejanus, his praetorian prefect, managed to find a pretext to expel them. During the reign of Tiberius, a sexual scandal involving priests of the Temple of Isis led to a further tightening of the Emperor's restrictions against all the Eastern religions, among which the Romans included Judaism. Tiberius' eventual pretext, however, was provided by a lesser scandal involving a shady type who had swindled a Roman matron who had converted to Judaism. The Jews were expelled from Rome in 19 C.E. Four thousand men of military age were sent to Sardinia, but many others were tortured for refusing military service rather than transgress their religious laws (*JA*, XVII, 84). After Sejanus' downfall, Tiberius allowed the Jews to return to Rome; in the reign of his successor, Caligula, Philo discovered there a repopulated district, along the Tiber. Although in his fits of insanity the young emperor dreamed of erecting his statue in the Temple at Jerusalem, he never disturbed the Jews living in the capital.

The sparse references to the Jewish presence to be found in Latin writers of the period reflect a certain contempt for exotic customs. Seneca cannot understand how one can indulge in "laziness" one day out of seven, and that on that day it was forbidden to extinguish the reeking oil lamps. Petronius, astonished that the Jews ate no pork, concluded that they must worship swine. It may have been during the reign of Claudius that outsiders began to notice a rift within the Jewish community. When Suetonius wrote that the emperor "expelled the Jews who were constantly rising up at the behest of a certain Chrestos," he was probably referring to the early Christians, for Claudius was actually fairly well disposed toward the Jews: he reaffirmed the rights of the Alexandrian Jews and personally supervised the education of the young Agrippa II. This information serves to support that provided in the Acts of the Apostles (18:2), when, in Corinth, the apostle Paul meets a Jew named Aquila and his wife, Priscilla, both victims of the expulsion of the disciples of "Chrestos" during Claudius' reign.

Nevertheless, Jewish proselytism continued to be active in Rome and throughout the Mediterranean region. We are familiar with Matthew's outburst against the Pharisees who "compass sea and land to make one proselyte" (23:15). Such missionary zeal spread Judaism to the point that, according to some estimates, nearly one out of ten inhabitants of the Roman Empire (with a population of between six to eight million) was Jewish.[16] "The masses have long since shown a keen desire to adopt our religious observances; and there is not one city, Greek or Barbarian, nor a single nation, to which our custom of abstaining from work on the seventh day has not spread, and where the fasts and the lighting of lamps and many of our prohibitions in the matter of food are not observed" (*AA*, II, 282).

The spread of Jewish customs Josephus describes does not necessarily entail actual conversions. Many of the pagans who were drawn to Judaism hovered on the threshold of commitment (later they were called "doorway proselytes"). Without submitting to either the circumcision or baptism necessary for conversion, they observed those rites to which they were attracted, most likely the ones Josephus mentions. They were referred to as "God-fearing" folk (*metuentes* in Latin). Not having made any irrevocable commitment, they could always back away if they found that they lacked "the necessary endurance" (*AA*, II, 123). On the other hand, Pauline preaching, which encountered considerable resistance among born Jews, was very favorably received by these half-proselytes after the Church of Jerusalem ceased insisting that the faithful undergo circumcision and observe the dietary laws.

Josephus reports one of the better-known conversions in the first half of the first century, that of Helena, queen of Adiabene, and her son Izates (*JA*, XX, 17-52). The missionary who had converted them need not necessarily have been a priest or rabbi—in this instance he was an ordinary merchant named Ananias, who, having access to the royal gynaeceum, converted the wives of King Izates, Helena's son, to monotheism prior to converting Izates himself. Izates then demanded to be circumcised, against the advice of both his mother and Ananias, who feared an uprising of the pagan population. However, a second Jew, Eleazar of Galilee, expressed a contrary opinion, and the king was duly circumcised. His elder brother Monobazius, who succeeded him, also became a convert. It was he who ordered built in Jerusalem the monumental tomb for Helena and Izates today known as the "Tomb of the Kings." This episode serves to demonstrate that Judaism often found a response first from women, who did not have to take circumcision into account. Throughout the Diaspora many women who had married Jews, in Antioch or Alexandria, for example, were converted. Josephus refers to the noblewoman Fulvia in the Rome of Tiberius as a true Jewish proselyte (*JA*, XVIII, 82).

The case of Poppaea is murkier. Josephus does not employ the word "proselyte" when referring to her. Writing about the intervention of the Jewish envoys sent to Nero by the procurator Festus, Josephus tells us that the emperor "showed favor to his wife, Poppaea, who was a worshipper of God and who pleaded on behalf of the Jews" (*JA*, XX, 195). The Greek word he employs, *theosebes,* can be understood to mean that she had accepted monotheism; Poppaea is therefore generally considered to have been a Judaist. If such be the case, all the Jewish delegations to Rome prior to the year 65, the date of her death, knew that they could count on her support. Josephus appears to have had prior knowledge of her sympathy, since he addressed her, through Aliturus. And he was not disappointed: "Through him I was introduced to Poppaea, Caesar's consort, and took the earliest opportunity of soliciting her and to secure the liberation of the priests. Having, besides this favor, received large gifts from Poppaea, I returned to my own country" (*L* 16).

THE ACCOUNT OF A VOYAGE AND A MISSION

We can imagine how proud the young Josephus must have been on his return from Rome around the year 65. At an age at which it was unusual (in antiquity as well as in our own day) to be named an ambassador, he had been chosen to undertake a politico-humanitarian mission to the capital of the Empire. After a dangerous journey he had immediately managed to knock on all the right doors; through his diplomatic skills he had been brought into contact with the empress Poppaea and had obtained even more than he had thought to ask ("large gifts" is all he says, without being more precise). He returned at once to Jerusalem accompanied by the two released priests, men older than himself and whom he venerated; had they not fed throughout their captivity on nothing but figs and nuts to avoid coming into contact with any impure food?[17] So Josephus quite rightly looked forward to being greeted as a hero, if not by the general populace at least by members of his own class, whose opinion meant the most to him. He must have dreamed of becoming the Romans' privileged spokesman in Judea, someone who would smooth out the inevitable problems when they arose and perhaps manage to ameliorate the life of his compatriots living under Roman domination.

It was a domination he did not expect to end soon. His trip must have opened his eyes and convinced him of Rome's power. The words of the prophets were still valid, of course, and the era of the Messiah would surely follow upon that of this world. Verily, as the prophet Daniel had foretold, a stone would smite the image with its golden head, silver breast and arms, belly of brass and legs of iron, but this last Empire seemed more solidly installed than the others, "through its iron nature, which, he said, is harder than that of gold or silver or bronze" (*JA*, X, 209).

Josephus had obviously been as dazzled as any young man from the provinces by his visit to the largest city of the known world. Rabbis less well disposed toward Rome than he have handed down to future generations impressions to which the Talmud has given the hue of legend: the sounds of the capital could be heard from a hundred and twenty miles away; its buildings were of unheard-of height; it had countless baths and markets; and its storehouses contained enough food to feed the entire world.[18] Yes, Jerusalem did have a universally admired Temple, magnificent palaces, impregnable walls, but this traveler returning to his native city could not have helped but notice its smallness, its crowded conditions—without necessarily losing his affection for it thereby —just as he must have been struck by the smallness of Judea, which had not been any more able to escape Rome's appetite than had its neighbors.

Nor could one's pride at being the possessor of a religion vastly superior to the vulgar paganism of the dominators remain completely unshaken. If the idolaters had been allowed to gain sway over the entire world, it must have been done in accordance with some divine plan: who makes and unmakes empires, if not the Lord? Thus, the empire would endure as long as God willed it should, always bearing in mind the fact that its power was but ephemeral and illusory and that the turn of Israel, as the most just of nations, would come at some future day. This Jewish doctrine, which is contained in a great deal of later rabbinical literature, was surely being developed at the time and must have attracted Josephus.

But still, it was a doctrine that called for patience and that posited a possible *modus vivendi*. It is likely that this was Josephus' inner conviction upon his return from Rome. During his absence, however, new local confrontations had occurred, and in the year 65, war was at the gates.

IV

GOVERNOR OF GALILEE

*The two Galilees have always resisted any hostile inva-
sion . . . for never did the men lack courage nor the country men.*

THE JEWISH WAR III, 42

When he returned from his mission in the year 65, Josephus was certainly not a partisan of a confrontation with Rome. Had he not benefited from the support of the imperial court? Had he not been impressed by the number of his coreligionists resident in the world's capital? Yet, in but a few months, he was to find himself not only caught up in the war against Rome but entrusted with a heavy responsibility—the command over all of Galilee and the region of Golan.

In later years he was to feel such an imperative need to justify his actions at this time of his life that his attempts to do so have made him somewhat suspect ever since. Nine-tenths of his autobiography is devoted to the few short months during which he exercised the functions of governor-general of Galilee in 66–67. Nor does the autobiography relate the conclusion of his tenure, which we know from the *War*—the siege of Jotapata, which culminated in Josephus, as commander, surrendering to the Roman general Vespasian.

The great number of details about this period is even more baffling because Josephus gave us two parallel narratives (a twenty–year gap between the two)—one in the *War* and the other in the autobiography, the first written in the third person and the latter in the first—that differ in some very important respects. Which is true? And might there be a third truth? In his overeagerness to justify himself, Josephus opened the door to the historian's worst enemy: a doubting posterity.

"THE JUDEAN WAR IS INEVITABLE . . ."

During Nero's reign (54–68 C.E.), Judea had been inflicted with a series of procurators—Felix, Albinus, and particularly the last in the series, Florus. If there is one point on which Josephus never contradicts himself, it is his description of the evil role played by the procurator Florus who, he tells us, "constrained us to take up war with the Romans, for we preferred to perish together rather than by degrees" (*JA* XX, 257).

In Caesarea, the large modern port city built by Herod, relations between Jews and Greeks, which had been shaky for some time, had now begun to worsen. When acting as arbiter in a dispute that had broken out shortly after the death of Poppaea, in the year 65, Nero had found in favor of the Greeks against the Jews. Florus, the procurator of Judea, took his cue from this decision and began to flout the most elementary tenets of the Law. Avid for gain, he was no longer content with the bribes he could extort from petitioners and began to dip into the Temple treasury. The people of Jerusalem reacted with scathing witticism and suggested a charitable fund be set up for the unfortunate procurator. This fairly harmless quip was met with immediate repression: soldiers charged into the crowd, massacre and pillage ensued. The famous Berenice, sister of Agrippa II, who happened to be in Jerusalem at the time in fulfillment of a vow, risked her life to intercede with Florus, but in vain. Her brother, sent as mediator by Cestius, the governor of Syria, attempted to calm his excited coreligionists. He delivered a long speech in Jerusalem, and Josephus' rewritten version of it obviously reflects his own opinions: "Admittedly, the Roman officials were intolerably harsh. That does not mean that all the Romans, including the emperor, will exploit you. The same procurator will not remain in his post forever. Why should you so protest at being the slaves of men who have conquered the entire world!

What army do you have? The only refuge is in God, but that too depends on the Romans, for without God Rome could never had realized such an empire" (*JW* II, 352).

Josephus must have relied on similar arguments many times during the troubled period that followed his return to Jerusalem. "I accordingly endeavored to repress these promoters of sedition and to bring them over to another frame of mind. I urged them to picture themselves the nation on which they were about to make war, and to remember that they were inferior to the Romans, not only in military skill but in good fortune; and I warned them not recklessly and with such utter madness to expose their country, their families and themselves to the direst perils" (*L* 17-18).

That is the analysis of a true political mind. Like King Agrippa, Josephus knew what Rome's power really was; he had recently seen it with his own eyes in the capital. Thus, while loathing Florus as much as did his compatriots, he tried to do all that he could to avoid a confrontation whose outcome would be disastrous. "There may be some who imagine that the war will be fought under special terms, and that the Romans, when victorious, will treat you with consideration; on the contrary, to make you an example of the rest of the nations, they will burn the Holy City to the ground and exterminate your race. Even the survivors will find no place of refuge, since all the peoples of the earth either have, or dread the thought of having, the Romans for their masters," he has Agrippa say (*JW* II, 397).

The machine had been set in motion, and it was already too late for anyone to stop it. In quick succession the moderate leaders learned that a group of Sicarii had driven the Romans out of Herod's fortress at Masada and retaken it and that a handful of young priests had decided to stop the practice, dating from the time of Augustus, of offering sacrifices in the Temple (at imperial expense) in honor of the emperor (*JW* II, 408-109). Obviously, Rome could not let such challenges go unpunished.

And there were plenty of purely human causes for the war that broke out in the year 66: there were the hotheads created by the "fourth philosophy," there were the taxes levied by the latest procurators, there was Nero's unfair arbitration of the Judeo-Pagan confrontation, there was the insult to the emperor and his chosen official.

Although Josephus mentions these reasons and emphasizes their importance, it is plain that for him there is another reason, one more important than all the others, one that makes historical analysis essentially nugatory, namely: Fate. Like most thinking men in ancient times, Josephus believed in Fate . . . with the one great difference that his Jewish piety led him to confuse Fate with the divine will, to view it as a kind of Providence. In retrospect, he was to reach the conclusion that the war had actually been ordained by God, that the Lord had permitted it. How could an event of such scope, an event that was to engulf and destroy His earthly capital, have occurred without His consent?

And indeed, there had been no lack of celestial warnings prior to the tragedy. But humans in their folly had been blind to them, had not known how to interpret them, and the catastrophe had been inevitable. Thus, as a good disciple of the Pharisees, Josephus sought to reconcile divine providence and human freedom. Once the tragedy was over, he was to recall all those signs that had so clearly predicted it. In the sky over Jerusalem had appeared a comet shaped like a sword that had shone for a whole year; in the Passover season preceding the outbreak of hostilities the Altar had been surrounded by an intense light for a half hour, a cow had given birth to a lamb within the Temple itself, and the Eastern Gate, which twenty men had difficulty closing, had opened of itself at the sixth hour of the night; shortly after the feast men had seen a heavenly battle in the setting sun (*JW* VI, 288-298).

Although the more optimistic might have been able to interpret such ambiguous signs favorably, there were two that were not equivocal at all: As the priests were entering the Temple courtyard to hold their service during the feast of Shavuot (the Pentecost), they heard a great disturbance and voices crying "Let us leave this place." It was the sound of the *Shekhina* (the Immanent Radiance of the Divine Presence) abandoning its home and leaving it vulnerable and unprotected (*JW* VI, 299). Report of this omen traveled as far as Rome, where at the end of the century Tacitus was to mention it with malicious delight, expressing his surprise that "that nation, as inimical to other religions as it was superstitious," had not seen fit to conjure away the bad luck "by vows or expiatory victims" (*Histories* V, 13).

Even more terrifying in Josephus' memory were the lamentations of an innocent—Jesus son of Ananias—who, four years before the war, i.e., before there had been anything to fear, had shouted out in the Temple in the midst of the Feast of Tabernacles, "A voice from the east, a voice from the west, a voice from the four winds; a voice against Jerusalem and the sanctuary, a voice against the bridegroom and the bride, a voice against all the people" (*JW* VI, 301). To any Jew, those words contained a clear echo of Jeremiah's awful prophecy: "Then I will cause to cease from the cities of Judah, and from the streets of Jerusalem, the voice of mirth, and the voice of gladness, the voice of the bridegroom, and the voice of the bride: for the land shall be desolate" (Jeremiah, 7:34).

The poor innocent, a pitiful prophet of doom, had roamed day and night through the streets of the city, crying out. Josephus mentions him as a familiar sight, and he must himself have often encountered this poor simpleton, known to all, treated roughly by some and with charity by others. It is perhaps to such a character that we owe the emergence in the Talmud of a new notion: Now that there were no longer any prophets in Israel, the gift of prophecy had passed to the simpleminded and to children. Although flogged to the bare bone by the Romans, Jesus son of Ananias still persisted in crying out the only thing he knew: "Woe to Jerusalem!" Then, in the midst of festive days, did his cry ring out. Josephus viewed as proof that God himself was speaking through his oracle the fact that "for seven years and five months he continued his wail, his voice never flagging nor his strength exhausted" (*JW* VI, 308). In the year 70, during the siege of Jerusalem, the same innocent was back wandering about the ruined ramparts and lamenting, "Woe once more to the city and to the people and to the Temple!" And at the moment he cried out his last word: "And woe to me also!" he was struck down by a stone hurled from the ballista and killed on the spot (*J W* VI, 300–309).

The voice of reason told Josephus, fresh from Rome, that in political terms the war was madness. The voice of the oracles—if, indeed, he really listened to them as he tried to make posterity believe—told him that it was an even greater folly, but around him things continued to go on as though God were warning of disaster and giving fools free rein.

This, to explain why, in the midst of the bellicose excitement he could feel mounting on all sides, Josephus opted for a far from glorious way out: "I now feared that my incessant reiteration of this warning would bring me into odium and the suspicion of siding with the enemy, and that I should run the risk of being arrested by them and put to death. I therefore sought asylum in the inner court of the Temple; the fortress of Antonia being already in their hands" (L 20).

FATAL SUCCESS

In the meantime, the partisans of peace at any price were attempting to counteract the underground maneuverings of the revolutionaries. They found an ally in King Agrippa II, who promptly dispatched troops to Jerusalem. Once there, they occupied the Upper City, where the palace-fortress built by Herod was located. During the week preceding the Feast of the Xylophora[1] in the year 66 they opened battle against the insurgents who were occupying the Lower City and the Temple, where some young priests had launched the insurrection.

The feast day saw victory for the insurgents, who, in an attempt to win popular favor, set fire to the archives containing the records of indebtedness. On the following day they succeeded in investing the Antonia Fortress, to the north of the Temple, which was held by a Roman garrison. This was the moment Josephus chose to take refuge in the Inner Temple. What he purports to have been merely an act of prudence can be interpreted as a rallying to the side of the war party, which was headquartered in the Temple at the time. Josephus' subsequent connection with the war is probably due to this misunderstanding.

The civil war reached into the very sanctuary of the Temple itself. A certain Menahem (a descendant of Judah the Galilean), who was already in control of the fortress at Masada, had now come to give the Jerusalem insurgents a hand. However, Menahem had also committed the first murder in this merciless struggle by having the high priest Ananias and his brother, Ezechias, who had rallied the royal troops, put to death. The priest Eleazar, the actual leader of the uprising, grew increasingly impatient at the attempts that were being made to replace him. Menahem even went so far as to ascend to the Temple dressed in royal robes, symbolizing his desire for power. He and his followers were caught in a torrent of stones thrown by Eleazar's partisans. A few managed to escape the city and make their way back to Masada, but some, including Menahem himself, were executed (*JW* II, 433-448).

From inside the Temple, where he had taken refuge, Josephus could now foresee the fratricidal dimensions of a war he had never wanted.

According to Josephus' account the early military successes of the insurgents created an intoxication that was to lead to catastrophe. In a few short days a handful of hotheads, who had armed themselves with whatever they could lay their hands on, had managed to force the capitulation of the royal troops, followed by those of the Roman garrison, who were massacred. Two months later, Cestius Gallus, governor of Syria, who had finally been alerted, marched on Jerusalem; he suffered a number of reverses *en route* and finally, despairing of being able to retake the city as easily as he had hoped, he beat a retreat and let his army be cut to pieces. It was a brilliant victory for the Jewish combatants, who had suffered very few losses while accounting for nearly six thousand dead among the Roman ranks and amassing an enormous booty of redoubtable and fearful engines of war (*JW* II, 553-555).

The clear-sightedness upon which Josephus prides himself, all the while deploring this lamentable victory, is very like an optical illusion after the fact, one of which he himself may have been the first victim. In fact, his position at the heart of events is far from clear. It even appears that he may have purposely acted in an ambiguous manner in order to avoid falling victim to one of the two camps.

Rejoining the Pharisee notables after Menahem's execution, he was no less embarrassed than they at the decision now facing them. To go against the insurgents was to invite execution; the most one could hope was to calm their militant ardor and wait for the Romans to force them to adopt a more reasonable course, which seemed inevitable. Looking back on the events, Josephus states that he and his friends were counting on Cestius' victory to restore order: "We had hopes that ere long Cestius would come up with a large army and quell the revolution" (L 23).

Thus, far from feeling proud of his people's victory over an enemy who was technologically far superior, Josephus bemoans the illusion of power the victory had instilled in the insurgents: in the normal course of events, Cestius should have won and the war been over in the first months of the uprising, November of the year 66. The insane notion that the insurgent movement might actually have a chance of success had caused the fighting to drag on for more than three years, at the price of incalculable misery. Josephus eventually came to believe that these early military successes, which had been almost unbelievable given the balance of forces involved, were evidence of the hand of God meting out punishment to his impious people: "But God, I suppose, because of those miscreants, had already turned away even from His sanctuary and ordained that that day should not see the end of the war" (JW II, 539).

Following Cestius' disastrous defeat, "many distinguished Jews abandoned the city as swimmers desert a sinking ship" (JW II, 556). Those Josephus cites by name were overt partisans of King Agrippa. As for Josephus, he had elected to remain in Jerusalem even though it was obvious that the war was going to go on with even greater ferocity. Perhaps, in spite of what he says, he had begun to believe that Rome could indeed be defeated, or perhaps he had merely given in to the prevailing exultant mood: "Those who were bent on war were thereby still more elated and, having once defeated the Romans, hoped to continue victorious to the end" (L 24).

And even he admits that "those bent on war" were extremely persuasive: "The Jews who had pursued Cestius, on their return to Jerusalem, partly by force, partly by persuasion, brought over to their side such pro-Romans as still remained" (JW II, 62).

Josephus, who clearly had not wanted war in the beginning, kept his profound misgivings and apprehensions to himself for a time and apparently allowed himself to be won over by the contagious high spirits of his compatriots. How else explain his acceptance of the command of Galilee, a key region, when it was offered to him by the rebels?

JOSEPHUS' MISSION IN GALILEE

By joining the rebel cause, Josephus achieved something very difficult to refuse when one is barely thirty years old, namely, power.

Clear as the purpose of his mission in Galilee seems from a reading of the *War,* the account he gives in his autobiography, written twenty years later with, as we know, an eye to self-justification, is fairly hazy. The earlier narrative, written with less confusion, is therefore clearly preferable to the later.

Josephus' duties were at once administrative, judicial, and military, evidence that the rebels had entrusted him with the powers hitherto exercised by the Roman prefect. Clearly, then, his mission was hostile to Rome. Up until now, we have dealt only with the situation in Jerusalem. The state of the rest of the country and surrounding regions was no less disturbing. Since the establishment of Roman dominion the old rivalries between Jews and pagans had grown sharper in all the cities with mixed populations, from Alexandria to Damascus, and including the coastal cities attached to the province of Syria and those in Cisjordan. Upon learning of the events that had taken place in Jerusalem, the pagans in many of these cities drew the conclusion that Rome now regarded their Jewish fellow citizens as veritable outlaws and that there was thus very little to stop them from massacring them. Caesarea, where intercommunal conflict had become especially bitter, managed to rid itself of its Jews "in less than an hour" (*JW* II, 457).

In Alexandria a confrontation between Jews and Greeks had degenerated into a bloody riot, and Tiberius Alexander, the then Prefect of Egypt, had fifty thousand of his former coreligionists massacred by the army (*JW* II, 487-498). In Damascus, 10,500 unarmed Jewish males assembled in a gymnasium were massacred unbeknownst to their wives, most of whom were converts. Elsewhere, the Jews destroyed the pagan cities, but at Scythopolis (Beth-Shan) those who had not hesitated to take up arms against their coreligionists who were laying siege to the city were later to be slaughtered by the pagans they had been assisting (*JW* II, 466-476). Thus, Galilee was surrounded with hostile cities that had rid themselves of their Jewish inhabitants by the end of the summer or autumn of 66. And to the east of the Lake of Tiberias lay the lands of King Agrippa II, who was still loyal to the Romans.

On his way from Antioch—the seat of the governor of Syria—to Jerusalem, where he had hoped to crush the uprising, Cestius Gallus had secured Galilee. Sepphoris, the capital of the Jewish-populated region, had hailed the arrival of his troops, while Rome's enemies had taken to the hills. When Josephus arrived, the city was to all appearances a pro-Roman enclave in a region rife with insurrection. Three parties were faced off against each other in Tiberias, one of which was openly favorable to Rome.

The indications are that Josephus had been entrusted by the faction in power in Jerusalem to raise the territory as a whole against Rome. The region was divided geographically into two parts, Lower and Upper Galilee, to which was added the impregnable fortress of Gamala in the Golan. According to Josephus' second and more enigmatic account of his mission, he was to persuade "the brigands"—that is, those who had gone into hiding—to "lay down their arms" and use them solely against important members of the population (*L* 29) or "to ensure peace in Galilee"(*L* 78). More probably, Josephus had been entrusted with bringing under his command all the disparate groups that had sprung up spontaneously. Nor does this aspect of his mission contradict the other. Indeed, he had first to establish his authority over an area in which anarchy was fast gaining a foothold, and this was all the more urgent in that Galilee, which abutted directly onto the Roman province of Syria, would in all likelihood be the first to be attacked.

ORGANIZATION OF THE TERRITORY

In carrying out his unifying mission Joseph was to rely on persuasion rather than force: indeed, this was an immutable part of his character. Above all, he tells us, he tried to win the affection of the Galileans, and his account of how he went about it is not entirely devoid of vanity.

Aware that he was a newcomer to the region and fearful of not being accepted owing to his youth—he was only twenty-nine years old—he decided to concentrate on the local notables, win them over to his side, and then, with their help, persuade the rest of the population to follow. He began by appointing a council of seventy Galileans selected from among a group of mature men known for their good judgment. This council, a kind of local Sanhedrin over which he himself presided (thereby making up the total seventy-one members required under Jewish law), exercised administrative and judiciary functions. All important matters, including criminal proceedings, were brought before it. Josephus took particular care to maintain friendly relations with the members of this council so as to control the rest of the region through them (*L* 79).

Above all, Josephus strove to organize the territory's defenses—indeed, such was his primary task. He fortified the cities and larger towns. He supervised this work personally, both assisting in and directing the operations (*JW* II, 575). He also saw to laying in supplies of corn and arms "for their future security" (*L* 188). In all Galilee he managed to raise an army of one hundred thousand young men. The region was a fertile and densely populated one—the smallest town had at least fifteen thousand inhabitants—and its men were famous for their strength and their bravery in combat. However, Josephus was not unaware that in one area the Roman army was unmatchable: its organization. Knowing the enemy he was to face, he tried to organize his army "as much like the Roman as possible." He set up a complex military hierarchy, taught his troops the elements of military tactics, and tried to instill them with a rigorous discipline.

Where had Josephus learned the art of war? On this he is silent. True, in those days any young, healthy man was a potential soldier, just as any nobleman was expected to be a leader of troops. To a large extent Josephus owed his post to his social status, but he may also have owed it to the knowledge he had gained by observing the workings of the Roman army, a knowledge he could have displayed to others in Jerusalem prior to assuming his command. Indeed, he gives a precise and lucid description of this army that is equaled only by the one provided by the Greek historian Polybius, who, writing a century before Josephus, was also attempting to understand the inner workings of the power that had conquered his homeland.

Thus, Josephus mustered a considerable army (60,000 foot soldiers and 350 cavalrymen, plus 4,500 mercenaries and 600 personal bodyguards) without having to disorganize the cities, in which a part of the able-bodied population was made responsible for supplying food to all, civilian and military.

If Josephus actually behaved as he says he did, why then did so many suspicions about him begin to spring up at this time? Was it really only because, at barely thirty years of age, "it is hard, especially in a position of high authority, to escape the calumnies of envy" (L 80)?

THE TIME OF SUSPICION

Proud of his name, his title, and his status as Jerusalem's representative in that agricultural province, Josephus expected to rally all of Galilee to his side. But in defense of what cause? Throughout this period, he describes himself as the Romans' adversary, but did he ever really seriously plan to go against them? Once away from the fanatical atmosphere of Jerusalem, which had caused him to be given his command, did he perhaps begin to have doubts? In any event, he did not behave as expected, and he quickly began to arouse suspicions.

As he relays them to us, the orders received from Jerusalem could not have been more imprecise: "They advised me to remain at my post and take precautions for Galilee, retaining my colleagues, if willing to stay" (L 62). Given the circumstances, it is difficult to understand why his first move turned out to be that of a religious fanatic: he set out to raze the palace of the tetrarch Herod on the pretext that it contained "representations of living things," forbidden by Jewish law. To do this, he seems to have needed the authorization of the Council in Tiberias, and he made every effort to persuade its members that the operation was necessary. While the pro-Roman party, which favored the Herodian family, was reticent, the anti-Roman faction quickly fell in with Josephus' plans and, after having pillaged the palace, set fire to the structure. Josephus, furious at this precipitate act, quickly took steps to lay hands on the booty, which he discreetly turned over to the pro-Roman notables with the intention, he tells us, of returning it later to King Agrippa II, the legal owner of the pillaged goods. Was his fury due only to moral scruples?

There is a similar account of another incident that occurred shortly afterward. Some young men from Dabaritta had ambushed the wife of a certain Ptolemy, one of Agrippa II's lieutenants. Proud of their exploit against the opposing party, they brought the booty to the governor-general as a prize of war, expecting to receive some reward in return. They were dumbfounded when Josephus preached morality to them (Jewish law forbade plunder, even of one's enemies) and refused to give them even the smallest part of the booty, maintaining that the money must go to reinforce the ramparts in Jerusalem. Even Josephus, however, admits that such was not the case, for the fruits of their kidnapping were secretly handed over to notables who were close friends of King Agrippa II. Although the secret of the exchange was well guarded, word began to spread through the villages around Tiberias that the young governor sent from Jerusalem was a traitor. In both these instances, then, although purportedly inspired by religious scruples, Josephus was really acting in the interests of King Agrippa II, who was still allied with Rome.

Similar behavior created a breach between Josephus and a well-known figure in the region, John of Gischala, who was to become his implacable enemy. John had wanted to take control of the imperial corn stored in the region in order to sell it and use the money to rebuild the walls of his city with the money. Faced with Josephus' firm refusal, he applied to the two priests from Jerusalem who had accompanied him, obtained their agreement—by bribing them—and acted counter to the instructions of Josephus . . . who, at one against two, was obliged to give in. But what did the governor-general of Galilee want with this corn? "As the authority entrusted to me by the Jerusalem authorities extended to that district, I intended to reserve the corn either for the Romans or for my own use" (L 72). An admission of treason? It is not that simple. In that early organizational period Josephus was obviously not eager to enter into conflict with the Roman army; the confiscation of the imperial corn gave the governor of Syria a pretext for intervening in Galilee. The formulation "reserve the corn for the Romans" is suspicious, but we must not forget that Josephus, who was writing about the event thirty years later in Rome, may have had some reason for altering the motive of his actions after the fact.

Aware that he had aroused John's suspicions by his first refusal, Josephus was nevertheless obliged to provide him with the means to fight by agreeing to go along with what he describes as a "base" dealing. Oil cost ten times less in Gischala, a region of olive trees, than it did in Caesarea Philippi. Since in those days the Jews refused to use the pagan's oil of unction, which was deemed impure, the Jews of Caesarea Philippi ordered some from John, who was making a considerable profit thereby, to Josephus' immense chagrin. On the surface there was nothing wrong with the transaction, but years later Josephus was still enraged by it. If he allowed it to occur, he writes, it was "for fear of being stoned by the mob if I withheld it" (L 76). In fact, it was easy for John to rouse the people against a leader they already suspected of treason.

Although he maintains that he was constantly being assured of the people's favor, there were several occasions on which Josephus nearly perished because of the Galileans. After the Dabaritta affair, the perpetrators, furious at Josephus' reaction, had gone around the countryside rousing the populace against the "traitor." Their suspicions matched John's, as well as those of the anti-Roman party in Tiberias, which was led by the city's archon, Jesus son of Saphias. Overnight, the coalition managed to assemble a hundred thousand armed men in the city of Taricheae, where Josephus was then residing.

While Josephus slept, his personal bodyguards and soldiers were summoned to the hippodrome where, in the absence of the accused, a kind of impromptu trial for treason was being held. Jesus son of Saphias was the most assiduous prosecutor. Brandishing a scroll of the Torah, he invoked the interests of the fatherland and respect for the faith. The popular verdict was unanimous: death to the traitor! The only disagreements were on the method of execution: should Josephus be stoned or burned alive? The second solution was probably the one preferred (at least by the most fanatical, led by Jesus), for Josephus was awakened at dawn to find that his house had been set afire.[2] Although Simon, his faithful bodyguard, urged him to kill himself (the only death worthy of a general), he instead gave a striking demonstration of his principal quality, the key to his survival throughout all this tumultuous period, namely, an extraordinary presence of mind.

Determined to stake everything on one throw, Josephus dressed himself as a penitent (black robes, according to one version; torn clothing, head strewn with ashes, according to another). Wearing a sword hung round his neck, he took an indirect route to the place of trial, the hippodrome, where his unexpected appearance created a sensation. Prostrating himself, weeping, he showed all the signs of immense contrition. Some were immediately moved; hoping to turn the fickle crowd in his favor, Josephus then asked to speak: Yes, he had sequestered the precious articles stolen by the young men from Dabaritta, but he had never intended to return them to their rightful owner; no, he had set them aside to pay for the building of a rampart at Taricheae: "If this does not meet your approval, I am prepared to produce what was brought to me and leave you to plunder it; if, on the contrary, I have consulted your best interests, do not punish your benefactor" (*JW* II, 607).

The tense silence that had accompanied his speech was followed by a wild uproar. Josephus had won: the grateful people of Taricheae had come over to his side; the crowd was now divided.

In order to win over the rest of the Galileans, their governor-general promised that they too would have new ramparts. Sensing that he was regaining the advantage, Josephus even went so far as to reproach the crowd, which an instant before had been calling for his death, for being so precipitate. He then persuaded the people to disperse and return to their homes. A few diehards (six hundred or two thousand, according to the version) remained unconvinced and returned to surround his house.

Once again Josephus gave proof of his prime quality—let us give it the same name he does, with no hint of the pejorative: guile or cunning. Throughout antiquity (we need only think of Ulysses), cunning is synonymous with intelligence—thus Josephus' propensity to brag about his cleverness. Barricaded in his house, he addressed the besiegers from the roof: they wanted to recover the booty? Then let them send someone in to get it! "The most enterprising of them" was delegated to do so, but a while later he was returned to his friends in pitiable condition: he had been flogged to the bone and sent back with one of his own severed hands hung around his neck.[3] The mob, cowed, withdrew.[4]

The quarrel with John soon turned into open war. Assured of the support of Gischala, his birthplace, John attempted to raise Tiberias, Galilee's largest city, against Josephus; of the three parties vying for power in Tiberias, two were already hostile to the young governor sent from Jerusalem. Ignoring the anti-Roman party led by Jesus son of Saphias, Josephus in his writings attacks the leader of the second party, Justus son of Pistos, with unparalleled violence, maintaining that by pretending to be hesitant about entering into the conflict, he had been hoping to take advantage of the situation to seize power for himself. To make things worse, Justus (as we shall see) was later to commit the crime of writing his own history of the war, one that did not completely agree with Josephus' version. (That work, like so many others, has disappeared, and its loss is most unfortunate for the objectivity of our data.)

John, who had not so far come out openly against Josephus, now asked for (and easily obtained) permission to go to Tiberias to take the waters, and in two days there he fomented his plans. As soon as he had been informed of John's activities by his own representative in the city, Josephus set out for Tiberias by forced march. As Josephus prepared to address the populace in the stadium, John's henchmen surged toward him. Warned by the shouts of the crowd, Josephus on this occasion owed his life to his own physical prowess: from the knoll on which he was standing he jumped down onto the bank of the lake below, leaped into a boat, and managed to escape with two of his bodyguards.

Now fully aware of John's enmity toward him, Josephus set out to undermine his adversary's credibility with the Galileans. He launched what amounted to a negative publicity campaign against John and, using both persuasion and intimidation, won many over to his side. He even resorted to denunciation: he demanded a list of John's supporters in every city and demanded that those whose names appeared on it either defect to him or have their property confiscated and their houses burned to the ground.

Galilee was now very close to civil war.

THE COMMISSION OF INQUIRY

John, bereft of his troops, decided to appeal directly to Jerusalem. Convinced that the governor-general was not faithfully performing the mission for which he had been appointed, John dispatched to Jerusalem a delegation led by his own brother, Simon, with instructions to make a full report. Josephus maintains that he was accused of being ambitious and aspiring to play a tyrant's role; here, by suggesting a patently absurd grievance, he may be trying to conceal the real complaint made against him, i.e., treason.

John's envoy made an immediate splash in Jerusalem. Instead of addressing the military leaders of the revolt he sought out a universally respected spiritual authority, the Pharisee Simon son of Gamaliel, who was also a friend. Simon, whom we know through the Talmud, was the son of that Gamaliel whom we know as the teacher of Saul of Tarsus, the apostle Paul (Acts 22:3). Although he was certainly not on his side in this affair, Josephus expresses great respect for Simon and pays a tribute to his intelligence, a proof of the unquestioned prestige he enjoyed (*L* 192).

Persuaded by John's report, Simon son of Gamaliel took steps to have Josephus recalled by the high priest Anan, who, with Joseph son of Gorion, wielded supreme power. He did not have an easy time of it: Josephus could rely on wide support in priestly circles and among the important Pharisees. When in the end Anan finally agreed to dismiss him, Josephus tells us, it was because he had been bribed to do so by John's brother.

Fearful, nevertheless, of the hostile reaction of Josephus' followers, the high priest appointed a delegation of four men,[5] two of whom were from priestly families, to look into the activities of the governor-general of Galilee and to ask for his resignation or, if he resisted, to kill him on the spot . . . all in the greatest secrecy. However, the high priest Joshua son of Gamala, who was one of Josephus' oldest friends, was close enough to the seat of power to be informed of everything. He warned Matthias, Josephus' father, who wrote to his son posthaste.

The messenger arrived before the delegation that had been sent. The latter, led by the Pharisee Jonathan, was escorted by six hundred soldiers and a suite of three hundred, not counting the small band accompanying John's brother, an additional hundred armed men.[6] By now, the Commission of Inquiry had begun to take on the appearance of a military expedition; it also had a considerable budget, allocated to it out of public moneys—forty thousand pieces of silver.

Josephus' first reaction was to return at once to Jerusalem to justify his actions, leaving behind the problems that were besetting him on all sides. Events, however, were to take a very different turn: three years were to pass before Josephus would see his native city again, from the camp of its Roman besiegers, and the next time he would enter it he would enter a city in ruins, a city where he knew more of the dead than the living.

What kept Josephus in Galilee? He says it was popular pressure. Hordes of men, women, and children came from throughout the land to beseech him to remain, not out of fondness for him personally, he tells us, but for fear that they would be left without protection: the people believed in him!

The other reason Josephus gives seems even odder to a modern mind, for it is based on a dream, or vision. In fact, the dream was not "visionary" in the true sense of the word, for there was nothing visual about it. It consisted simply of a friendly voice telling Josephus to abandon all fear, promising him success and adding: "Remember that thou must even battle with the Romans" (*L* 209). It was actually more like a moment of inspiration, a lucky notion dressed up as a dream . . . but are dreams not credited with being divine messages? Was the wise counsel given Josephus by his guardian angel merely another ruse born of our author's insomnia? He had gone to bed "upset" and confounded by his father's letter, and in the depths of his sorrow the solution had miraculously emerged. His mission was to protect Galilee against the Romans. Of course he had not managed to do so yet, but he still had a while before the commission from Jerusalem would arrive. When it did, it had to find him deeply engaged in action.

The very next day Josephus assembled five thousand men (including three thousand foot soldiers) and marched on Ptolemais (Acre). What was he trying to provoke? At least the semblance of a confrontation with the Romans, which he had hitherto so carefully avoided.

The port city of Ptolemais was a Hellenistic city populated by pagans and situated in land under Roman control. The governor of Syria had sent a certain Placidus to Ptolemais with two cohorts of infantry and a squadron of cavalry. The city was to serve as a base for attacking the Jewish lands in the interior. Ptolemais was already protected by a trench moat against possible incursions, even though there had never been any sign of such so far. Josephus set up camp a few miles from the city near Chabulon, but he took care not to make his intentions too clear so as not to provoke any enemy response. In fact, his sudden bellicose posturing was less for the benefit of the Romans than for the imminent Commission of Inquiry. He was well aware that the Commission would summon him to come to meet it (which, indeed, it did) and sensed a trap. Following the age-old Hebrew proverb, "Where wine enters, secrets emerge," he managed to get the Commission's envoy drunk and induce him to talk, and upon hearing his words he realized that his suspicions were only too-well founded. Were he to proceed alone to the meeting with Jonathan and his colleagues, he would be seized; if he went with troops, he would be viewed as guilty of high treason. He had, however, a pretext already prepared for disobeying the summons, and he promptly wrote the Commission: "I am here at Chabulon, keeping watch on Placidus, who is meditating an incursion up country into Galilee" (*L* 227).

Much irritated, Jonathan and his friends continued to press Josephus: they summoned him to appear in Gabara within three days, unescorted. Instead of obeying this second order, he set out with three thousand men for the fortress at Jotapata and sent back a firm message: "If you seriously desire me to come to you, there are two hundred and four cities and villages in Galilee. I will come to whichever of these you may select, Gabara and Gischala excepted: the latter being John's native place and the former in league and alliance with him" (*L* 235).

The Commission, seeing that its real intentions had been unmasked, now broke off the correspondence. At John's urging, its members prepared to raise the whole of Galilee against its governor-general. Josephus, who was alerted to these plans by a deserter, intercepted a letter on its way to Jerusalem and discovered that he was to be proclaimed a public enemy. Other missives were intercepted that called upon the towns of Galilee to arm themselves against him.

Taking the initiative, Josephus then began to incite Galilee to rise against the foe. He recruited reinforcements in the villages and proceeded to Gabara surrounded by a large troop of loyal followers. Carefully bypassing the castle where the Commission of Inquiry was awaiting his visit, he only made a pretence of sleeping in camp with his troops. His adversaries attempted to seize this opportunity to rally his troops against him. But Josephus had been keeping a weather eye open, and his unexpected reappearance thwarted the maneuver and allowed him to provide another illustration of one of his prime qualities: eloquence. He had a wonderful ability to sway a crowd: producing the letters he had intercepted, he aroused his audience to great indignation by reading out their contents. In demanding that the Commission of Inquiry proceed according to the rule of law and allow him to call witnesses on his behalf, he was only calling for simple justice; by gaining the applause of the listening Galileans, he was showing the Commission how dangerous it would be to lay hands on such a popular man. Next, he magnanimously protected his adversaries from the aroused mob and offered them a pardon, which they grudgingly accepted.

The least one can say of Josephus on this occasion is that he could well have seized the occasion to wreak vengeance on his foes and that, by mastering his resentment, he avoided civil war. Calming the crowd after having roused it to a frenzy, he led the mob off to another village and prepared to proceed via diplomacy rather than arms. He selected a hundred notables of respectable age and sent them to plead his cause at Jerusalem and to demand the withdrawal of the Commission of Inquiry. There is, however, one disturbing element: to save time, the delegation was instructed to proceed through Samaria, where Josephus had friends to protect it. Now, Samaria was totally under Roman control; the Commission of Inquiry had probably avoided the region, since it had taken several days to get from Jerusalem to Galilee. Josephus' delegation, however, made the trip in the other direction in only three days. Who were these friends entrusted with protecting its security when it crossed Samaria? Another highly suspect detail.

The Commission of Inquiry, for its part, while pretending friendship, did not lay down its arms. Its members, supported by two leaders of local parties, Jesus son of Saphias and Justus son of Pistos, began to try to turn the people of Tiberias against Josephus, taking advantage of the Sabbath when all the faithful were assembled in the synagogue. Warned by his spies, Josephus arrived in Tiberias at dawn the following day, foiling his adversaries' ruse and catching them in the act. He found them publicly accusing him of spending his time carousing and doing nothing to protect Galilee against the imminent Roman attacks. With his usual presence of mind, Josephus once again succeeded in putting his enemies in a bad light: the Romans were attacking the borders at four points; to stop them, he was prepared to entrust the command of a division to Jonathan and his three colleagues on the Commission, while he himself would command a fifth: "It becomes brave men (I urged) to give not merely advice but practical assistance by assuming the lead in an emergency" (L 288).

Having been thus brought up short, Josephus' foes resorted to trickery. One of the members of the Commission proposed that the young Ananias be proclaimed general on the following day. Everyone was to assemble in one place, unarmed, to beseech divine assistance. Suspecting a plot, Josephus went to the synagogue the next day wearing a breastplate and sword beneath his cloak and accompanied by two faithful bodyguards who were also armed with concealed daggers. In the event, of his party only he and his two guards were allowed to enter the precincts. The archon Jesus son of Saphias then attempted to pick a quarrel with Josephus over the booty seized at Dabaritta. Sensing the growing impatience of the assembly, which had no notion of the real purpose of the meeting, Jonathan finally revealed his true intentions. On this occasion Josephus owed his life to his forethought in bringing armed bodyguards.

Fleeing his other enemy, John, who was now on the march in his pursuit, Josephus fled by boat to Taricheae, where he awaited the return of the delegation he had sent to Jerusalem. Its arrival brought the fulfillment of all his hopes: his mandate over Galilee was confirmed, and the Commission of Inquiry was recalled to Jerusalem. Josephus rejoiced and quickly disseminated the decision that had been brought from the capital. At John's instigation, his adversaries, much chagrined, tried one last maneuver. Of the four members of the Commission, two were to remain in Tiberias, where they were in control of the city, and the two others, Jonathan and Ananias, would return to plead their cause in Jerusalem. Josephus managed to intercept them at the southern border of Galilee and take them prisoner. He tricked a third member of the Commission, capturing him in Tiberias itself, and rapidly took over that city after threatening a siege. He does not tell us the number of victims, but this time there had actually been a beginning of civil armed conflict.

Thus, after a dramatic struggle Josephus had finally managed to rid himself of the Commission of Inquiry once and for all.

With the four culprits in chains and at his mercy, he then made the noble gesture of freeing them and dispatching them back to Jerusalem under guard. Confirmed in his post, he would hence-forth have a free hand in Galilee, but the time had now come for him to give proof that he was indeed performing the mission with which he had been entrusted.

FIRST FRUITS OF THE MISSION

For a few months, from the autumn of 66 to the spring of 67, Jose-phus governed Galilee without having any real confrontation with the Romans. Although he tells us how popular he was, his narra-tive of this period serves to demonstrate how shaky that popularity was in fact. He often reveals his need to justify himself by frequent remarks about his moral integrity and humanity:

"Yet I preserved every woman's honor; I scorned all presents offered to me as having no use for them, I even declined to accept from those who brought them the tithes which were due to me as a priest. On the other hand, I did take a portion of the spoils after defeating the Syrian inhabitants of the surrounding cities, and admit to having sent these to my kinsfolk in Jerusalem. And though I took Sepphoris twice by storm, Tiberias four times and Gadara once; and though I had John many times at my mercy when he plotted against me, I punished neither him nor any of the communities I have named, as the course of this narrative will show" (*L* 15).

It is significant that the feats of arms Josephus mentions are all victories against Jewish cities, not against the Romans. And indeed, he had encountered opposition and had not been able to rally to his side Galilee's two largest cities, Tiberias, considered the region's natural capital, and Sepphoris, which had been granted that title in return for its submission to the Romans.

Upon his arrival in the region, Josephus had taken measures to appease Sepphoris, which was under threat from the Galileans because of its pro-Roman stand. The city's inhabitants had sent a band of mercenaries against him, but it was quickly disarmed. They then pretended to join the revolt and to build ramparts against the

Romans, as Josephus had ordered the other fortified cities to do. In reality, they invited Cestius Gallus, the governor of Syria, to come and take possession of the city, or to send them a garrison. Learning that he had been tricked, Josephus attacked the town and occupied it. With an eye to the future, he attempted to save those Sepphorians who had taken refuge in the fortress; seeing that it would be difficult to restrain the fury of his troops, he spread the rumor that the Romans were about to arrive and gave it credence by creating a stampede. Sepphoris was saved, but immediately appealed to the Romans for help again, thus forcing Josephus to make another assault, which earned him but an indecisive and short-lived victory.

The situation in Tiberias was complex and unstable. None of the three parties in the city favored Josephus, which explains why he was forced to take it four times. Upon his arrival the governor-general had found it entangled in the machinations of Justus son of Pistos, a clever demagogue whose veneer of Greek culture made him even more formidable. While Josephus was hoping to avoid any provocative gesture that might have justified a Roman attack, Justus defied him by attacking the pagan towns of Gadara and Hippos, located on the border between Tiberias and Decapolis. Jesus son of Saphias, even more extremist than Justus, had to Josephus' fury burned and pillaged the palace that Herod the tetrarch had built in the region and had then massacred every Greek in Tiberias. These were the two men who were later to support John of Gischala in his attempt to get rid of the governor-general he viewed with such great suspicion.

Josephus, as we have seen, had always handled King Agrippa with kid gloves. After the pillaging of Herod's palace, he had turned what royal possessions he had been able to save over to Tiberian notables partial to the king. Nevertheless, the city twice rose against Josephus and went over to the king. On the first occasion, aware of his numerical inferiority, Josephus resorted to trickery. He made a show of arriving in force: the lake was filled with his ships, but they all kept a careful distance from shore to conceal the fact that they were empty (*JW* II, 635-637). Josephus, sailing forward on one of them, managed to capture six hundred members of the Council and two thousand other citizens without firing a shot and carry them off to Taricheae. Clitos, who had been largely responsible for the defection and who now realized that he would not escape punishment, elected to cut off his left hand himself (*JW* II, 644).

Some time later, the city once again attempted to go over to Agrippa II. Josephus learned of it from an intercepted letter. On this occasion, his indulgence to the arrested royal messenger reveals his desire for conciliation: after imprisoning him as a matter of form, he then personally helped him to escape.

However, confrontation with the royal troops became inevitable. Josephus began by sending his lieutenant, Jeremios, accompanied by two thousand soldiers, to the town of Julias, on the northernmost edge of Lake Tiberias, where the king's army had set up camp. On his arrival the following day, Josephus once again preferred ruse to a head-on battle and succeeded in ambushing and routing the enemy without undue bloodshed. Josephus had good reason for avoiding combat. His horse had fallen in a swampy area and he had broken his wrist. He had to be carried to Capharnaum, where he spent a day confined to bed with a fever. When night fell, the doctors allowed him to be moved back to his headquarters in Taricheae (*L* 404). Thus ended what had been one of the most serious military engagements of his campaign so far.

Notwithstanding all Josephus' efforts to depict his actions in a favorable light, the net result of these few months is wholly negative. Not only had he not been able to unify the region under his command, he had even provoked new divisions. He had aroused fierce enmity, escaped several assassination attempts, and had managed to retain his position thanks only to friends in high places. His only victory had been a purely personal one, although political in nature: he had managed to remove John from a position in which he could have injured him by getting rid of the Commission of Inquiry he had had created. John, who had gone to ground in Gischala and been deserted by part of his troops, was left to sit "completely cowed, in his native town" (*L* 372). And Josephus had won this victory not against the clique hostile to the rebellion, which he was supposed to win over, but within what was theoretically his own camp.

What was that camp? Thanks to Josephus' ambiguous
behavior, the question was being asked all over Galilee. There were
several reasons for his ambiguity. First, there is his own interpretation of his mission. For him, as we have seen, it was not so much to
wage war as to "keep peace in Galilee." Peace, first, meant domestic
peace and preventing confrontations between Jews and attacks by
armed bands against the pagan population—anything, in short, that
might work against order and unity. Peace meant refraining for as
long as possible from provoking intervention on the part of Rome
or its allies. Josephus' only role was to protect the territory under
his jurisdiction—for example, by fortifying the cities to dissuade
possible future attacks—and thus purely defensive, and, indeed, he
was far too familiar with Roman power to take the offensive.

Clearly, his personal enemies, like John, reproached him
with a degree of spinelessness, which they soon began to regard as
treason. Minds inflamed with an almost-mystical ardor were unable
to understand the temporizing tactics of a prudent and calculating
mind. "What man is wise? He who can foresee the consequences."[7]
Josephus appears to have taken the Talmudic maxim very much to
heart.

Nor was Josephus seen as being unduly zealous during the
military operations in which he did engage his enemies in Galilee.
On numerous occasions he preferred trickery to armed struggle.
However, in this instance the charge of cowardice seems a bit exag-
gerated. Josephus explains his motives on several occasions: his mission was not to foment civil war and shed Jewish blood, his first
duty was to protect his compatriots, whatever their current position. It is for those reasons that he called a halt as soon as possible
to the battles he was sometimes compelled to wage against them;
he preferred to order one person's hand chopped off to set an
example than to engage in a wholesale slaughter of his opponents;
never was he to execute an adversary who had fallen into his hands.

As for his circumspection toward King Agrippa II, there is a
further but unstated reason that should probably be considered,
namely, caste solidarity. Josephus was allied, albeit fairly tenuously,
with the Hasmonean dynasty, and he could not bring himself to do
battle with this great-grandson of Herod who, through his great-

grandmother Mariamne, was also descended from the Hasmoneans. In Jerusalem, where Agrippa had a palace, Josephus had probably met him frequently. Since they were personally acquainted, Josephus could not countenance men theoretically under his orders pillaging or sacking the king's possessions. He probably also realized that sooner or later the majority of Jews would be reconciled to the last king remaining to them.

Thus, Josephus' behavior in Galilee, which does indeed appear ambiguous to an outside observer, followed a perfectly rational inner logic. The problem was that the Galilean insurgents were unwilling to go along with it: they had been looking for a soldier driven by an unwavering faith and they had been sent an intellectual as tricky as he was eloquent, and unwilling ever to dirty his hands.

V

THE ART OF
SURVIVAL

What would you have had him do?
CORNEILLE, *HORACE*

Up until the spring of the year 67 Josephus had been engaged mainly in dealing with the civil disorders in the turbulent region over which he had been appointed governor-general. The Romans took care to remain out of sight, lurking as it were in the shadows to gather the fruits of the disunity rife in their enemy's camp. As a matter of fact, however, such cynical patience was not in the Roman character. Their apparent passivity was due solely to the distance that separated them from the supreme fount of all decisions, their emperor. As soon as Rome had selected its champion on the ground, in the person of Vespasian, Josephus found himself plunged into a fateful battle in which, unable to win, he was forced to practice the only art available to him: the art of survival.

THE ARRIVAL OF VESPASIAN

The monstrous portrait Latin historians have left us of Nero can make us forget that he sometimes acted as a true emperor of Rome. The news of Cestius' defeat in Judea had plunged him into a state of deep and lasting depression. The empire's majesty had been flouted by a handful of Eastern barbarians. A check must quickly be put to their pretensions if Rome intended to continue to reign over the world and Nero over Rome. And indeed, Nero's time was growing short, for he was to be assassinated a few months later. However, there can be no doubt that in entrusting the command of the Judean campaign to Vespasian he had ensured the empire's survival. In his later awareness of the decisive importance of Nero's selection of Vespasian, Josephus was to write that in his choice Nero must have been inspired by God (*JW* III, 6).

Now fifty-seven years of age, Vespasian was a general who had gone gray in the job. During the reign of Claudius he had distinguished himself in campaigns against the Germans and the Bretons. The empire owed to him its expansion beyond the confines of the European continent to southern Britain. When the imperial favor fell upon him, he was accompanying Nero on a voyage to Achaia in Greece. His appointment, which was dictated by necessity, pulled him back from the brink of disgrace. The Bard-Emperor had noticed that Vespasian had a habit of napping through his recitals, when he couldn't manage to avoid attending them altogether. To punish him, he had been banished from the court and forbidden to attend public ceremonies. Vespasian was keeping out of sight, expecting the worst, when he suddenly found himself pulled out of retirement. Nero considered the situation in Judea serious enough to merit the dispatch of his most experienced general. He also knew that Vespasian had a valuable assistant in Titus, one of his sons. He therefore invested Vespasian with the command with all the good feelings a despot can display when forced to call upon his last resource. Nor was Nero stingy when it came to supplying his general with the wherewithal for his task, putting three Legions at Vespasian's disposal.

As soon as Vespasian had received his command at Nero's hand, his considerable organizational gifts came into play. Titus was dispatched to Alexandria by sea, whence he was to bring the XVth Legion up to the field of operations. Vespasian himself crossed the Hellespont and marched by land on Antioch, the capital of the province of Syria and seat of its governor, the third city of the empire after Rome and Alexandria. At the head of two legions, the Vth and the Xth, he effected a rendezvous in Antioch with the troops of King Agrippa II, who had come to pledge his allegiance, and then descended toward Ptolemais (today Acre), in Tyre, on the western border of Galilee. The Roman camp continued to grow: squads of cavalry arrived from Caesarea and Syria, and, in addition to Agrippa, the other kings of the region—Antiochus of Commagene, Soaemus of Emesa (Homs, Syria), and the Arab Malchus, all eager to please Rome, sent elite troops of archers and knights, making an effective total of sixty thousand men, not counting servants. To this must be added considerable advantages on the ground, the main one being the support of the city of Sepphoris, in the heart of Galilee.

Sepphoris, in the beginning overtly favorable to the Romans and later somewhat shakily supportive of Josephus, could not have helped but be impressed by the arrival of such a leader at the head of such a host. The city was already the headquarters of a Roman garrison. Now it offered its services to Vespasian, in return requesting troops to ensure its security, a request that was quickly granted. Thus, immediately upon his arrival, and without having met any resistance, Vespasian found himself being offered the largest city of Galilee and one of its strongest fortresses, protected both by its natural site and by its ramparts.

Even before Vespasian's appearance, however, Sepphoris had become the center of all the harassment operations against Josephus' troops. It had harbored six thousand foot soldiers within its walls, and a thousand horsemen were camped outside it on the plain. Incursions led by the tribune Placidus had kept Josephus on continual alert: if his troops attempted to make a sortie they were repulsed, and if they remained quietly inside some town its approaches were laid waste. When Josephus had finally attempted to retake Sepphoris by force, he found it "so strongly fortified as to render it practically impregnable even to the Romans" (*JW* III, 61).

Placidus ravaged the countryside of Galilee with fire and sword, like some outlaw chief. He reduced peasant families to slavery and massacred any battle-weary stragglers he happened to encounter, but he was brought up short when he attempted to take the best-defended fortress: Jotapata. There, he experienced a defeat at Josephus' mocking hand, a grotesque foretaste of the awful combat of leaders in which Josephus himself would later confront Vespasian.

Vespasian delayed his arrival only to ensure his eventual success. With Titus' assistance he organized his forces in Ptolemais and drew up his plan of campaign. When he finally gave the signal to march, the deployment was a superb one wholly in keeping with the fame of Roman arms. In the vanguard were the units furnished by his kingly allies—light infantry and archers—which acted as scouts; next came the heavily armed Roman troops, which were followed by the corps of engineers and a cavalry detachment to protect the impedimenta. Vespasian rode at the head of the elite troops of foot soldiers, cavalrymen, and lancers. There followed the legionary cavalry (with a hundred and twenty horsemen per legion), war machines transported by mule, officers escorted by elite soldiery, and, finally, preceding the bulk of the army marching in columns of six and commanded by centurions, came the insignia of all the legions grouped around the eagle, the symbol of the empire, and accompanied by trumpeters. The end of the procession was brought up by military servants in charge of the beasts of burden laden with military equipment, mercenaries, and a rear guard of foot soldiers and horsemen.

Thus accoutred, Vespasian left Ptolemais and crossed the entire region to set up camp on the border of Galilee, confident of the psychological effect that such a vast deployment of forces would surely have on his enemy.

DEMORALIZATION

Josephus elected to place his description of the functioning of the Roman army at the head of his narrative of Vespasian's campaign, intending thereby, he tells us, "not as much to extol the Romans as to console those whom they may have vanquished and to deter others who may be tempted to revolt" (*JW* III, 109).

The sight of the Roman army and news of its exploits had given Josephus much food for thought. Order, training, discipline, equipment—everything about it was impressive. It was an army in which each man knew his role and his place, an army with a strict chain of command, an army that followed a rigorous training schedule when not engaged in actual fighting. Each soldier was equipped with a weapon proper to his corps, each had a helmet and breastplate. The fighting units were accompanied by a corps of engineers that could hew down forests and flatten hills in the twinkling of an eye. The war machines that were transported with the troops or constructed on the spot—scorpions, catapults, ballistas, battering rams, assault towers—were awesome. The Roman soldiers, notwithstanding all this technological superiority, never engaged in battle lightly; reflection always preceded action and rash actions were severely reproved. Josephus' highly complimentary words conclude with a veritable hymn of praise: "No wonder that the empire has extended its boundaries on the east to the Euphrates, on the west to the ocean, on the south to the most fertile tracts of Libya, on the north to the Danube and the Rhine. One might say without exaggeration that, great as are their possessions, the people that won them are greater still" (*JW* III, 107).

Undue attention to the flattery contained in those lines can distract us from their essential point: behind this description is the shadow of another, tacit one, a description of the existing Jewish army.

Josephus had tried to organize his own troops in the Roman manner, but lack of time had made that impossible. How can a national temperament be altered overnight? How can passion be disciplined, ardor channeled, obedience instilled? One might as well try to tame the mountain stream or domesticate the wild ass. Whereas the Jews believed above all in courage and daring—which they had in abundance—the Romans had discovered one of the great moving forces of our modern societies: rationalization. Their entire military organization was wholly rational. That of the Jews was quite the opposite; indeed, it could even have been said that they had no organization at all. Once in a while an act of senseless bravery or some flaw in the enemy's tactics might vouchsafe them a victory, but it could not be maintained.

Josephus was to become increasingly aware of this as the war approached. He had been kept informed of events in the south following the deceptive and all-too-easy victory over Cestius. In the ensuing euphoria an expedition against Ascalon led by three outstanding Jewish generals had come to a sorry end, with two of them—Silas the Babylonian and John the Essene—slaughtered. The third, Niger the Peraean, after a valiant struggle, had managed to survive only by hiding in a cave. Yet the Jews had been superior in number and had demonstrated an unparalleled determination. The news of this defeat inspired Josephus to make a frighteningly lucid diagnosis:

"It was a case of novices against veterans, infantry against cavalry, ragged order against serried ranks, men casually armed against fully equipped regulars, on the one side men whose actions were directed by passion rather than policy, on the other disciplined troops acting upon the least signal from their commander" (*JW* III, 15). Thus, the professional army prevailed over the citizen army, and, in the long run, it could not have been otherwise. While continuing to do battle with pro-Roman Sepphoris, therefore, Josephus could not help thinking that the city, with a perfect appreciation of the balance of forces, had chosen the better side.

Now, Vespasian's impressive progress only fed Josephus' fears. He, who ruled over a divided population, at the head of an improvised army whose numbers were in constant flux, what chance did he have against sixty thousand men led by a great conqueror? The approach of the Roman army gave him much to ponder, especially since the majority of his own troops assembled at Garis, near Sepphoris, had fled at the news, "not only before any engagement, but before they had even seen their foes" (*JW* III, 129). Had he not himself once brought low the most hotheaded among the Galileans who had rallied around his mortal enemy, John? Now he had nothing but timid and indecisive men, men who were prepared to rally to either side. The few faithful who had remained with Josephus in Garis would most likely have welcomed capitulation, but their general was the prisoner of his role.

Vespasian's conduct in the field left no room for illusions. He was determined to make the Jews pay dearly for the disaster they had inflicted on Cestius. The town of Gabara was put to the torch, along with all the surrounding villages, and the population was slaughtered or reduced to slavery.

While this was happening Josephus, eager to avoid waging a losing battle, withdrew to Tiberias, in the interior of Galilee. Inside the city, where dissent had been rife since the beginning of hostilities, the population interpreted his flight correctly: no less a personage than the governor-general himself had lost hope as to the outcome of the war. Only a short time before, Josephus had been accused of treason in that very town. Thus, notwithstanding his present difficulties, he took pains to avoid a further accusation by obtaining Jerusalem's sanction. Each sentence in the report he sent off posthaste to the leaders in the capital is carefully weighed. To display terror when confronted with the enemy's strength would have been undignified; a show of overconfidence would have had an effect opposite to the one intended, namely, a cessation of hostilities.

Josephus thus elected to return the ball to his employers' court by forcing them to face up to their responsibilities. He was merely a disciplined executant; if higher powers decided to treat with the enemy, he would be glad to go along; if the struggle was to continue, then let them send him real reinforcements. He was well aware that after the unfortunate incident at Ascalon, and given the fact that Jerusalem would have to prepare for a siege sooner or later, it was highly doubtful that any such reinforcements would be sent. In drafting his letter, Josephus was disclaiming in advance all responsibility for an inevitable setback while hoping that his hints would be acted on and that he would receive an order to lay down his arms rather than expose himself to a crushing defeat. Did such an answer ever come? We do not know.

Josephus was soon to be forced to act, not by orders from on high but because of Vespasian's actions on the ground. Once he had protected his rear, Vespasian had imperturbably proceeded to move eastward and was now preparing to deal with the fortress at Jotapata. He managed to flatten the rocky terrain surrounding the city and facilitate access for his troops in only four days. Next, he set up camp north on a highly visible rise where he would clearly be seen by all. By so clearly broadcasting his intentions he was almost compelling the region's governor-general to come in person to defend the threatened fortress, and (according to the person most interested in the matter) he was greatly pleased to learn that the man reputed to be his cleverest enemy was indeed about to fall into the trap (*JW* III, 144). Josephus, whose morale could not have been lower, was forced to set off posthaste for Jotapata to raise the morale of its beleaguered population.

THE SIEGE OF JOTAPATA

Jotapata was one of those impregnable fortresses the Romans always seemed good at taking. Built on a peak and protected by a ring of surrounding hills, the city also had natural defenses in the form of deep ravines that surrounded it on every side but the north, where it could be reached by sloping ground. Josephus had also fortified the fortress' ramparts at the beginning of his mandate in Galilee.

After Vespasian had disposed his forces, the inhabitants of Jotapata found themselves encircled by a double line of infantrymen backed by a line of cavalry. On the northern slope some seven stadia distant (a stadium equaled around six hundred feet) they could see drawn up a glittering and seemingly countless host. The city's defenders reacted with the energy born of despair. A preliminary Roman assault was repulsed by the Jews, after which attacks and counterattacks continued for five days. Vespasian, now realizing that the task would be harder than he had expected, then decided to throw up immense siege works. He began by building an embankment on the northern, most vulnerable, side of the city.

It is here that Josephus probably witnessed for the first time the workings of a corps of military engineers of a quality unheard of in the Jewish army. The mountains in the vicinity were soon cleared of trees and a huge pile of stones assembled; protected by palisades, the Roman soldiers threw up a vast earthwork, working at quick cadence and passing all the necessary materials along to each other in brigades. When the Jews attempted to impede the work by launching various projectiles from the walls, Vespasian countered with his war machines: catapults hurled javelins, and ballistas launched stones weighing as much as a talent (approximately fifty-eight pounds), which made whistling sounds before landing and leveling the crenelated battlements, often bringing down several men at a time. Attempting to describe the power of the ballistas, Josephus tells us that later, during the siege, one of its stones decapitated a man and carried his head nearly three stadia away, and that a pregnant woman had her child torn from her womb and thrown a half stadia's distance. Nor were the javelinists, the troops armed with slings, or the Arabian archers idle. The besieged stopped showing themselves on the walls and exposing themselves to such heavy fire and instead sent out raiding parties to try to destroy the earthworks and set fire to the palisades. Nevertheless, the works continued to rise to the north.

Josephus came up with increasingly clever stratagems, affirming his reputation as the "most intelligent man among the enemies." There was only one way to parry the inexorable rise of the Roman earthworks: the town ramparts would have to be raised. The procedure was a dangerous one, given the enemy's ballistas; to protect the laborers Josephus came up with a new trick: he stretched the hides of freshly slaughtered cattle over the palisades behind which the men were working. The taut, dampened surface caused the stones to bounce off, deflected javelins and extinguished flaming arrows.

The besieged were beset by another enemy, thirst. The city had sufficient foodstuffs, but its water reserves were nearly exhausted and the season—this was the month of July—was not a propitious one for abundant rainfall. The rationing Josephus imposed on the population only added to the general anxiety. The besiegers had located the place where the water was being distributed, and it quickly became a prime target. Josephus, who had learned to his cost the importance of good morale among his troops, now turned to psychological warfare, something at which Vespasian too was fairly practiced. Josephus staged an astonishingly daring bluff to deceive the enemy: under the eyes of the stupefied Romans, wet cloths were hung over the ramparts and the water was allowed to trickle down the sunbaked walls of the city as it sweltered beneath the sun amid the bare hills of the parched Galilean countryside. Tired of waiting for the city's surrender, which now began to seem even more uncertain, Vespasian held his fire . . . which suited the besieged, who had no illusions about their fate and preferred to die in battle rather than perish from thirst.

Josephus' innate cleverness, inspired by the desperate situation in which he found himself, enabled him to come up with some other unconventional ideas. Noting that the ravine to the west of the city was badly guarded, he sent messengers and men to bring in supplies from that direction. To deceive the Roman sentries, the men draped themselves with animal skins and went on all fours. The trick was soon discovered and the ravine was better guarded henceforth.

Perhaps because he sensed he was running out of inspiration, Josephus was tempted to flee the city—indeed, he made no secret of it. He explained to the appalled inhabitants that his presence in the city was no longer of any use, but that if he were to escape he could collect additional troops and open another front against the Romans, thereby lightening the siege. With astonishing frankness, however, he does not conceal from his reader the fact that his principal concern was for his own safety. However, when he heard the wild supplications of the crowd—women with babies, old men, children, all weeping at his feet—he was quick to understand the tacit threat underlying their emotional response: he would not be allowed to leave. Always ready to accommodate himself to circumstances, he gave in to their pleas, adopted a heroic posture, and immediately began to preach fighting on until death, exclaiming: "Now is the time to begin the combat, when all hope of deliverance is past. Fine it is to sacrifice life for renown and by some glorious exploit to ensure in falling the memory of posterity" (*JW* III, 204) . . . such was, in essence, his speech as he reports it. He then suited his actions to his fine words and set out to burn what he could of the Roman earthworks.

The final stage of the siege now began, for the Romans' earthen platform continued to rise in spite of the Jews' ceaseless efforts to destroy it. Vespasian had been holding in reserve a war machine that Josephus was to describe with a certain awe even years later: the battering ram. A huge metal head cast to resemble that of a ram was attached to the end of a thick beam of wood, which was worked by a number of men, and no rampart was long able to withstand its repeated blows.

Had Josephus not been present, the besieged would probably have been frozen with terror when the awful machine began its work. Apart from their inability to countenance the flight of a leader in time of peril, they were also well aware of why they were so eager to retain his presence: Josephus could always be counted on to come up with something unexpected to keep their minds off their imminent death. This time, he got them to fill sacks with straw and lower them over the walls to the spot where the battering ram was at work so as to cushion its blows. The sight of the besiegers' mortification at finding their most formidable war machine thus rendered harmless must have been the last pleasure afforded the inhabitants of Jotapata. The parry inspired another thrust, and the Romans produced long scythes with which they cut the ropes that were holding the sacks in place.

The regalvanized Jewish fighters responded with individual acts of heroism, which Josephus dutifully reported to posterity. Three of them are given posthumous citations: Eleazar son of Samaeus of Sabah, in Galilee, for having cracked the head of a battering ram by throwing a huge stone from the ramparts, descending to the base of the wall to retrieve it and then, although pierced with five arrows, climbing back up with his prize before being cut down; Netiras and Philippus, two brothers from the village of Rumah, for having single-handedly managed to make a breach in the ranks of the Xth Legion.

A few other anonymous heroes, brandishing torches, continued to throw themselves against the Roman war machines and platforms, which the troops attempted to protect by covering them with dirt. One of them, taken prisoner by the enemy, withstood all kinds of torture and died crucified, a smile on his lips, without having uttered a word about the real state of affairs within the city.

History is filled with episodes that enable us to imagine how differently things could have turned out. The Roman general was struck by an arrow . . . but only in the foot. Vespasian quickly quelled the dismay caused by the sight of his blood, and the siege went on.

Josephus' description of the night before the final assault takes on an epic tone. On the ramparts the besieged fought with fire against the war machines that were drawing ever closer; at night, they became easy targets for the attackers. Stones cast by the ballistas swept their ranks, bodies began to pile up, and over the dull thudding sounds of falling bodies could be heard the screams of the women. "The echo from the mountains around added to the horrible din; in short nothing that can terrify ear or eye was wanting on that dreadful night" (*JW* III, 250).

At dawn, a section of the ramparts had given way and the defenders filled the breach with their bodies. The triple belt of troops surrounding the city had not yet moved; weapons glittered in the distance. At the foot of the breaches the elite legionnaires, wearing breastplates and with lowered lances, were backed by a cordon of cavalry. Behind them were stationed archers and slingmen, ready to fire. On the flank where the ramparts still held, assault ladders had already been moved into place. Seeing this awful sight, the women and children emitted the poignant cries that always seem to accompany great catastrophes. Josephus had them shut away so as not to exacerbate the tension already rampant within the fortress. He tells us that he had then decided to offer his own person and had betaken himself, not to that part of the ramparts being defended by "the fatigued and older men," but directly to where the breach had been made, accompanied by the youngest and most vigorous defenders, drawn by a lot, whom he had formed into groups of six, and "among whom he himself drew for his place to bear the brunt of the battle" (*JW* III, 258).

The ensuing hand-to-hand combat was merciless. The defenders had nothing left to defend but were wreaking vengeance for their lost cause, for the slashed throats of the elderly, for the murder or enslavement of their women and children. Their bravery was fruitless against the strength of the opponent; while their numbers were steadily decreasing, the Romans kept bringing up fresh relief troops. Josephus came up with one final expedient, born of despair. There was an abundance of olive oil, a local product, and Josephus had boiling oil poured down on the besiegers. We his readers are not as amazed at this defense technique as he seems to think we will be, for from our later perspective we immediately think of the sieges of the Middle Ages, but our author describes it as his own invention. Nor were his companions totally devoid of ideas: they poured fenugreek over the footbridges on the lower levels and fired down upon the Romans as they slipped and staggered across.

It took ten more days for Vespasian to invest a city he had believed already conquered. He was forced to raise the embankment he had constructed and build three siege towers, iron-clad to resist fire. These loomed over the besieged, who now had no way of avoiding the missiles being hurled down upon them. Weakened by days of constant battle and guard duty, the defenders saw their numbers dwindle day by day. Vespasian learned of all this from a deserter (the only one of the entire siege), who had a hard time convincing him of his veracity. However, his intelligence turned out to be correct, and the attack was ordered for the last watch, when the defenders would be most exhausted. The scene of slaughter that brought the siege of Jotapata to an end is like a preview of the final days of Jerusalem, which Josephus was to witness exactly three years later. The Romans rampaged and massacred through all the towers, alleyways, hiding places, and basements of the city, sparing only women and small children, who were allowed to live only to be enslaved.

The death toll of the siege amounted to forty thousand Galileans. The city was then razed at Vespasian's orders, and the memory of Jotapata was lost for centuries.

BETWEEN SUICIDE AND SURRENDER

On the day Jotapata fell, "at the new moon of Panemos in the thirteenth year of Nero's reign"—July 20, 67 C.E., Josephus, the leader of the besieged, was nowhere to be found. For three days he was sought in vain, even among the dead. Josephus had not committed suicide, as had many of his elite troops, nor had he fallen in combat in the breach. When the enemy had surged in, he had managed to jump into a deep cistern that communicated with a lateral cavern through an entry that was invisible from above. Forty of the city's upper-class citizens had already taken refuge there, supplied with ample food and water. On the third day, however, his luck turned, and one of the captured women revealed Josephus' hiding place.

It was not in the Roman tradition to kill an enemy general on the spot. It was customary to take him back to Rome and hold him for a future triumph, after which he could be executed. However, aside from the fact that he was not commander in chief of the entire Jewish army, which would have afforded him some reprieve, Josephus was afraid that the prolonged resistance Jotapata had offered might have exacerbated Vespasian's anger toward him. And indeed, the Roman soldiers would have set fire to the cave had Vespasian not been firm. What he wanted was Josephus' surrender. The first two emissaries he sent returned empty handed. The third, the tribune Nicanor, was a better choice: he was, Josephus tells us, "an old acquaintance and friend" (*JW* III, 346). We know nothing about the origins and circumstances of this friendship.

Nicanor's skillful speech and protestations of loyal friendship succeeded in moving Josephus, who appears to have been somewhat uneasy about admitting to his interlocutor his readiness to give in to pressure. He sought a nobler motive, one that would later give him an opportunity to recall his noble birth, his vast ancestral culture, at a time in which he could well have seemed to have lost claim to either. We have already noted his inclination to confuse his own inspiration with divine inspiration. Thus, at this moment he just happened to recall that he had had several premonitory dreams—of divine origin, he tells us. For the benefit of any dubious reader, he again vaunts his priestly lineage and his outstanding knowledge of Holy Scripture, guarantees of his ability to interpret the divine will, even if expressed in dreams.

Josephus is obviously trying to impress his contemporaries, all of whom, Jews and pagans, believed in the premonitory value of nocturnal visions. He is both dreamer and a self-described "interpreter of dreams," and he cleverly links himself with his biblical homonym. He also says that he is "skilled in divining the meaning of ambiguous utterances of the Deity" (*JW* III, 352).

On the surface, this would seem to refer to dreams, but Josephus, who also vaunts his skill in exegesis, is probably thinking of something else. The term "ambiguous utterances" emerges from his pen on another occasion when, evoking the fatal blindness that had led the Jews into the war, he recalls that one of the motives for the revolt had been the exegesis of a biblical passage promising empire over the world to someone from their land.[1] It is not very clear to which passage he is referring, but it is probably one of the Prophets who announced the reign of the Messiah. Hard times increased the ardor of the expectations of the arrival of a Messiah-King who would usher in a new world; some even identified him with a Galilean called Jesus, who had been crucified under Pontius Pilate.[2] Many, by taking up arms against Rome, the symbol of Evil, had thought to hasten the advent of the Good.

Josephus had never been wholly convinced of all this; now that he who had believed so strongly in his star was a mere defeated general, he suddenly found illumination. The Messiah's day was probably still far distant, but for the moment the ruler of Judea was the man who had conquered it. So be it, such was the law of history. And every empire that had ever subjugated the Jewish people—Babylonian, Persian, Greek—had gone on to rule the world. When He had some reason to punish them, the Lord would deliver His people only unto the most powerful. Thus, if Rome was the new Babylon, Vespasian might well be the new Nebuchadnezzar, and Josephus might then play the role of Jeremiah. He too would be a prophet, a prophet preaching surrender before the Babylonian army led by King Nebuchadnezzar came to lay siege to Jerusalem.

The role suited him; it cleansed him of any suspicion of treason and made him the servant of the divine plan. Such is the sense of the silent inner prayer Josephus then improvised, and which he reconstituted as follows when he came to write it all down: "Since it pleases Thee, who didst create the Jewish nation, to break thy word, since Fortune has wholly passed to the Romans, and since Thou hast made choice of my spirit to announce the things that are to come, I willingly surrender to the Romans and consent to live, but I take Thee to witness that I go, not as a traitor, but as Thy minister" (*JW* III, 354).

By clinging to the figure of Jeremiah, Josephus was also reassuring himself: he was no traitor. He would have had more trouble
convincing his companions in defeat, if indeed he tried. All of his
interpreted dreams, his biblical exegeses, his historical parallels, everything he calls his "prophetic inspiration," tended to a single goal,
namely, survival. His companions were no fools, and seeing him
about to give in to Nicanor's pleadings, they interrupted indignantly:
a true Jewish general would die with his troops rather than surrender.

Liberty or death! seems in those days to have been the
favorite Jewish motto. Anything, rather than fall alive into the
hands of the enemy. Indeed, young healthy men were well aware
that by surrendering they would only be putting off the inevitable,
and at the price of their honor. If by some extraordinary chance
their lives were spared, it would be only so that they could be
thrown to wild beasts or forced to fight a brother in some arena to
the jeers of the crowd. Obviously, this fear was not their only
motive, since one of Josephus' lieutenants had urged him to commit suicide when threatened by the Jews, not by the Romans.

In such circumstances suicide was the culmination of a certain ideal of honor: to kill oneself with one's own hand rather than
give the enemy that pleasure. In the time of the Maccabees (see
Chapter One), a noble patriot named Razis had thrown himself
from the walls to avoid falling alive into the hands of the Syrian
enemy;[3] his was a much-venerated example. The collective suicide
at Masada in 73 is what we remember most from Josephus' narrative, but his works are full of similar gestures.[4]

When fortresses were under siege, as had just happened at
Jotapata, the suicide of groups of entrapped defenders was common. Historians have not dwelt on the fact, and such suicides are
usually represented as reflecting stoicism. But how many thousands
of unknown Jews there were for each Cato of Utica!

The Jews' careless attitude toward death probably had to do
with their belief in the immortality of the soul, a belief that enabled
them to accept martyrdom unflinchingly. When a man was in mortal danger, suicide only served to speed up the separation of the
body and the soul and enabled the latter to survive unblemished
when its honor was threatened.

Thus, forty threatening daggers were pointed at Josephus, ready to run him through if he made Nicanor the slightest sign of consent.

Once again, Josephus was within a hair of losing his life for wanting to save it. But with the amazing self-control we have already witnessed, he managed to bring all the available arguments against suicide together in one fine speech.

First, he demonstrated suicide's absurdity. Yes, it was a fine thing to die for freedom, but in combat—and then at the hand of the foe who was trying to deprive you of it. And if one rejected surrender for fear of death, why then mete out death to oneself? If one rejected surrender for fear of slavery, what was so free about the situation in which they now found themselves? Josephus then took up the so-called grandeur of suicide and drew an impromptu comparison: far from being heroic, suicide was a cowardly deed, as cowardly as that of a pilot who would allow his ship to sink because he feared the storm. He also dealt with suicide in general, apart from some situation of extreme danger that might justify it. It was an act against nature, for every animal had an inborn instinct for life, and no animal killed itself voluntarily. His religious argument was his most elaborate: man owes his existence to God and has no right to dispose of that gift as he pleases; his recompense or punishment in the afterlife will be based on the respect with which he treats his life in this one. As his final argument Josephus called upon the common wisdom of nations, as set forth in their laws: the Jews left a suicide's body unburied until sunset, the Greeks cut off the death-dealing right hand of the suicide: *ergo,* suicide is a crime.

We do not know whether Josephus actually gave voice to all these scholastic arguments in the dramatic situation in which he found himself. After the fact, at least, he lays out a well-constructed speech, with an inevitable peroration: they must resign themselves to living if the Romans allowed them to, and he for his part would never have been a traitor. However, he did not exclude the possibility that in promising him his life the enemy might be laying a trap for him.

Whether taught in the school of the Pharisees or in that of the Greek philosophers, Josephus had learned to plead the most contradictory of causes with considerable skill. One of the high points in Book VII of the *War* is the section in which Eleazar ben Jair, the leader of the Masada defenders, delivers his poignant speech in favor of suicide.[5]

From these two amazing speeches we come away with a high estimate of Josephus' agile mind and a certain skepticism with regard to his interpretation of what everyone believed to be divine providence. For Josephus' companions, in any event, the answer was plain, and the eloquence with which our hero had already saved his life on several prior occasions fell this time on deaf ears. Josephus managed only to irritate his listeners. In their view, all his arguments were just that, mere pretexts, unable to conceal his growing hope that he might come out of things alive while abandoning the others to their sorry fate. Insults rained down on him, daggers were again drawn. Attacked on all sides, Josephus faced up to them all, in his own words, "like a wild beast surrounded by the hunters" (*JW* III, 385) and again managed to deflect the blows: "He, addressing one by name, fixing his general's eye of command upon another, clasping the hand of a third, shaming a fourth by entreaty, and torn by all manner of emotions at this critical moment, succeeded in warding off from his throat the blades of all." No one dared strike at him, the governor-general's prestige was still intact, even in defeat.

He now had to play his trump card. The final act of this tragicomedy consisted of a kind of lottery Josephus had thought up. Alone against them all, he pretended to go along with the collective decision, and even further: if they were to allow each person to kill himself with his own sword, some irresolute persons might just pretend to do so without his companions' knowing. In order to be sure, it might be better if they slit each other's throats in order, to be determined by drawing lots. The person who drew number one would be slain by number two, and so on until the end.

Josephus drew the highest number. He himself attempts to justify this to the reader by suggesting a miracle and blesses the good fortune, chance, divine providence, which saved him. In olden times some cynics found a more logical explanation for the "miracle": Josephus was a mathematician of genius. Thus, he managed to organize the drawing in such a way as to ensure that he got the highest number. Here is the form this ploy has been given in a recent French mathematics textbook:

Flavius Josephus' Permutation[6]

>In the year 67, in the course of a Jewish revolt against the Romans, forty Jews were taken prisoner. Unwilling to be taken as slaves, they decided to form a circle and number themselves from 1 to 40. Every seventh man was then to be killed until only one was left; the last man left was to commit suicide. Flavius Josephus, the future historian, positioned himself so that he would be the last, and then did not commit suicide. Determine the number Flavius Josephus chose.

As things turned out, Josephus was not the only one left alive. He was no fonder of killing than he was of being killed. When his turn came to slit the throat of the last survivor, he refused to do so and promised to do all he could to save him along with himself. He then surrendered to Vespasian, the victorious general. Thus, to use his own words, he "survived both the war with the Romans and that with his own friends" (*JW* III, 392).

THE PREDICTION TO VESPASIAN

In the custody of his friend the tribune Nicanor, Josephus made his way through the throng of soldiers and officers crowded around the entrance to the cavern in which he had taken refuge. We can imagine the enormous curiosity and joy that must have been aroused by the capture of the commander of such a valiant foe and fortress; there were also some voices that clamored for revenge. Josephus maintained his dignity superbly in the center of the hostile crowd. Most astonishing of all was his youth: a Jewish general of thirty had held his own against a Roman general of nearly sixty!

To the shouting of his soldiers Titus, Vespasian's son, watched his enemy move toward him, and as he watched the first thing that may have struck him was that they were the same age. Josephus marks this moment as the beginning of Titus' firm and faithful friendship toward him, and it is probably true that their shared age counted heavily in their affection for each other.

Josephus bases that affection both on the merits of his own personality and on the young Roman conqueror's mental acuity. Titus was a man of feeling and intellect. He would have viewed the enemy general's failure as an illustration of the capriciousness of the goddess Fortuna, who raised up and cast down according to her whim. In much the same way the Greek historian Polybius depicts his friend the Roman general Scipio the Younger standing in the still-smoking ruins of Carthage and weeping at the thought that Rome would one day inevitably suffer the same fate. The sight of Josephus may even have made Titus imagine himself in the prisoner's place. That, at least, is the impression we get from reading Josephus' account of this episode.

Vespasian's first words to his prisoner were to inform him that he would soon be dispatched to Nero himself in Rome. For Josephus, the news meant another long journey to Rome, no less dangerous than the first, and this time to be made in humiliating conditions. His supporters in Rome had vanished with Poppaea's death. As for Nero, his increasingly unstable and cruel behavior and his wrath at the Jewish uprising meant that it would be difficult to expect any pardon from him. Josephus far preferred dealing with the old soldier before him, a man with a reputation for integrity and generosity.

Vespasian, indeed, was a solid bourgeois whose origins had not prepared him for high places. Nero's choice had fallen upon him not only because of his military qualifications but because of his lowly origins as well, origins that prevented him from being a potential rival. Vespasian had not even tried to enter upper-class Roman society through marriage. Instead, he had been content to rise—often with difficulty—through the stages of the *cursus honorum:* military tribune, edile, praetor. Successes against the Germans and Bretons had won him the insignia of triumphs, two priesthoods, and even a consulate. He had returned from his time in Africa, where he had been Roman proconsul, without the vast wealth amassed by his predecessors. Nero had then sent him to Judea.

Having risen so high through his own merit alone, Vespasian had begun to believe that he enjoyed the special protection of Fortuna, and he was always avid for signs to confirm that belief. His biographer, Suetonius, was to draw up an impressive list of verifying omens. Thus, prior to leaving Achaia for Judea, Vespasian had had a dream that he and his family would enter into a period of prosperity when Nero lost a tooth. The very next day the palace physician had shown him an imperial tooth he had just extracted. Josephus was probably unaware of this omen, as of the others. Nevertheless, he could have learned that immediately upon arriving in the region Vespasian had made a point of going up to Mount Carmel, the ancient holy mountain of the Canaanites still worshipped by the pagans, just as earlier, in Egypt, Alexander the Great had consulted the oracle of Amon. The response had been highly encouraging: all of his plans would come to fruition, all his dreams would come true. As a much-decorated general, what else could he have been dreaming of but empire? This was a conclusion at which Josephus could have arrived by simple deduction.

Ever since he had sensed that the uprising was doomed to failure, Josephus had been haunted by another idea, the idea that, as had been proved in the past, God never chose an unworthy conqueror to punish his people. Josephus was applying to the present situation a widely held opinion that was well founded in scripture and historical precedent. He describes his interpretation of Holy Writ and history as "prophecy." The great conquerors of the past were not mere soldiers, they were kings. Through a process of "prophetic" deduction, therefore, Josephus reached the conclusion that his conqueror was destined for royalty.

To Vespasian's astonishment his young captive immediately requested a private audience in order to communicate his revelation. The request was granted. Only five persons remained in the victorious general's tent: his son Titus, two of his friends, and Josephus. Josephus began by attempting to cleanse his surrender of dishonor. He had surrendered not because he wished to live but because of a more pressing need—indeed, a mission—to deliver a divine message: Vespasian was soon to become emperor himself. There was thus no need to send Nero his prisoner! Vespasian would soon reign, and his son after him, over "land and sea and the whole human race" (*JW* III, 402).

There was every chance that Vespasian might regard this prophecy as some kind of trick. Yet his interlocutor spoke with such conviction, his knowledge of old Eastern scripture lent his words such authority—and then, his prophecy coincided with so many earlier omens! A brief survey among the other Jewish prisoners confirmed the fact that their vanquished governor-general was thought to be a kind of wise man, many of whose earlier predictions (concerning the length of the siege, for example) had already come true. Both Vespasian and his son Titus who was not without ambition himself, were awestruck. Both wanted very much to believe in this new omen, which was far more explicit than any of the others. What did they have to lose by treating this unusual captive with special care?

Josephus was put in chains, but in every other respect he was to enjoy a very special treatment and was to be showered with presents by his protectors.

He had managed to survive.

JOSEPHUS AND HIS DOUBLE

The news of the fall of Jotapata was considered a disaster in Jerusalem and greeted with universal gloom. The extent of the defeat was so great that for a time people refused to believe it—easy to do in that there were no survivors. However, soon additional details began to filter in, passed from village to village, and it became impossible to avoid facing the facts. The prospects for the future were horrifying: it was said that Galilee would not be able to hold out much longer, that the Roman army would soon invade the south and lay siege to the Holy City. The sorrow, too, was intense, for many mourned a relative or friend fallen in defense of the fortress. Since there was no news of Josephus, he was believed to have perished in the battle; he became an instant national hero, and the entire city of Jerusalem went into mourning for the ritual thirty days.

With time, still other news began to trickle in. Not only was Josephus very much alive, but his captors were treating him with more consideration than were he merely some ordinary prisoner. How could men help but think him a traitor? The mourning for the hero was suddenly replaced with invective and curses hurled at the cowardly betrayer.

In Jewish tradition, Josephus has a "double," a man as venerated as Josephus was anathematized. His name is Johanan ben Zakkai, and he is credited with having ensured almost single-handedly the survival of Judaism following the awful catastrophe of the destruction of the Temple in the year 70. Although almost nothing is known of the biographies of most of the rabbis quoted in the Talmud, we do have some few details about the actions of Johanan ben Zakkai during the siege of Jerusalem, and they remind us strangely of Josephus' behavior. The rabbinical writings in which they are recounted make no pretense of being historical records; indeed, they were written some two centuries after the events they record. Thus, we can easily excuse their patent inaccuracies: for example, Vespasian, not Titus, is purported to have laid siege to Jerusalem, whereas in fact at that date the former had already been emperor for a year.

However, the error is not insignificant—it is even necessary to the tale. Johanan ben Zakkai, we are told, made up his mind to go over to the Romans during the siege of Jerusalem because he saw that the city was in danger of famine and could not hold out for long. Since the leaders of the revolt prevented anyone from leaving, Johanan ben Zakkai had himself shut up in a coffin and, carried by his closest disciples, who pretended they were leaving the confines of the city to bury their master, he managed to pass through the guard posts on the walls. Once outside, he presented himself to the leader of the besiegers, Vespasian, and hailed him (in correct Latin) as emperor: *Ave domine imperator.* When Vespasian evinced surprise at the title, the pious rabbi informed him that he was soon to succeed to the empire's throne, and shortly afterward the prediction came true. As his reward, Johanan ben Zakkai was given permission to found an academy on the coastal plain at Jamnia (Yavneh) for the teaching of the Pharisaic doctrine, on which he was a great authority. Clearly, in this story his surrender is viewed as an act of the highest wisdom, one without which Judaism might well not have survived. And indeed, the two other schools, Sadducee and Essene, were to perish in the catastrophe.

Johanan's prophecy to Vespasian, like that of Josephus, relied on Scriptural exegesis. However, although our historian neglects to cite the particular biblical passage that inspired him, which is somewhat unusual, the rabbinical writings make a great point of giving the source for Johanan's prediction. In answer to the Roman general's expressed incredulity, he refers to a verse from Isaiah: "By us it is written that only a king shall destroy the Temple, for it says: Lebanon[7] shall fall by a mighty one" (Isaiah 10:34).[8] It is possible that when Josephus realized defeat was inevitable, like his rabbinical homologue, ben Zakkai, this same exegesis may also have leaped to mind.

We are intrigued by this coincidence involving the two men, and we cannot exclude the possibility that the posthumous biography of the Pharisian sage may be a distant echo of the life of Josephus. The historical accuracy of Johanan's prediction, as we have seen, is spoiled by several chronological impossibilities. On the other hand, Josephus' account is confirmed in his own autobiography, as well as by Suetonius, who adds to an account of the omens foretelling Vespasian's accession the following:

"Furthermore, a noble captive named Josephus, when cast into prison, stated with the greatest assurance that he would soon be delivered by Vespasian himself, who would be emperor."[9]

The prediction must have created quite a stir in the Roman army in the East. Who can say that it may not even have influenced Vespasian's eventual election to the office, since in the event he was borne to power by his own troops? Thus, Josephus could have had a hidden influence on the course of history.

There is a fundamental difference between Josephus and Johanan ben Zakkai: by his prediction, Josephus was attempting to save his own life, whereas his rabbi "double" was thinking above all of his people's spiritual patrimony. Nevertheless, by writing the history of his time Josephus too saved at least a part of that patrimony, the memory of it, for without him we would know almost nothing of these events. Thus, even if there were cowardice or treason in the aftermath of the fall of Jotapata in 67, the historian can only rejoice.

VI

THE CAPTIVE
OF CAESAREA

And they shall deride every stronghold; for they shall heap dust, and take it.

HABAKKUK, 1:10

With Josephus' capture in July 67, we turn to the second panel of his life, which is the one about which we know the least. Indeed, the remainder of his career can be summed up as follows: freed when Vespasian was named emperor, he followed Titus to Judea, witnessed the siege of Jerusalem, and, following the fall of his native city, returned to live in Rome with his imperial protectors.

Beginning in his thirtieth year, Josephus was no longer an active player on History's stage, but merely a witness.

IN CAESAREA

For the two years of his captivity (July of 67 to December of 69), Josephus is absent even from his own narrative. He not only ceases to occupy center stage, as before; he vanishes completely, leaving to his biographer the delicate task of finding him.

Throughout the period, Vespasian was pursuing his victorious progress through Galilee and, later, Judea. By the time he was called to the empire in July 69, the entire region had fallen to him with the exception of Jerusalem and a few fortified places, one of which was Masada. There is a hypothesis that the Roman general must have profited from his prisoner's knowledge of the terrain and the local language and had taken Josephus with him as a member of his entourage. However, if we think about it, that hypothesis does not stand up. Vespasian had so little need of Josephus that his first impulse had been to dispatch him to Nero forthwith. His armies included many auxiliaries native to the region who knew the countryside and could speak Aramaic. In addition, in Galilee he could rely on the close cooperation of King Agrippa II, whose lands stretched to Lake Tiberias.

These reasons, added to Josephus' own silence about himself, tend to support a second hypothesis, namely, that Josephus did not accompany Vespasian on his campaigns but instead spent this entire period under guard in Caesarea, the city that served as both headquarters for the Roman administration and the home base and supply port for its troops.

After his victory at Jotapata, Vespasian had made haste to return to Caesarea, which he had selected as the winter headquarters for two of the legions under his command, the Vth and the Xth. The XVth Legion was sent to Scythopolis (Beth-Shan) "in order not to burden Caesarea with his whole army" (*JW* III, 411).

Nearly a hundred years earlier, Herod too had selected the coastal site of the ancient Tower of Strato to construct a large Greco-Roman town. The work had taken twelve years. In addition to a magnificent port (today under water), even larger than the one at Piraeus, Herod also had built a theater, an amphitheater, and a large pagan temple dedicated to Rome and Augustus that was furnished with colossal statues and so situated that it was visible from far out at sea. Herod named the town, which turned out to be a masterpiece of urban planning, Caesarea in honor of the emperor,[1] thereby demonstrating both his allegiance to Rome, whence his power flowed, and his determination to conciliate his kingdom's large pagan population, for whom he organized many magnificent games. We can understand why the pagans should have called him Herod the Great, while the Jews, scandalized by his many acts of cruelty and his contempt for "ancestral customs," referred to him (behind his back) as Herod the Impious. We can also understand why, after the annexation of Judea, the city had been chosen as the seat of the Roman administration.

Around the middle of the first century the Jews still made up approximately half the local population of Caesarea. The city's territory also took in the exclusively Jewish suburb of Narbata, located at some 60 stadia distance (*JW* II, 291). The political friction between Caesarea's Jews and pagans had been partly responsible for the war. At the earliest outbreaks of trouble, which had occurred in the year 66 in the time of Florus, the pagans had felt free to fall upon the Jews that remained in their part of the city: "Within one hour more than twenty thousand men were slaughtered, and Caesarea was completely emptied of Jews," Josephus informs us (*JW* II, 457).

It was into this city rife with unrest that Josephus entered in chains at Vespasian's side in late July of the year 67. The inhabitants acclaimed the victor and howled "Death!" at the sight of the conquered governor-general. Vespasian was unperturbable, however; aware of the impossibility of reasoning with a mob eager for blood; his only reply was silence (*JW* III, 411).

From this moment on all trace of Josephus vanishes from his own narrative. However, a passing reference at the end of his autobiography throws an unexpected light on the period of his captivity in Caesarea. We learn that Vespasian not only continued to treat his prisoner with great consideration but even offered him a wife, a young prisoner from the region.

Although Josephus may have been married a first time in Jerusalem, as we have supposed earlier, this second marriage was very different from the first. It took place not in the Holy City but in the military encampment in Caesarea; the bridegroom's family was represented by a Roman general and both of the newlyweds were prisoners: given those circumstances, there was no ceremony. Why, therefore, refer to it as a marriage? At the time, both Roman and Jewish law recognized a union of simple concubinage as being perfectly legal.

The legal impediment to Josephus' marriage had a different origin. The biblical priestly code banned the marriage of a *cohen* with a "profaned" woman (Leviticus 21:7). Female captives of war were included in the latter category, since it was presumed that they had been raped; and Josephus' wife was a captive. However, as a prisoner himself, he had no choice. In this case the girl—she must certainly have been very young—may have been spared rape, since she had not been taken following a siege. The only Jews who had suvived the massacres in Caesarea in 66 were those who had managed to flee the city in time. The procurator Florus had had them arrested, brought back, and herded into the arsenals. This is probably where Vespasian had found the young bride he offered his prisoner.

In any event, Josephus knew that from now on he would have to forgo many of the "ancestral customs" that were woven into the daily life of a free man. Fate had placed him in a situation over which he had no control, a status not unrecognized in Jewish law. There were only three instances in which a Jew should prefer death: to avoid committing murder, to avoid committing idolatry, or to avoid engaging in one of the sexual couplings condemned in the Bible (incest, sodomy, zoophilia). With those exceptions, a man had no choice but to live as best he could, and Josephus had always shown himself determined to do just that.

NEWS FROM GALILEE

Josephus probably spent most of his time as a captive reflecting on the situation in the world around him and making the notes on which he would later base his composition of the *War*. The description of the fall of Jotapata, for example, reads as though it had been based on fresh information that had probably been written down very shortly after the event.

During this time, however, the war was continuing, and news of military operations must surely have reached Josephus' ears in the camp in Caesarea. In the autumn of 67 he learned of the tragic end of another coastal city, Jaffa. Cut off from the interior after a preliminary battle, the city's inhabitants had decided to continue the war from the sea, and their pirate vessels had been imperiling navigation between Egypt and Syria-Phoenicia. At the approach of Vespasian's troops they had left the city and sought refuge in their ships. At dawn, a fierce north wind had risen and the ships, which were anchored off the unprotected coast, had been smashed to smithereens. It is unlikely that Josephus had been an eyewitness to the scene, but his account vividly depicts the agony of the pirates, caught between the fury of the waves and the armed Roman soldiers drawn up on the shore. He describes—as the Talmud was later to describe the Battle of Bar Kokhba (the second Jewish revolt against Rome) in the second century—the sea red with blood, cadavers tossed on the waves.

Vespasian, who was absent from these battles, did not resume his campaign immediately. Sometime toward the end of winter he left for Caesarea Philippi (Paneas, today Banias), in northeastern Galilee, in lands subject to Rome's ally, King Agrippa II. After the harsh conditions of military life, he must have enjoyed Agrippa's luxurious Oriental hospitality, which flattered his nascent ambitions. Twenty days were spent in pleasure and distractions in honor of the victorious general. From such a guest, Agrippa II also expected a few favors in return. His heterogeneous and servile kingdom was on the point of disintegrating following the secession of two predominantly Jewish cities, Tiberias and Taricheae, on the shores of Lake Genesareth. Helping the king to regain his possessions would also strengthen Rome's control in Galilee, and Vespasian did not hesitate to fall in with plans that reflected such obviously convergent interests.

After concentrating his troops in the pagan city of Scythopolis (Beth-Shan), Vespasian moved to the western bank of Lake Tiberias, a region all too familiar to Josephus. Tiberias, over which Josephus as governor-general had never managed to gain real control, had fallen into the hands of the anti-Roman faction led by Jesus son of Saphias, while the leader of another faction, Justus, who had begun by favoring the uprising, had now rejoined forces with Agrippa II. Had Josephus been present, Vespasian would probably have made use of him to launch an appeal to a third faction still active in the city, that loyal to Agrippa, and to discourage Rome's enemies by showing them the ex-governor of Galilee vanquished and in chains. A decurion named Valerianus was sent to parley without much success, since he was forced to abandon his horse and flee on foot. Shortly after that, a group of important citizens made a conciliatory gesture to Vespasian, the war faction fled the city, and Agrippa was able to reoccupy it nearly intact.

The anti-Roman party had taken refuge north of Tiberias in the large town of Taricheae (Magdala, today's Migdal) on the lakeshore. Its forty thousand inhabitants were already hard pressed to accommodate the many people from outlying districts who had flooded into the city for protection. Josephus, who had fortified Taricheae while governor-general, although not to the same extent as he had its neighbor, had stayed there frequently at the time. When he comes to describe its sad fate he takes a moment to bid farewell to a place where everything had seemed to combine to make life pleasant and livable: fresh air, pure water, luxuriant vegetation, and an abundance of fruits and fish of all kinds.

It is at this point in Josephus' narrative that we most clearly see how his perspective on military operations had changed. Henceforth, everything is seen from the victor's camp. Josephus' voice seems suddenly to have become a Roman one—indeed, it is the voice of a hagiographer of Titus. This is the guise he assumes for us, for example, when he re-creates (following the purest Greco-Roman historical practice) the speech in which Titus, who had been detailed, with only six hundred elite cavalrymen, to do battle against a much larger enemy, masterfully roused his own troops, frustrated at the late arrival of reinforcements sent by Vespasian. Titus then led the assault against the enemy force, a part of which was drawn up outside the walls. And it was he who first entered the city in pursuit. Josephus describes him performing caracoles on his horse, invincible, sparing innocent inhabitants and saving his rigor for the "real culprits" (*JW* III, 501); his achievements impressed his father. He did not play an active part in the third phase of the battle, which was waged on the lake: Roman rafts laden with armed and armored soldiers battled with light skiffs manned by exhausted men. Once again, Josephus imagines for us the water red with blood and the stench of rotting bodies strewn along the once-enchanting shores.[2]

The Roman slant of Josephus' narrative is also evident in the manner in which he attempts to absolve Vespasian of base treachery. After the victory at Taricheae, the general had sent its inhabitants home and pretended to grant amnesty to the foreigners, in reality leaving them no choice but to go to Tiberias. There, he assembled them in the stadium, massacred some twelve hundred of the "unserviceable" among them, selected six thousand of the healthiest, and sent them off to Nero for the construction of the canal across the Isthmus of Corinth[3] and sold the rest (numbering 30,400) into slavery. Having done so, he regained his camp at Amathus (Hama), located near two famous watering places, across from Tiberias. In justifying his protector's actions Josephus very nearly makes these prisoners of war seem like common criminals (*JW* III, 542).

When reading Josephus' narrative we must not forget that at the time he published the final version he took care to pay grateful homage to two successive emperors, Vespasian and Titus, nor that he had accounts to settle with certain Jewish factions (in this case the one led by Jesus son of Saphias). He also depended heavily on Roman reports, to which he was privy both at the time and later on, in Rome, where he was allowed access to the Imperial archives. We are thus dealing with a Roman narrative, especially with regard to incidents where the military chronicle is not counterbalanced by any other eyewitness testimony.

We get the same impression from his description of the taking of the three fortresses that continued to stand against Rome in the northern part of the country: Mount Tabor, Gamala, and Gischala.

The taking of Mount Tabor—another of the fortifications Josephus had established during his time as governor-general—is described in a few lines. True, the task was performed by the tribune Placidus, who succeeded through trickery.

Although located on the other side of the Jordan on the Golan Heights, the second fortress, Gamala, had also been a part of the territories entrusted to Josephus. The former governor-general, who had equipped it with ramparts and tunnels, gives an extraordinarily precise description of the site and convinces us that it was to all intents and purposes impregnable. Even today, when we see this peak shaped like a camel's hump (*gamal* = camel in Hebrew; whence its name, Gamala) rising out of its rock-strewn plateau, we are amazed at the audacity of anyone's having elected to live on it. "The houses were built against the steep mountain flank and aston-

ishingly huddled together, one on top of the other, and this per-
pendicular site gave the city the appearance of being suspended in
air and falling headlong upon itself" (*JW* IV, 7).

King Agrippa II, who wanted to regain possession of the
town, had been unsuccessfully laying siege to it for seven months.
When Vespasian arrived with his three legions, Agrippa turned to
intimidation and attempted to obtain a surrender by addressing the
defenders of the fortress from the foot of the ramparts. Their
response was very like the one Josephus was later on to receive in
similar circumstances during the siege of Jerusalem: a stone hurled
at him by a sling (which only struck the king on the right elbow).
Once again, the Roman army's engineers worked wonders: earthworks were rapidly thrown up and the ballistas went into action.
The battering rams were then brought forward and opened a
breach through which soldiers poured into the fortress amid the
tumultuous sounds of trumpets and the clash of arms. Yet the city
was far from taken. Its configuration was highly unfavorable to the
attackers, for the defenders, entrenched above them in the upper
town, was able to repel them with ease, hurling rocks and weapons
down upon them. The attackers were squeezed in the narrow alleyways and crushed in the lower city as the roofs of buildings in
which they had sought protection collapsed on them. Even Vespasian found himself in difficulties and owed his life only to his
prompt withdrawal outside the walls. In a high-flown speech to his
troops Vespasian admitted that they had suffered a disaster,
reproached them for having given in to "barbarian" impetuosity,
and counseled them to act in future with a more Roman discipline
(*JW* IV, 39-48).

Unlike Jotapata, the town did not lack water, for there was
a spring inside the walls. After a month of siege, however, food
supplies were very low. Prey to hunger, many of the besieged had
fled through the tunnels. Three events were to contribute to the
eventual fall of the fortress. A handful of legionnaires succeeded in
undermining one of the towers, which collapsed, causing a terrible
panic of which the Romans took full advantage to begin massacring the population. Then Titus, who had been on a mission to

the governor of Syria, arrived and gave new impetus to the attack. Lastly, a sudden windstorm—it was the month of November—came up and threw the defenders, who had taken refuge high in the fortress, off balance at the same time as it propelled in their direction the arrows released by the Romans. Here too, the carnage was horrible: the victors, enraged at the lengthy siege, are reported to have tossed even nurslings into the ravines. There were no survivors.[4]

Here too, Josephus' account has a partiality that can be explained, at least in part, by his reliance on Roman sources. Vespasian's retreat is described as a divinely inspired action, Titus' timely arrival as a stroke of Providence. As for the heroes, they are no longer the valiant Jewish defenders, as had been the case in Jotapata, but intrepid legionnaires like the decurion Aebutius, killed in combat, or the Syrian centurion Gallus, who, profiting by his knowledge of Aramaic,[5] had managed to upset plans of which he had gained knowledge by overhearing a dinner-table conversation.

The last site of resistance in Galilee, Gischala, did not require such a great deployment of forces. Vespasian sent the Xth Legion off to Scythopolis and himself returned to Caesarea with the Vth and XVth, leaving Titus to take Gischala with a thousand horsemen.

Gischala had been the birthplace of John son of Levi, Josephus' sworn enemy, about whom he cannot find harsh enough words: "A traitor, a scoundrel, a cheat even with his dearest friends, a rascal, a bandit" (*JW* II, 585). For that reason his account of the fall of Gischala has become a model of extreme historical partiality. Following Josephus' usual line, the inhabitants of Gischala were purportedly peaceloving folk in the grip of a handful of miscreants, among them John. Titus the compassionate had hoped for a prompt surrender. John used the pretext of the Sabbath to beg the magnanimous young leader for a suspension of hostilities and basely used it to flee to Jerusalem, taking with him not only his comrades-in-arms but whole families. According to Josephus, Titus found "solace" for having been so tricked by killing six thousand fugitives and reducing nearly three thousand women and children to slavery

(*JW* IV, 115-116); as for the inhabitants who had remained in the city, they were treated with exceptional indulgence. "Galilee was thus now wholly subdued."

Such passages, in which Josephus seems to be settling strictly personal accounts while indulging in the most arrant flattery, are the most difficult for his modern reader to read without discomfort.

NEWS FROM JERUSALEM

Vespasian brought his campaigns to an end in the autumn of the year 67 with the taking of Jamnia (Yavneh) and Azotos (Ashdod), in the southern part of the coastal plain, and then returned to his winter quarters in Caesarea, where Titus had arrived before him. Admitted to the company of these leaders, Josephus was able to glean a steady stream of information about what was going on in Jerusalem. The events of that winter plunged him into despair, while at the same time reassuring him that he had made the right choice.

Refugees from all over the province were flowing into Jerusalem. In spite of the ominous precedents, they believed they would be safer in the Holy City than anywhere else. Among the newcomers, John of Gischala reminded the city's population of the difficulties the enemy had encountered in Galilee and used them to inspire resistance: "Even had they wings," he remarked, "the Romans would never surmount the walls of Jerusalem" (*JW* IV, 127). Such words found a special response among the young: families were divided.[6]

From its beginnings, the anti-Roman revolt had been accompanied by a veritable social revolution. After the insurgents set fire to the house of the high priest and the palace of Agrippa and Berenice—both of whom had Roman connections—they burned the city archives to destroy records of indebtedness. At least some of the insurgents seem to have been engaged in a battle of poor against rich. This faction was led by an aristocrat, Eleazar son of Simon, whose partisans called themselves "Zealots." The name was apparently intended to be complimentary, for it managed to arouse Josephus' ironic comment: "so these miscreants called them-selves, as though they were zealous in the cause of virtue and not that of vice in its basest and most extravagant form" (*JW* IV, 161). The name quite obviously refers to the ideal of zeal in the service of the Lord to which the Maccabees had earlier been loyal. The Zealots regarded themselves as the soldiers of God and believed that, as such, they were entitled to special protection. Whence their ardor and intransigence. At the beginning of the war the Zealots had eradicated another faction that was close to them ideologically, the Sicarii, whose leader—a certain Menahem related to Judah the Galilean—had been excessively arrogant.

In the year 66 when, following the defeat of Rome's party, an oligarchic power had been established in Jerusalem under the leadership of the high priest Ananus (Hanan), care had been taken to keep power out of the hands of Eleazar son of Simon because of his well-known despotic tendencies. Soon, however, lines of com-munication had to be reestablished with him for reasons of public finance: Eleazar was in possession of the booty seized from the Romans.

The flood of refugees that had converged on Jerusalem in the summer of 67 had served to strengthen the Zealot faction. Many of those from the countryside who had come to seek refuge in the Holy City believed that they would be better protected there than elsewhere both because of the city's strong ramparts and because of the existence in its midst of the Temple. Where would the living God be more present than in His dwelling place? This is probably the real meaning of the words of John of Gischala quoted earlier, with their reference to wings. Thus, Eleazar, who was already occupying the Temple, saw his troops increase.

These hotheads regarded the attitude of many of the city's notables as singularly lukewarm. Three members of the royal family were living in Jerusalem, and when this was discovered they were quickly executed. Suspect persons were taken prisoner and then basely murdered in their cells by a hired assassin. Finally, all privi-leges were abolished by decree: the high priests were no longer to be chosen from among the members of a few great families but were to be selected by lot from among all the priestly families, whatever their social standing: ironically, the post eventually fell to an exceptionally uncouth villager named Phanni (Phineas) son of Samuel, who had some trouble understanding what had befallen him. Historians of the Jewish war in the last century were not far off the mark in drawing from such occurrences all kinds of analogies with the French Revolution.[7]

The oligarchy in power, led by two aristocratic high priests, Ananus and Jesus (Joshua) son of Gamala, was scandalized. Furthermore, it regarded it as unbearable that the Temple should be occupied by Eleazar's troops—as if they had some monopoly on the Lord God—and profaned by fighting men with fresh blood on their sandals. Ananus had no trouble arousing the people against the Zealots, who were compounding sacrilege with murder. Josephus has him deliver a long and moving harangue, which the historian slants to suit his own purposes: the Romans were at once less cruel and less sacrilegious than the Zealots. This is a notion Josephus was often to return to later as he witnessed the turn events were taking. Faithful to his social class, he was no less shocked than the rest of his caste upon learning of the Zealots' actions. His hatred of them was further stoked by the fate they reserved for his former friends.

However, it must be said that Ananus, by arousing the people against the Zealots, was the person perhaps most responsible for unleashing civil war. He managed to gain control over the outer precincts of the Temple and forced his adversaries to take refuge in the inner precinct, whither his religious scruples prevented him from pursuing them. At this point in his narrative, Josephus makes a passing comment that brings out the social aspects of the confrontation: Ananus had the gate to the second precinct guarded by his men, but he authorized persons of rank "to hire some of the lower classes and sent them to mount guard in their stead" (*JW* IV, 207).

What were the true motives of the upper-class faction led by Ananus? It is true that after a moment's hesitation the High Priest had also participated in the anti-Roman revolt that had led to Cestius' defeat. But times had changed and Galilee had fallen, and the Roman forces would soon be moving on Jerusalem. We cannot exclude the possibility that the party in power might now have considered coming to terms with the enemy. We can imagine that such a possibility might have suited Josephus, since it would have justified his actions, but he raises it, admits it, or denies it to suit the demands of his narrative. However, all rabbinical tradition concerning the flight of Johanan ben Zakkai would seem to support it, if we grant those writings some basis in historical fact.

Further confirmation can be found in the attitude of John of Gischala. The Galilean leader enjoyed the solid support of the Jerusalem power structure. We will recall that the Pharisee teacher Simon son of Gamaliel had taken his side in his quarrel with Josephus and had persuaded the high priest Ananus to appoint a commission of inquiry. Upon his arrival in Jerusalem, John had undoubtedly immediately rejoined his friends' camp and had later begun to have doubts about their true intentions, making him more sympathetic to the Zealots. He was thus drawn into playing a double game and removed his mask only when he could be certain that Ananus had indeed dispatched emissaries to Vespasian. Josephus seizes upon John's actions as a pretext to brand his old enemy with the same opprobrious name so often used against himself: "traitor."

John's information forced the Zealots to seek help from outside. They drafted a letter "concisely stating that Ananus had imposed on the people and was proposing to betray the capital to the Romans; that they themselves having revolted in the cause of freedom were imprisoned in the Temple" (*JW* IV, 228). The letter was addressed to the Idumaeans.

As their name implies, the Idumaeans, or Edomites, were descendants of Edom, another name for Esau, which made them brothers to the sons of Jacob-Israel, at least in theory. Brothers, perhaps, but originally enemy-brothers, as witness the biblical history of their relationship, which is fraught with incessant quarrels and confrontations. In 129 B.C.E. John Hyrcanus—the son of Simon, the last of the Maccabean brothers—had annexed to Judea, recently freed from the Syrian yoke, the southern plains where the Idumaeans were still following their ancestors' nomadic way of life. In a step rare in Jewish history, he converted the Idumaeans by force, making them what the Talmud describes as "lion proselytes,"[8] who were far less highly regarded than the "just proselytes" who had converted because of some inner spiritual desire. A few decades after this mass conversion, the Idumaeans were to produce two important political figures: Antipater, who was to be the real master of the country during the reign of the weak Hyrcanus II, and his son, Herod, as seen in Chapter One.

However solid their conversion may have been, the Idumaeans, who retained their ethnic separateness, were henceforth regarded as wholly Jewish from the point of view of faith. Thus, the Zealots were able to rely on their devotion to the Holy City. The Idumaeans' bellicosity was also well known; Isaac's blessing upon their forebear Esau in Genesis 27:40 had not been in vain: "By thy sword shalt thou live." No sooner had the Idumaean leaders received the summons from Jerusalem than they called for a mass levy and set out to place their swords in the service of the Lord.

Their arrival reversed the situation on the ground. Ananus' party was now caught in the middle, but his followers were determined not to open the city gates to admit the Idumaeans. Jesus son of Gamala vainly attempted to convince the Idumaeans of the Zealots' bad faith and to persuade them either to lay down their arms or to turn back. Speaking through one of their leaders, Simon son of Cathlas, the Idumaeans responded with all the sensitivity of the newly converted: So, the very party that was ready to welcome the Romans would shut the gates to them, true followers of the Lord, who had come to defend the Sanctuary!

During a nocturnal storm, and while the sentinels slept, a handful of Zealots slipped out of the Temple and opened the city gate nearest the Idumaean camp. The Idumaeans, after having delivered their allies in the Sanctuary, took possession of the outer precincts and hewed down their adversaries: at dawn, Josephus reports, there were 8,500 dead. Their fury was not spent until they had executed the two principal leaders of the aristocratic party, Ananus son of Ananus and Jesus son of Gamala. The bodies of the two high priests were left unburied.

The news upset Josephus more than it did anyone else. Ananus and Jesus had been men he deeply restored, in whose wisdom he had trusted to spare his fellow citizens from the worst.

Their disappearance was not only a source of personal sorrow given the close ties of friendship between the families; it was also a fatal historical event, signifying for Josephus the triumph of crime over virtue.

And there are all the feelings to which Josephus did not give voice, for he was writing a history, not a private journal—his anxiety over the fate of his own family. Not only was his father, Matthias, known to be a close friend of the murdered leaders, but the Zealots regarded him as the father of a traitor. Matthias was thrown into prison; that is the last trace of him we have.

The Zealots and Idumaeans created in Jerusalem an atmosphere strikingly like the one that prevailed in Paris during the Reign of Terror. Twelve thousand young aristocrats were imprisoned and summarily executed. For certain prominent citizens, like Zacharias son of Baris, a mock trial was held, but the seventy-one member tribunal—the required number for criminal trials—refused to pronounce the death sentence. Zacharias was thus simply murdered in the presence of his judges; the others, at least, were spared.

Soon, however, the Idumaeans, who were ashamed of the role they were being made to play, returned to their lands, leaving the field free for the Zealots. The massacre of the nobles continued apace. Josephus learned with horror of the execution of two prominent persons—Gorion, the son of the Joseph ben Gorion[9] who with Ananus had led the revolt in 66, and Niger the Peraean, ex-governor of Idumaea and the only general to have survived the Ascalon expedition early in the war. Thus, the early great leaders of the movement were being ousted by the extremists, a process that can be observed throughout recorded history.

From beneath this mountain of corpses, a new political authority was to emerge: John of Gischala, Josephus' worst enemy.

During the winter of 67–68, not a day must have passed for Josephus without its burden of tragic news. His feelings during this period must have been vastly different from those of the Romans among whom he was living. For them, the civil war in Jerusalem must have seemed like an unexpected blessing. Some generals wanted to attack the capital at once to take advantage of the windfall. Acting with the authority of his experience, his age and his past victories, Vespasian reined in their impatience: the enemy factions might well join forces against the Romans; better let them fight among themselves for as long as possible.

Listening to the tales of the refugees who had managed to escape from the capital, Josephus now had but one wish: that the Romans should take Jerusalem without delay.

ENCIRCLING JERUSALEM

As soon as the winter was over, Vespasian set his new tactical plans in motion. Instead of marching directly on Jerusalem, he encircled it from a distance, and with the help of the tribune Placidus he took the region of Peraea, across the River Jordan, with its capital, Gadara, which left only the fortress of Machaerus, farther to the south. In order to operate more freely in Judea itself and in Idumaea, in the spring of 68 he transferred the bulk of his army to Antipatris, not far from Jaffa. Moving from there to the south, he took Lydda (Lod) and Jamnia (Yavneh) where, Josephus tells us, he installed "an adequate number of residents from those who had surrendered" (*JW* IV, 444). We recall the school of Yavneh, founded, rabbinical tradition tells us, by the Pharisee Johanan ben Zakkai with Vespasian's benevolence. Vespasian then moved south again and ravaged the western borders of Idumaea. In reaching Jericho, which was one of his goals, he was eager to avoid crossing the rest of Idumaea and the Judean desert to the east, both of which regions were extremely hostile to him. Instead, he made a flanking movement to the north, came to the Jordan valley, and, after a forced march across its burning expanse, arrived at the legendary palm-filled oasis of Jericho, all of whose inhabitants had fled.

The fertility of the site, which produced such rare plants as the balsam or balm tree, enchanted Vespasian.[10] He was also fascinated by the amazing and unique properties of the "Asphaltic Lake" (the Dead Sea) and tested them by throwing bound men into it and watching them rise to the surface. An echo of the wonderment of the Roman legions and their commander can be found in the pages of the *Natural History* of Pliny the Elder, who collected their observations with great interest; after all, he was one of Vespasian's confidants.[11]

Not far from Jericho at a site known today as Qumran, there lived a community of Essenes, which Pliny also mentions.[12] It was probably on this occasion that its members, fearing the Roman advance, fled into the surrounding mountains, bearing with them their most precious possessions, their sacred scrolls, which they concealed in jars and hid deep within the hillside caves, where they were to remain for some nineteen centuries undiscovered. They are known today as the Dead Sea Scrolls.

Thus, by the beginning of June 68, Jerusalem was encircled in the southwest, the west, the north, and the east by a line of troops forming a perimeter some thirty-six to sixty kilometers distant, the two nearest Roman positions being Emmaus to the west and Jericho to the east.

The south, which was still in the hands of the insurgents, was far from secure. The Sicarii held the fortress of Masada and were gradually growing bold enough to make incursions into the surrounding countryside to bring more territory under their control. During Passover of the year 68 they got as far as the oasis of En-Gedi, near the shores of the Dead Sea. With them was a certain Simon bar Gioras ("Son of the Proselyte"), from Gerasa in northern Judea, a young man of uncommon physical strength and a temperament more warlike than politic. Simon viewed his friends' expeditions as exercises in timidity owing to their refusal "to venture far, so to speak, from their lair" (*JW* IV, 507). After the death of the high priest Ananus he decided to organize the defense of the whole area up to and including Jerusalem. He raised an army, made up at first of slaves he had freed and later joined by the inhabitants of the villages of the region, and supplied it by sending out raiding parties to plunder the countryside.

For the moment, Simon's new army worried the Jews more than it did the Romans. A dangerous firebrand, Simon was inordinately ambitious, and his men already regarded him as tantamount to a king. The Zealots launched a sortie against him to keep him away from Jerusalem, whereupon he fell back on Idumaea. The defection of Jacob, one of the Idumaean leaders, who had been seduced by Simon's hospitality and promises, brought the entire region under the latter's control virtually without a struggle. He entered the age-old city of Hebron, where even in those early days the marble tombs purported to be those of the Patriarchs were being displayed to the curious. The road to Jerusalem lay open. Simon's forty thousand men ravaged the countryside through which they passed like a plague of locusts; the most fertile land became a desert beneath their feet. The Zealots, terrified at their approach, attempted another sortie and managed to capture Simon's wife along with her attendants. Aware of her husband's great affection for her, they hoped by holding her hostage to force the hot-blooded warrior to give in. However, he reacted more "like a wounded beast" (*JW* IV, 540), and his threats so terrorized the Zealots that they returned her to him.

In Jerusalem, John of Gischala's Galileans, allies of the Zealots, were presiding over a reign of terror. So successful were they that a delegation led by the high priest Matthias, of the famous line of Boethos, was dispatched to Simon to ask for help. The latter entered the capital to the acclamations of the mob, and the terror was replaced by renewed civil war.

Through all these fratricidal confrontations the Roman troops continued to move forward. Cerealis, one of Vespasian's generals, took Hebron, where Simon had left a garrison, and burned it. The Romans also succeeded in occupying the Judean mountains to the south. They were now within thirty-five kilometers of Jerusalem.

In the spring of 69 the situation on the ground could be summed up as follows: Jerusalem was totally cut off from the rest of the country. The Roman vise had been tightened to a line some thirty kilometers from the city in every direction save the southeast, toward the desert, where three fortresses were still holding out: Herodian, Masada, and, across the Jordan, Machaerus. Vespasian and his troops now turned their eyes toward Jerusalem, which the civil war was making weaker day by day.

But some unexpected events that were occurring thousands of miles away were about to give the Holy City some respite.

NEWS FROM ROME

Since June 68, Caesarea—even more, perhaps, than the rest of the Roman world—had been hanging on the news coming from the Empire's capital. Vespasian, who had returned to his headquarters between campaigns, was preparing his great offensive against Jerusalem when he received astounding news, news that reawakened all his hopes: on the ninth of June Nero had committed suicide in a Roman suburb. Josephus awaited further news as anxiously as did Vespasian himself. The Julian-Claudian dynasty had come to an end. Who would inherit the empire? Would his prophecy come true? For both Roman general and Jewish captive, wild hope was quickly followed by despair. Back in Rome, Vespasian's name was not even mentioned, in spite of his victories; the theater of operations was too far away.

The uprising against Nero had begun in Gaul, where Vindex, the pro-praetor in the province of Lyon, had been the first to proclaim the emperor's deposition. He had offered power to Galba, an elderly general of famous lineage and the governor of Spain-Tarascon, who, at the age of seventy-three, was still waiting to be raised to the supreme magistracy that had so often been predicted for him. Galba's election as emperor plunged Vespasian into disappointment mingled with anxiety. He believed that Galba—perhaps aware that he had a rival—had secretly dispatched men from Spain with orders to assassinate him in Judea. He therefore kept close to Caesarea, leaving the city only on brief expeditions and returning frequently.

After several months had passed, Vespasian decided to send his son Titus to Rome, ostensibly to hail the new emperor and seek his orders but actually to sound Galba out as to his intentions with regard to himself. This is implicit in Josephus' narrative. And in fact Titus did take to sea, despite the winter weather (it was now January), accompanied by Agrippa II, who was in duty bound to pay homage to the emperor like any other vassal ruler. At Corinth they received news of Galba's assassination after a reign of seven months and seven days. While Agrippa calmly continued on his way to hail the new emperor, Otho, Titus hastened back to Caesarea to be the first to bring the news to his father.[13]

Back in Caesarea, Josephus may have been privy to the lengthy conversations that now ensued between father and son, conversations in which each weighed Otho's chances of holding on to power. In fact, at the very moment Otho had been having Galba assassinated in the Forum, the legions in Germania had been electing their own leader, Vitellius, as emperor. To conciliate Vitellius, Otho had offered him the hand of his own daughter, but Vitellius' lieutenants were already marching on Rome. It was civil war. Defeated at Bedriac, near Verona, Otho was to commit suicide after reigning for only three months.

The choice of Vitellius had been an unfortunate one. His character has been summed up in a single sentence. While walking through the battlefield where his troops had fought so valiantly for him in his absence, he observed his companions holding their noses because of the smell and remarked: "The corpse of an enemy always smells sweet, and particularly if it is that of a fellow citizen."[14] It was soon realized that in Vitellius the country had saddled itself with a new Nero: cruel, gluttonous, and depraved, the new emperor brought the Roman orgy to its apogee, while the city of Rome fell prey to the greed of his hardened troops.

Vespasian could not help but compare his own merits with those of the new emperor, for whom he felt a boundless contempt. He believed himself worthy of power, but his innate prudence kept him from presenting himself for the post. The pitiful situation in Rome was paralyzing his actions in Judea: was he to lay his dearly achieved conquests at the feet of an unworthy and dissolving empire? Josephus, a witness to Vespasian's dejection, anxiously awaited his decision. However, Vespasian decided not to set out for Rome. It was still winter, the sea was dangerous, and who knew what might not happen in Rome before he could get there? His uncertainty lasted until June of the year 69. Rome's fate was to be determined in the East.

During the past year (June 68 to June 69), known to history as the Year of the Four Emperors, the army had already thrice made and unmade an emperor. Throughout the empire, the army had become aware that it was not just a military force but a political one as well. The Army of Judea was deeply attached to its leader. It knew he was capable of governing and felt that it had more right to appoint the new emperor than did corrupt praetorian guards or units of the Army of the West, which had not waged so harsh a war. Three legions strong, not counting auxiliaries, Vespasian's army had the means to impose its choice.

If the candidate of the Army of the East were to become emperor, the future seemed assured. Vespasian had a worthy heir in the person of Titus, a fact that would help to solve the problem of succession. In Rome, he also had another son, Domitian, who would rally the aristocracy, and, more importantly, a brother, Sabinus, who was head of the police and who would do what was necessary to see that his brother did not meet with any resistance.

Such were the arguments Josephus must have often heard in the camp at Caesarea—we cannot go so far as to say he inspired or instigated them. There were doubtless those who recalled his prediction after Jotapata and regarded it as a favorable omen. Nevertheless, Vespasian insisted on being begged and persuaded . . . he was a prudent man by nature. Two emperors, Nero and Otho, had been forced to commit suicide in the space of a year, and a third, Galba, had been murdered. Vitellius' present position was shaky, true, but there might still be some other general waiting in the shadows, someone who could steal a march on Vespasian. The road from Caesarea to Rome was a long one. Josephus tells us that to force Vespasian to make up his mind the soldiers even gathered around their leader and threatened him with drawn daggers.

Roman historians were to prefer other versions of events: According to Suetonius, shortly after Otho's death two thousand legionnaires in the Army of Moesia, assembled in the town of Aquileia, had decided to select an emperor themselves.[15] They had reviewed all the possibilities among the longtime consular legates, and some soldiers who had served in Syria had brought up the name of Vespasian . . . and that, for the moment, had been that. Some time later, Tiberius Alexander, the prefect of Egypt, had got wind of this and, approving the idea, had his legions pledge themselves to Vespasian on the first of July. Ten days later the Army of Judea had followed suit. Another contemporary Latin historian, Tacitus, has the movement beginning in Alexandria and attributes the initiative to Tiberius Alexander, telling us that it was enthusiastically welcomed by the Judean legions two days later, on July 3.[16]

Josephus' version reverses the chronological order of those two narratives and has Vespasian elected first by his own troops. And indeed, what is more likely, given the times, that Year of the Four Emperors? It should be added that Josephus has the advantage over the two Latin historians in that he was actually present. His re-creation of the excitement in Caesarea at this moment in history and of the legionnaires' arguments in favor of Vespasian has great vivacity as well as the ring of truth. Although present-day historians rarely turn to Josephus for the answers to purely Roman questions, his testimony should in this case be given preference.

Mucian, the legate to Syria—to which Judea was still attached for administrative purposes—was secretly wildly jealous of the Roman general who had begun as his subordinate, but managed to keep his feelings to himself in the face of the army's acclaim. His adherence erased Vespasian's last vestiges of hesitation.

Assured of the backing of the large province of Syria, Vespasian turned next toward the other part of the Roman East, Egypt. That rich province was of the utmost importance, for from its principal port, Alexandria, with its famous lighthouse, sailed the ships laden with corn for Italy.[17] The man who controlled Alexandria could starve Rome.

Thus, as soon as he had taken the decision to stand as emperor, Vespasian wrote to Tiberius Alexander, the prefect of Egypt. He informed him of his own army's enthusiasm and offered him high posts if he could obtain Egypt's support for his candidacy. The reply was not long in coming. On July 1, Tiberius Alexander had the two legions of Egypt and its people swear allegiance to Vespasian. So important did Vespasian consider this backing that he was to date the beginning of his reign from July 1 (thereby, perhaps, misleading the two Latin historians mentioned earlier). Vespasian thus openly recognized that he owed his throne to a prefect of Jewish birth born in Alexandria, Tiberius Julius Alexander, the son of the alabarch[18] Marcus Julius Alexander—himself a Roman citizen and practicing Jew—and nephew of the philosopher Philo who, despite his arguments, had been unable to persuade him to remain faithful to

Judaism.[19] In his youth Tiberius Alexander had renounced his faith for the sake of his career—and he had succeeded.

Thus the "ambiguous oracle" so well known throughout Judea seemed to have been fulfilled, but in a manner much different than some might have hoped: a new master of the world seemed now to have emerged in the East.

FREEDOM REGAINED

The first time Vespasian had heard this prophecy applied to himself had been two years ago, from the lips of an enemy general captured at Jotapata—Josephus son of Matthias, a native of Jerusalem. Now, as Fortuna smiled upon him, he remembered his prisoner. Two years earlier, he had not yet dared believe a prediction he suspected of being a mere fabrication prompted by fear. Now, however, he regarded Josephus as being endowed with a supernatural power, the "minister of the voice of God" (*JW* VI, 626). Was it right that such a man remain in chains?

Thus, one day in the summer of the year 69, Josephus was summoned to appear before the new emperor and his son Titus. In the presence of Mucian, the governor of Syria, and other generals to whom he had bragged about his prisoner's oracular gifts, Vespasian commanded that Josephus' chains be removed (*JW* IV, 626). Titus felt that this was insufficient reward: for two years, they had held prisoner a man who should never have been subjected to such an indignity. Such an injustice must be effaced; the humiliation must be wiped out by the symbolic gesture of having the chains publicly struck off. Vespasian acceded to his son's wishes. Before all present, the captive's chains were struck off with an ax. Josephus was a free man once more, his lost honor restored, his two years of captivity erased.

The new emperor needed a few more months to consolidate his power. Vitellius still reigned in Rome, but few of the Legions remained faithful to him. Mucian, on Vespasian's orders, was already advancing on Italy with an imposing army. In mid-December, Sabinus, Vespasian's brother, felt the time was ripe to invest the Capitol. The hill was soon retaken by German soldiers loyal to Vitellius, however; the Temple of Capitoline Jove was burned to the ground[20] and Sabinus was executed on the eve of the entry into Rome of the first of Vespasian's supporters. The ensuing battle produced more than fifty thousand dead. Vitellius' throat was slit as he left a banquet at which he had drunk and eaten even more than usual. On the following day, December 20, Mucian entered Rome and had Vespasian acclaimed as emperor.

Vespasian received the news of Vitellius' demise at Alexandria. If the messenger who brought the news had made the dangerous winter crossing, he would have reached the Egyptian coast around the first of January of the year 70. All the habitual presents the Romans offered each other to celebrate the January kalends— dates or honey to make the year sweet, pieces of silver or gold to make it prosperous—must have been viewed as favorable augurs for Vespasian's new reign. Indeed, upon arriving in Egypt the Roman had consulted the oracle of Serapis, and rumor had it that under the aegis of the god of healing he had publicly performed two miracles, restoring the sight of a blind man and causing a cripple to walk.[21]

The new emperor had traveled from Caesarea to Alexandria with a large train of attendants, which included not only Titus, but Josephus and his wife as well. The young woman must also have benefited from the imperial clemency and been freed, but she was to derive only a fleeting pleasure from her refound liberty, for she died on the way to Alexandria. Josephus tells us nothing more; we will never know the cause of her death or whether her husband mourned her. In any event, he must have recovered rapidly, for shortly after his arrival in Alexandria he took another wife (L 415).

Josephus was awestruck by one of the empire's most beautiful cities, the largest after Rome. He describes its port, the famous Pharos, the ceaseless bustle. He was probably presented to the Prefect of Egypt, Tiberius Alexander. He almost certainly knew him to be an apostate, and in spite of the necessary deference he must have paid him, he was undoubtedly shocked. Indeed, Josephus is our only source for the Prefect's true origins. In *Jewish Antiquities,* after mentioning his family, Josephus was to add: "Alexander's piety

was far different, for he was to abandon the customs of his fathers"
(*JA* XX, 100). Nor was Tiberius Alexander content to be a mere
apostate. He seems to have been fated to act against the Jewish people. As procurator of Judea in 46, he had crucified both of the sons
of Judah the Galilean,[22] and it was also he who, in the year 66, had
crushed the Jewish uprising in Alexandria with a bloodbath.[23] Josephus could have heard tales of those awful massacres from the survivors; his disapproval seeps through the studiedly neutral tone of
his narrative. Tiberius Alexander was to continue to contribute to
Jewish misfortunes, for as he left for Rome, Vespasian asked him to
accompany his son Titus to lay siege to Jerusalem.

During the months of January and February 70, Josephus
was present for the parade of ambassadors who came "from the
world over" to congratulate the new emperor. There were governors of provinces and royal allies whose lands were an integral part
of the empire. There was Vologesius, the king of Parthia, which
bordered the eastern regions subject to Rome; he placed forty
thousand archers at Vespasian's disposal.[24] The world's second city
did not have room enough to accommodate all the visitors.

The winter over, Vespasian set sail from Alexandria for
Rome. But he did not forget Judea. Had he not been elected
emperor, he himself would have laid siege to Jerusalem. Now, he
entrusted that task to Titus, even though he felt that his son was
still too young to confront so many problems without help. He
therefore placed at his side Tiberius Alexander, a mature, experienced man who was familiar with the terrain. And the party
accompanying the young heir, who already bore the title of Caesar,
also included Josephus son of Matthias.

VII

BENEATH THE WALLS OF JERUSALEM

He hath abhorred his sanctuary, he hath given up into the
hand of the enemy the walls of her palaces . . .
LAMENTATIONS OF JEREMIAH, 2:7

In Josephus' life certain months are more important than entire years. Such was the case with the six months he spent in Galilee. Such was also the case of the half year he was to spend in the daily company of Titus at the time when Titus was preparing, organizing, and achieving what was to be the crowning Roman victory: the taking of Jerusalem.

While the youthful prince set out to win fame by great deeds, Josephus watched his native city crumble day by day, knowing that persons dearer to him than all the world still resided within its walls and aware too that within it stood the one Temple of his God.

THE MARCH ON JERUSALEM

Josephus reports Titus' itinerary from Alexandria back to Judea with astonishing precision, and this sudden exactitude is highly significant. It cannot be explained by his possible recourse to one of Titus' campaign diaries at the time he was writing, for in narrating other events he does not appear to have used other pertinent documents that would have been at his disposal. Josephus is precise because the return to Judea occurred in conditions that were quite different from those of the journey to Alexandria. On the trip out, he had been a newly released prisoner, still getting used to feeling his limbs freed from the weight of his chains, a man concerned about the health of his young wife, who was about to die. When it came time to make the return trip, he had grown used to being a free man once again, and the friendship of Titus, the heir apparent and new head of the armies, protected him from evil wishers and even made him privy to some decisions. As a result, he became a more knowledgeable and attentive witness.

When he came to look back on it, the Roman army's implacable progress toward its goal must have seemed to him like the progress of fate. And as for the fate of the Holy City, he feared the worst. The man who had vanquished the Jews, who had vanquished him, Josephus, was now Emperor. Was that not itself a sign that God had pronounced an awful sentence against His people?

Terrible things had been happening in Jerusalem. Although the city was empty of Romans, blood had flowed like a river in its streets to the very portals of the Holy Temple. The flower of the nation was being slaughtered with no thought for age or merit. A handful of irresponsible men were battling each other in a struggle for power.

Josephus was in Alexandria when Vespasian received news that civil war had again broken out in Jerusalem. Once the moderates had been got rid of, the three extremist factions in the city had been unable to reach agreement. Eleazar son of Simon, who had led the Zealots from the beginning, had no intention of serving under the orders of John of Gischala, a relative newcomer to the city, and younger to boot. As for Simon bar Gioras, he felt that if the gates were opened for him, it was because he was to be given power. Thus, instead of preparing to withstand the coming siege, the three factions had begun to fight among themselves.

Eleazar, who had recruited the last of his remaining noble friends, was now left with a very small number of men. However, their position on the ground was relatively favorable. Careless of sacrilege, they had installed themselves in the inner precinct of the Temple, where they had access to the large reserves of foodstuffs intended for the priests. Their position overlooked that of John's men, more numerous, who had set up camp in the outer precinct below and who were themselves fighting on two fronts, since they were also exposed to the projectiles launched by Simon's troops. From time to time John was even forced to form his men up back to back so that they could fire in both directions; as a rule, however, the fighting took the form of skirmishes rather than fixed battles, and was waged in spurts, with missiles or arrows. Indeed, combat was not intense enough to prevent the faithful from going up to the Temple Mount to sacrifice; worshippers were occasionally brought down by a stray arrow.

In their attempts to sap each other's strength John and Simon could do no better than set fire to stores of foodstuffs laid up in case of a siege: "All the environs of the Temple were reduced to ashes, the city was converted into a desolate no-man's-land for their domestic warfare, and almost all the corn, which might have sufficed them for many years of siege, was burnt up" (*JW* V, 25). In the distant echoes of these days that are still to be heard in the rabbinical accounts written at least two centuries after the fact, no note sounds more clearly than this: thanks to the wise precautions of a few notables, for example Gorion, the city had enough supplies to hold out for years (three, ten, twenty-one, or twenty-two, depending on the source),[1] but certain extremists had set fire to the stores in an attempt to compel the inhabitants to fight with the fury and determination of despair. Whatever the arsonists' motives, the Holy City was now forced to prepare to face famine as well as siege.

Marching on Jerusalem at his protector's side, Josephus—if we view him dispassionately and objectively—looks to us very like a traitor: he could envisage the inevitable outcome of the struggle and had gone over to the victor's camp. That, however, is far from how he saw himself. Trusting in his friend Titus, Josephus was hoping to salvage what could be salvaged, to bring his irrational brothers to see reason. As for those he deemed responsible for the ruin of his homeland, he hated them much more than any Roman could. Confident that they would receive their just punishment, and perhaps even eager to participate in it, he saw himself in the role of Justice pursuing Crime.

ROMAN ORDER AND FACTIONAL "FOLLY"

Books V and VI of *The Jewish War* contain the most complete and detailed account that we have of the siege of Jerusalem. Indeed, without Josephus we would know very little about it: one or two pages by a few Greco-Latin historians,[2] and the edifying reinterpretation set forth a century or two later in the Talmud. The principal difference between those sources and ours is that the latter is a contemporary account by a person who was deeply moved by the spectacle to which he was a powerless witness.

Josephus, without ever bearing arms, was henceforth to be a part of the Roman army, and everything about it only served to increase his admiration. Titus had four legions to use in the siege: the three that had served under Vespasian (Vth, Xth, XVth) and the XIIth from Syria, which had been dreaming of revenge ever since its setback at the beginning of the insurrection, along with sizeable allied and auxiliary contingents recruited in the region. This large force advanced in impeccable order and joined up not far from Jerusalem. Titus, aware of the importance of setting an example by taking personal risks, himself led the first reconnaissance mission around the city walls. The legions were then stationed on the hills surrounding the city, the Vth slightly to the rear to the north and the Xth on the Mount of Olives, while Titus himself set up camp on Mount Scopus with the XIIth and XVth. From there, he had a perfect view of Jerusalem and the "grand pile of the Temple gleaming afar" (*JW* V, 67). Josephus, at his side, now saw his city again for the first time in three and a half years.

When they saw this preliminary encircling of the city, the three factions inside it finally began to lay aside their fratricidal quarrels and return to their senses. Making up their minds to test their bravery against the enemy rather than against each other (*JW* V, 74), they managed to give the besiegers a bit of a struggle with a first sortie. However, the rivalry among them continued to be intense. John of Gischala took advantage of the Passover feast to wipe out Eleazar's Zealot faction and penetrate into the inner precinct, where the Temple provisions were stored.

Josephus gives a very exact estimate of the total number of Jewish combatants, which he sets at 23,400; Simon had 10,000 men with fifty leaders, the Idumaeans 20,000 with ten leaders, John 6,000 men with twenty leaders, who were eventually joined to Eleazar's 2,400 Zealots. There were now two factions confronting each other within the walls: Simon and the Idumaeans on one side, John and the Zealots on the other. While John occupied the Temple and its immediate environs, including the Cedron Valley, Simon held the lower city southeast of the Temple and all the upper city to the west. Entrenched in those positions, the two parties fell to fighting once again, as Josephus informs us with vengeful bitterness, "doing all their besiegers could have desired" (*JW* V, 255).

In the meantime, the Roman noose tightened. Titus was now camped at the northwest angle of the ramparts, near Herod's tomb. In four short days the entire area from there to Mount Scopus had been leveled. Every vineyard and kitchen garden had vanished. Josephus watched as the low stone walls and enclosures were destroyed and every tree chopped down to serve as filling to level the uneven ground. One part of his Jerusalem, the district outside the walls, had already disappeared. Soon, the entire surrounding landscape would be transformed. In constructing the siege works Titus had had the countryside cleared of trees. Henceforth, for two thousand years the hills of Judea were to be covered with nothing but bare rock and brambles.

The Roman army worked tirelessly to construct huge earthwork embankments. Simon tried in vain to stop them by hurling down rocks and javelins or by using the war machines that had been captured from the enemy during the very first battle of the uprising in 66, but which few of his men knew how to operate. As for the Roman side, their machines were formidably effective, especially those of the Xth Legion. The projectiles of its ballistas caused heavy damage to the ramparts, especially after someone got the idea of blackening the white stone missiles so that the besieged would not be able to see them coming at them from a distance and have time to take cover. The Romans acted with order and method in all things. Josephus watched as the engineers measured the distance from the embankments to the ramparts by throwing out a horizontal plumbline to ensure that the battering rams would be able to operate properly.

When the horrible thud of the battering rams suddenly began to resound against the ramparts on all three sides of the city, the two rival factions once more decided to set their differences aside temporarily. Now united against the common foe, John's and Simon's men began to toss burning brands down on the wooden war machines and to move out in small groups to tear off the hoods that protected the battering rams. They even attempted a mass sortie to set fire to the machines, and they might even have succeeded had it not been for the resistance offered by the elite troops from Alexandria and the rash bravery of Titus, who personally slew twelve of the fighters in the vanguard, forcing the remainder of the troop to withdraw.[3] Soon, ironclad assault towers were moved forward, and the first breach was opened in the outer wall. However, there were two inner ramparts, behind which the Jews now withdrew.

From the beginning of the siege proper, which lasted for fifteen days and ended with the taking of the outer ramparts, Josephus had witnessed the confirmation of what he already knew: his people had all gone mad. The war that had been begun with such unthinking excitement and exhilaration was now being waged with a self-destructive fury. After having slaughtered the nation's elite, the factions were now bent on destroying each other while the most formidably organized and equipped army in the world stood at the gates. Their belated return to sanity would mean nothing. *Quos vult Jupiter perdere dementat prius.*[4] Jerusalem had fallen into the hands of madmen. Had the Lord therefore willed its loss?

JOSEPHUS, A TOOL OF PSYCHO-LOGICAL WARFARE

Titus had not kept Josephus with him merely out of friendship. His former prisoner was an integral part of his plans.

Prior to any siege the Romans customarily issued an appeal for surrender. In most cases the leader of the expedition would personally exhort the besieged to give up. Titus had done so in Galilee before the fortress of Gischala, the tribune Placidus at Mount Tabor. When the Roman leader was accompanied by an important personage from the opposing camp who had sided with Rome, this task often fell to him. Thus, prior to Vespasian's siege of Gamala, Agrippa II had attempted—in vain—to treat with the besieged. Such a man had the advantage of being able to address Rome's enemy in his own language, but the sight of a compatriot who had gone over to Rome was liable to produce an effect opposite to the one hoped for: the only reply had been a stone hurled from a sling, which had injured Agrippa's right elbow (*JW* IV, 14).

Titus had known at the outset that the siege of Jerusalem would be long and arduous. Owing both to its site and its fortifications, the city appeared to be impregnable. Built on hills, it was surrounded by unpassable ravines. In the lower city was the abundant Pool of Siloam, and there were a number of capacious rainwater cisterns. The besieger could not rely on thirst to bring him victory.

Where Jerusalem was not protected by ravines, in the north and northwest, it was surrounded by a triple wall. The outer, third, rampart, whose construction had been begun in around 41 or 42 by King Agrippa I, was intended to protect the new quarter of Bezetha that had spread out to the north of the Temple at the foot of the Antonia Fortress, which had been retaken from the Romans at the very beginning of the war. The construction of the outer rampart had been quickly broken off so as not to arouse the suspicions of the Roman authorities. Had it been continued, Josephus tells us, the city would have been truly impregnable, for no machine would have been able to dislodge the immense stone blocks ten by five meters in size which had been set aside for its construction (*JW* V, 153). This wall was to have been located forward of the existing wall, next to the Damascus Gate. It was hastily completed when the war broke out and fell before the first assaults, on May 25, 70.

The second wall was located behind the third on the north side and joined to the Antonia Fortress, which protected the Temple.

The first—and oldest—wall is probably the one of which Israeli archeologists have uncovered some sixty-two meters in today's Jewish quarter in the Old City, a wall that is at least seven meters thick.[5] It surrounded all the other districts of the city, including the Temple. Its total perimeter was between five and seven kilometers.

Each of the walls was broken by massive towers. There were ninety of them on the third wall, fourteen on the second, and sixty on the first. Some of these deserve special mention. At the northwest corner was the Psephinos Tower, near where Titus set up camp; it was an octagonal tower seventy cubits (thirty-five meters) high, the summit of which afforded a panoramic view from Arabia to the Mediterranean. Grouped together a bit farther south on the west side (near the present Jaffa Gate) were three towers built by Herod: the Hippicos, named after a friend, the Phasael, named after his brother, and the Mariamne, named after his wife, the daughter of Hyrcanus II, whom he had murdered in a jealous rage. Today we can still admire the foundations of what is incorrectly called the "Fortress of David."

The Antonia Fortress, which dominated the Temple at the junction of its north and west gates, was built on a rocky eminence and had four corner towers. The Temple itself was also a fortress. Herod had rebuilt it with the immense stone blocks that can still be seen in all that remains of it, the Western Wall (known also as the Wailing Wall).

Under the Herods the city had been almost completely rebuilt. According to Josephus' nostalgic description, it was a vision of beauty allied with strength, its towers were veritable palaces, while Herod's palace itself was a true fortress. As for the Temple, which had also been rebuilt according to Herod's grandiose vision, it was a true marvel standing at the heart of that other marvel, the city itself. Built in record time thanks to the popular fervor that had helped to raise its immense stone blocks, its decor was continually being augmented by the contributions of pious Diaspora Jews, among them the alabarch Alexander of Alexandria, father of the Roman general Tiberius Alexander, who was even now one of the leaders of the siege of the Holy City, serving at Titus' side.

In having Josephus accompany him, Titus had been hoping to achieve by psychological warfare a victory that it appeared would be very lengthy and difficult to win by force of arms. Josephus spoke the language of the besieged. He was known to all the inhabitants of his native city; his example might give them cause to reflect. If he could manage to persuade them that there was no other course than the one he himself had chosen in Jotapata—surrender—then Titus might be able to conquer Jerusalem at the lowest possible cost.

The young prince knew he could count on the eloquence of his former prisoner. For that matter, Josephus assured Titus that the people were weary of war, that they loathed the faction leaders, and that they were looking forward to the arrival of the Romans so as to be delivered from them. Josephus could not stop thinking of the anguish and suffering of those, like his family, who were trapped in the city by the siege. He could not imagine that all the intelligent people he had frequented there could willingly be following irresponsible gang leaders called John of Gischala or Simon bar Gioras. Titus had no need to dictate to Josephus his address to the besieged. He was fully aware of what they needed to hear.

Josephus probably went into action for the first time in early May, after Titus had set up camp near the Psephinos Tower. His first harangue, about which he has little to say, was probably without result (*JW* V, 114). His failure, however, enabled Titus easily to see through the ruse when, the following morning, men suddenly appeared on the ramparts to call in loud voices for peace, promising the Romans that they would open the gates if they would first state their terms. Meanwhile, a small group of purported extremists was ejected from the city by the peace partisans, a trick to draw the Roman soldiers forward to meet them and thereby make them easy targets. Many Romans impetuously fell into the trap. Titus' wrath against the surviving Roman soldiers, all of whom had disobeyed direct orders, was terrible. However, he decided not to deal with them too severely, since it was in his own interests not to diminish his troops.

Josephus spoke a second time following one of Titus'

reconnaissance missions around the ramparts, to "endeavor to parley with those on the wall on the subject of peace" (*JW* V, 261).
On this occasion a friend, the tribune Nicanor, was wounded by an
arrow in the left shoulder. This second failure on Josephus' part
determined Titus to begin throwing up embankments for the siege.

His first two attempts had made Josephus especially wary.
He had begun to realize that the situation was quite different from
what he had at first thought. Yes, there were factions among the
besieged, but now they had all joined forces against the besiegers
and seemed to have many fighting men, despite their losses. He
took this as evidence that they now had the population's support.
When firm in his former belief that the party for conciliation was
in the majority, Josephus had been hoping that some Jew would
open the city gates to Titus—that had occurred before, in the time
of Pompey. However, today the case was quite the opposite. The
Jews, who were now entrenched behind the second wall, were
continuing to battle tooth and nail, which would seem to indicate
that they had not lost all hope. Josephus was once more being made
aware of a quality in his own people with which he had long been
familiar, namely, their extraordinary tenacity in adversity. Simon,
whom he considered to be no more than a common thief, was
behaving like a true leader, loved and respected; his men were prepared to die for him. The Jewish fighters were just as heroic as their
besiegers.

When a Jew named Castor, who with ten men was man-
ning the tower in the center of the northern ramparts, begged the
Romans for mercy while five of his comrades pretended to kill
themselves to demonstrate their disagreement, Titus was almost
taken in. He gave a tongue lashing to a soldier who had fired an
arrow at Castor, hitting him in the nose, and had been about to
send Josephus to continue to parley with Castor. Josephus knew
better and held back others who were tempted to try. Events
proved him right: no sooner had a foolhardy man named Aeneas
moved forward to the tower than Castor sent a huge stone flying in
his direction, which struck a Roman soldier. Furious at having
been taken in, Titus stepped up the pace of the battering rams. As
the tower fell, Castor and his comrades set fire to it and fled

through the tunnels, giving the impression they had thrown themselves into the flames.

Notwithstanding the resistance he encountered, it took Titus only five days to breach the second wall. He passed through the opening he had made with a thousand legionnaires and his elite troops only to find himself in a part of the city that was a maze of narrow alleyways inhabited by small craftsmen and shopkeepers. He magnanimously spared their lives. However, a daring charge by the defenders, facilitated by their being at the top of the steeply sloping street, caused him to beat a hasty retreat. When Titus returned to the assault, the Jews managed to close the breach with their bodies for three days. It was not until the fourth day that he was able finally to gain control of the second rampart. This time, he did not hesitate to have it razed at once.

However, Titus was not forgetting the importance of psychological warfare. Before attacking the rampart, he engaged in a two-part maneuver designed to intimidate. He began by offering the besieged a magnificent spectacle. The time had come to distribute the duty pay provided by the Roman army. Instead of having it doled out discreetly by his officers, Titus decided to make a grandiose and solemn ceremony of its distribution. The entire army was drawn up within sight of the besieged, who massed on the ramparts to witness the spectacle. The Roman soldiers fell out in full battle array, the cavalry magnificently caparisoned. Beneath the brilliant sun the scene was aglitter with silver and gold. The ceremony lasted for four days, the time it took to pay each man in each legion. The spectators on the walls were obviously awestruck by the display, but on the fifth day the plea for surrender for which Titus had been hoping did not come. And yet the Jews were now contending with new enemy: hunger.

Forced to undertake still another siege to bring down the last remaining rampart, Titus began to raise embankments at two points, one against the Temple opposite the Antonia Fortress, which was being defended by John and the Zealots, and the other to the northwest opposite the upper city occupied by Simon and the Idumaeans. By this show of stubborn determination Titus was still hoping to intimidate the enemy. However, the Jews had the advantage of their elevated position. Furthermore, they had finally learned how to work the machines they had captured from the Romans (three hundred oxybellum and forty stone throwers) and were thus able to impede the work on the embankments considerably. "Aware that speech is often more effectual than arms" (*JW* V, 361), Titus once again attempted to exhort the besieged to surrender. He assured them that their resistance was in vain because the city had already virtually fallen, and he promised clemency. Not sure of being understood, for he was far from able to address them in their mother tongue (he probably spoke to them in Greek rather than in Latin), he once again had recourse to Josephus' services.

At this point in his narrative Josephus dwells at some length on the speech he was called upon to deliver on this occasion. He spoke it while pacing below the ramparts, "endeavoring to keep out of range of missiles and yet within earshot" (*JW* V, 362).

The insertion of speeches in a narrative was a common technique employed by the Greco-Latin historians Josephus took as models for his own work. Each of the seven books of the *War* contains one or two speeches in either direct or indirect discourse. They are usually discourses of ideas rather than of character. Josephus has not put himself center stage to such a degree since his narrative of the events at Jotapata and his prophecy to Vespasian. Now, he emphasizes the importance he attaches to the harangue he delivered at that decisive moment in history by devoting considerable space to it (nearly a dozen pages, some sixty paragraphs in most current editions). In fact, what we have presented to us as a single speech is probably a synthesis of several successive harangues, for a bit further on Josephus mentions a "round" of "unremitting" exhortations (541).

Josephus begins by reporting his speech to the besieged in indirect discourse and only later switches to direct. This has a significance beyond mere stylistic interest. In fact, a purely Roman discourse is followed by a Jewish one. At the outset, Josephus is in fact speaking merely as Titus' spokesman, perhaps even as an interpreter translating the speech the latter had just made in Greek. He beseeches his compatriots to spare themselves and the people, "to spare their country and the Temple" (*JW* V, 362).

His arguments take several forms. First of all, knowing the importance of the Temple in the eyes of the Jews, he assures them that they can rely on the Romans' *religio,* that is, their much-vaunted respect for the sacred.[6] He then takes up the political argument already developed in the speech made by Agrippa II in the early days of the uprising: Roman power is invincible, it already extends over virtually the entire universe; there is no dishonor in surrendering to the masters of the world. Indeed, it is a law of nature that the weaker give way to the stronger.

We shall return to the next argument again—it concerned theology. Rome's successes prove it to be favored by Fortuna, the capricious goddess of the Greeks and the Romans, who was able to shift camps at will. However, Josephus (or Titus?) couches this notion in words that made it unacceptable to the Jews: "Fortune, indeed, had from all quarters passed over to them, and God who went the round of the nations, bringing to each in turn the rod of empire, now rested over Italy" (*JW* V, 367). The notion that the Lord had abandoned them and gone over to Rome touched the deepest part of their belief, and not only did it fail to convince them, it may well have succeeded in eliciting their rejection.

And indeed, as Josephus concluded his peroration, stressing the desperate character of the situation—two ramparts had already fallen, famine was beginning to ravage the city—and promising Titus' clemency, jeers (not to mention projectiles) began to rain down on him from the ramparts. Whereupon he launched into an entirely different kind of discourse, this one totally individual, a Jewish discourse, which he presents to us in direct voice.

This speech contains much to confound the historian versed in the Greco-Latin classic models. We might be listening to the homily of a rabbi rather than an exhortation on the field of battle, for Josephus shared with the besieged not only a common language but a common culture too, and it is in the latter that he searches for words capable of moving them.

He tries to prove to them the very thing they refuse to believe, namely, that God is no longer on their side. Arms are useless without divine support. This is the first point Josephus develops, with the help of many biblical examples. He begins by evoking all the times their forefathers had not needed to resort to arms since God had acted for them: when Pharaoh had seen that Sarah, Abraham's wife, was very fair and had her taken into his house, Abraham did not give in to the temptation to fight but let the Lord plague Pharaoh and his house with great plagues;[7] when the sufferings of the Hebrews in the land of Egypt became intolerable, the Lord sent ten plagues against their oppressors[8] and His people went forth "without bloodshed, without risk" (*JW* V, 383); when the Philistines bore the Ark of the Covenant into the Temple of Dagon they were smitten with "emerods in their secret parts" and forced to restore the stolen Ark and make all kinds of compensations;[9] when Sennacherib, the king of Assyria, laid siege to Jerusalem, "an angel of the Lord smote in the camp of the Assyrians an hundred fourscore and five thousand and when they arose early in the morning, behold, they were all dead corpses";[10] when the Jews were sent into Babylon, it was Cyrus who freed them after seventy years' captivity. Josephus' recourse to biblical history did not exclude his modifying certain details in passing, the better to buttress his argument, but that was also common practice among the rabbis of the Midrash, which was already taking shape at this date.

A contrario, his speech then turned to all the cases in which the Jews had futilely had recourse to arms instead of trusting in and relying on the Lord: under Nebuchadnezzar or in the early battles against Antiochus Epiphanus, or in two more recent episodes to which they owed their present servitude to Rome, the war of succession between Aristobulus and Hyrcanus II, and the retaking of Jerusalem by Herod in the short reign of Antigonus son of Aristobulus. And he concludes his historical panorama with the following words: "Thus, invariably have arms been refused to our nation, and warfare has been the sure signal for defeat" (*JW* V, 399); as a result, Josephus counsels the people of Jerusalem to "leave everything to the arbitrament of God and to scorn the aid of human hands [and] conciliate the Arbiter above" (*Ibid.*).

At this point in the speech moral preachment gains the upper hand. Josephus inveighs against the hidden sins of the factions as well as against the most obvious sin of all, the profanation of the Temple they are purporting to defend. In such circumstances, what help can they expect from the Lord? Had He intended to intervene, He would have done so long ago, hence it is not for His people but for the Romans that He is now working His wonders: abandoned springs in the outskirts of Jerusalem have begun to produce water again for the benefit of Titus' army. He returns to the theme of Israel's abandonment in favor of Rome, but this time it is couched in Jewish terms. Now it is not capricious Fortuna who has changed sides, but a haughty Providence that punishes and rewards. When Josephus reiterates his conviction that "God has fled His sanctuary," he is taking up a familiar notion in rabbinical Judaism, that of the exile of the *Shekhina,* God's immanent presence that cannot reside among sinners.

In a final emotional appeal Josephus exhorts his compatriots to repentance, which alone can move God and suspend His decree.[11] He shows them the last chance they have to spare the Temple and their families. Aware that there are those who would accuse him of thereby trying above all to save his own family,[12] he theatrically offers the life of that family along with his own: "Slay them, take my blood as the price of your own salvation. I too am prepared to die, if my death will lead to your learning wisdom" (*JW* V, 419). Josephus' rhetoric rises out of a real anguish, and he sheds real tears. He is sure that his arguments have touched at least a part of the populace, but they are not the ones with the power to decide. The combatants remain inflexible.

Shortly afterward, while continuing to pace beneath the ramparts, Josephus was struck in the head by a stone and fell senseless (*JW* V, 541). The Jews attempted to drag his body into the city but were forestalled by Titus' vigilance. Nevertheless, the besieged emitted shouts of joy, believing they had slain the traitor. Hearing the false news of her son's demise, Josephus' mother told her warders that her son had been dead to her ever since Jotapata, but in private, in the presence of her handmaidens, she wept (*JW* V, 544-545).

Josephus quickly recovered from his injury, and when he reappeared in public it was to cry for vengeance.

This new setback in the psychological war, in which Josephus was the principal weapon, forced Titus to return to the siege.

CRIMES AND PUNISHMENTS

The situation of the besieged became increasingly desperate. Each day the famine spread, and the number of desertions grew ever larger. John and Simon, however, were determined to fight on to the end. In another attempt to bring them to surrender, Titus sent back captured fighters whose hands had been hacked off; he was unable to break their spirit. True, the daily sight of some five hundred prisoners being publicly whipped, tortured, and crucified—often headdown—by the Romans was hardly likely to inspire confidence in the enemy's promises. "So great was their number, that space could not be found for the crosses nor crosses for the bodies"(*JW* V, 451). The four earthworks the Romans had thrown up with such difficulty in seventeen days were mined and burned by John's and Simon's men, who made daring raids outside the walls that amazed and baffled their opponents.

At this point, at least according to Josephus' account, Titus made a decisive move. He convened a council of war and listened carefully to the different opinions expressed. Rejecting the two extreme solutions—an immediate and massive assault or a lengthy siege to let famine do its work—he decided upon a middle ground that avoided both exposing the army to danger and letting it stand idle for too long: another wall would be built around the remaining ramparts to ensure a total blockade of the city. Then the siege could not possibly drag on unduly.

Estimates were that the building of the wall would take months; however, the zealous soldiers, urged on by their leader, labored so mightily that it went up in three days. It was thirty-eight stadia long (nearly seven kilometers) and flanked by thirteen guard posts between which the Romans constantly patrolled at night. A trap had closed around the Holy City.

Here, Josephus' narrative is replete with a mixture of merciless hatred and desperate compassion: hatred for the rebel leaders, compassion for the civilian population he felt to be their victim. The long list of the crimes he imputes to the instigators of the uprising can be reduced to one: they did not heed him, they did not give up when there was still time. Thus, they alone are held responsible for all the sufferings their ridiculous obstinacy has caused.

Famine in a city under siege is not a matter of hunger alone. It affects every law and rule of moral conduct. It reduces men to the level of beasts. Without having seen the sights he describes, Josephus nevertheless tells of once-wealthy men trading all their goods for a measure of corn and shutting themselves away to gobble it down, raw or cooked; he writes of members of the same family tearing a few miserable scraps of food from each other's mouths, of the brutal treatment meted out to those suspected of concealing food. The Talmud (*Gittin* 56a) would later sum up such lapses in the tale of Martha, a great lady of the priestly family of Boethos: venturing out-of-doors barefoot after having sent her servants to the market for food in vain, she dies of disgust at having trod on the rubbish in the streets, or, according to another version, she strews her gold and silver in the streets, crying out: "What is all that to me!"[13]

In the end, the besieged were reduced to eating grass, straw,[14] and the leather of their belts or sandals.

Following the construction of the wall of circumvallation, the situation within the city could only grow worse. Again, Josephus describes, as though he had been present, the innocent victims of the famine: "The roofs were thronged with women and babes completely exhausted, the alleys with the corpses of the aged; children and youths, with swollen figures, roamed like phantoms through the marketplaces and collapsed wherever their doom overtook them. As for burying their relatives, the sick had not the strength. For many fell dead while burying others, and many went forth to their tombs ere fate was upon them. And amidst these calamities there was neither lamentation nor wailing: famine stifled the emotions, and with dry eyes and grinning mouths these slowly dying victims looked on those who had gone to their rest before them. The city was wrapped in profound silence and night laden with death" (*JW* V, 513-515). Such are the scenes his feelings and his imagination (buttressed by a few reminiscences of the Lamentations of Jeremiah or Thucydides' description of the Athens plague) enabled Josephus to reconstruct.[15]

His indignation and hatred led him to describe in detail the behavior of the "brigands"—in other words, the rebels—who stripped the dead piled up in the houses and exited laughing, or who thrust their swords into cadavers. Although it was decided to have the dead buried at public expense, Josephus tells us that it was only because the living had begun to find the stench "intolerable" (*JW* V, 518).

The corpses, indeed, soon became too numerous, and the only solution was to toss them into the ravines surrounding the city where, still according to Josephus, the rotting bodies aroused Titus to pity. "He groaned and, raising his hands to heaven, called God to witness that this was not his doing" (*JW* VI, 519).

Yet the worst horror was yet to come: a woman driven mad with pain killed her baby to eat it. On this occasion too, Titus proclaimed his innocence before God (*JW* V, 201-219).

Indeed, one of the recurring themes in the *War* is that the treatment the Romans meted out to the Jews was no worse than the treatment the Jews meted out to themselves. And although there was no dearth of Roman atrocities, the "good" Titus always learned of them too late to stop them. Thus, the few fugitives who attempted to come over to the enemy all met a horrible end. Since the Romans' Arab and Syrian auxiliaries knew that before being searched some of these men had swallowed gold pieces in an attempt to bring some of their wealth out with them, they took to slitting open their stomachs. In a single night, we are told, as many as two thousand were so disemboweled (*JW* V, 552). Titus waxed indignant at the cruelty of the foreigners in his army, which was imitated by some of the Roman legionnaires, but he was loath to punish them, and the practices continued. "Advancing to meet the fugitives before the troops caught sight of them, these barbarians would massacre them, and then, looking round to see that no Roman eye was upon them, rip them up and extract the filthy lucre from their bowels. In few only was it found: the bare hope of finding it caused the wanton destruction of most" (*BJ* V, 560-561).

But if Titus was never responsible for any of it, not even the atrocities of his own troops, Josephus knew who were: they were the "brigands," the "factious." They were responsible for every famine victim as well as for the deaths of the opponents they continued to cut down. On Simon's orders the high priest Matthias son of Boethos, the same who had earlier opened the city gates, had his throat slit after having been forced to witness the assassination of three of his sons. Several members of the aristocracy also perished in the same manner (*JW* V, 531-532), after which one of Simon's lieutenants attempted to foment a plot against him, which was soon foiled.

Crimes against men were accompanied by what Josephus considered crimes against God. John of Gischala was especially guilty of these latter. Early in the siege he had used timber intended for the Temple to construct war machines. Next, he had had all the sacred vessels melted down, including precious vases offered by the emperor Augustus and his wife. Then he had dipped into the Temple reserves of oil and wine.

Josephus' indignation seems far in excess of the "crime." His partiality eventually arouses our indignation, as it did that of the French historian F. de Saulcy.[16] "Indeed, Josephus' hatred of those who had sacrificed their lives to throw off foreign domination is often all too evident. The historian who had deserted his fatherland's cause imputes every crime to his political foes, and here he exercises his indignation against facts that I am unwilling to see with the same eyes as he. Men set upon dying and defending to their last breath the sanctuary of their cult and their patriotism drink consecrated wine and rest their exhausted limbs by anointing them with oil intended for sacrifice. A strange crime, it is true, for men ravaged with hunger, men fighting every hour of the day and night. I have no hesitation in saying that John of Gischala is the one who comes out of it well, and I cannot keep from feeling greater esteem for him than for Josephus. Yes, he was quite right to tell his companions that the Temple should nourish its defenders." However, when we react in this way we moderns overlook the weight sacred things exerted on the antique mind, not to mention the mind of a member of the priestly aristocracy of the time.

On several occasions Josephus calls down punishment on the rebels' heads: "Nor can I here refrain from uttering what my emotion bids me say. I believe that, had the Romans delayed to punish these reprobates either the earth would have opened and swallowed up the city, or it would have been swept away by a flood, or have tasted anew the thunderbolts of the land of Sodom. For it produced a generation far more godless than the victims of those generations, seeing that these men's frenzy involved the whole people in their ruin" (*JW* V, 566).

THE DREAM OF THE HEAVENLY JERUSALEM

Josephus is constantly describing the "brigands" who were acting against mankind and good sense. He never allows us to understand what has inspired them to act as they do. "Folly" and "blindness" are, according to him, their only motives.

He used such terms on another occasion when describing the emergence of the "fourth philosophy," which came into existence in the year 6, and in introducing us to it he declared it to be the cause of every ensuing evil. His presentation, however, was vague as to the doctrine's content: in essence, it was Pharisaic doctrine with the addition of "an irresistible passion for liberty" (*JA* XVIII, 23). Its watchword—"God alone is leader and master"— falls into the most authentic lineage of Jewish thought, in which God is sole king. Josephus himself, in *Against Apion,* uses the term "theocracy" (literally the "power of God") to define the law of Moses in all its purity, for "it places power and strength in God"; yet he finds the fourth philosophy a pernicious innovation, which he never takes the trouble to define in any detail.

The founders of this "philosophy," who were desirous of no master but God, obviously could not accept a Jewish king (Herod's reign was to leave a disastrous memory) any more than they could foreign control; nor did they want a theocracy in the modern sense of the term, which would have bestowed power on the priestly caste, of which they were not members. Although Josephus views this philosophy as a fourth trend within Judaism, it cannot have arisen merely out of a simple nationalistic desire for independence.

If we put ourselves back in the early first century we can perhaps dimly imagine the impatience with which men awaited in that anxious present the coming of the Kingdom, i.e., the advent of the Lord promised by the prophets and, after them, by the various Jewish apocalyptic writings that flourished at the time. In ridding themselves of the Romans, the followers of the fourth philosophy surely believed that they were hastening the advent of God's reign. They regarded Rome as the Evil Empire, which, according to the Book of Daniel—which had a considerable influence on contemporary Jewish thought—would be history's last and would in turn make way for the Messiah.

The fourth philosophy's "innovation" consisted in this linking of Rome and the Evil Empire, and it is this aspect of the doctrine that fomented the apocalyptic restlessness that was to lead inevitably to war. This is why Josephus accuses the fourth philosophy of having planted in the land "the roots of the evils that would spring up later" (*JA* XX, 10). Indeed, it gave birth to the Sicarii, who emerged around the year 50 and who were to distinguish themselves at war's end by their heroic stand at Masada. It also inspired the Zealots of Eleazar son of Simon and John of Gischala, who was ideologically very close to them.

If we want to unravel the motives of the "brigands," the only thing Josephus vouchsafes us is an interpretation of some of their rare utterances, which he repeats, and in the diatribes he directs against them. In his harangue to the besieged that we summed up earlier, Josephus repeatedly tells them that they are cruelly mistaken if they think God is their ally: "Can you persuade yourselves that God still remains with his household in their iniquity—God who sees every secret thing and hears what is buried in silence?" (*JW* V, 413). During the final moments of the siege, on the seventeenth day of the month of Tammuz (July), when the flames were already licking at the Temple and the perpetual sacrifice had been broken off, Josephus again apostrophizes his old enemy John as follows: "And do you hope to have God, whom you have bereft of His everlasting worship, for your Ally in this war?" (*JW* VI, 100)

This, then, is what inspired the combatants to fight on to the end, even when all seemed lost. They continued to believe in a miracle, they still expected some divine intervention, for as soldiers of the Almighty they were certain He would protect them. In that light, we are better able to understand the words spoken by John of Gischala upon his arrival in Jerusalem: "Even had they wings, the Romans would never surmount the walls of Jerusalem" (*JW* IV, 127). Later, when all was clearly lost, he was to shout to Josephus that he would never fear being taken, for the city belonged to God (*JW* VI, 98). What had weighed the most in convincing the insurgents that Jerusalem was a safe haven had been the fact that it was the Holy City wherein dwelt the divine presence. The argument of the exile of the *Shekhina* employed by Josephus persuades us *a contrario* that it was the faith in its presence that underpinned the insurgents' intransigence and paradoxical confidence at even the most critical moments. The most destructive aspects of their behavior—the eradication of the moderates, the burning of food-stuffs—can be understood as ways to arouse the ardor of their despised fellows who were men of little faith, for they themselves were firm in the belief that they were entitled to divine protection because they were fighting for the Lord.

As for John's actions in the Temple, which so shocked Josephus' sense of priestly tradition, they too must be understood within the eschatological perspective of Kingdom Come. After all, what had the besieged said? "The world is a better temple for God than this one" (*JW* V, 458). Josephus wished to save the earthly Temple; they were already thinking of the celestial Jerusalem.

Such a faith endowed the insurgents with the supernatural courage that so impressed their foe: "But worst of all was the discovery that the Jews were possessed of a fortitude of soul that could surmount faction, famine, war, and such a host of calamities. They fancied the impetuosity of these men to be irresistible and their cheerfulness in distress invincible" (*JW* VI, 14).

The enmity between Josephus and John, pro-Romans and insurgents, moderates and diehards, reflects the opposition between politics and mysticism. On the one hand were those who had correctly assessed Rome's power from the beginning or those who had become aware of the adversary's strength with time and tended to compromise. On the other were those who, strong in the Lord's support, rejected the purely human aspects of the conflict: God would bring about the triumph of His cause.

THE FATE OF THE EARTHLY JERUSALEM

The fate of Jerusalem and the Temple was decided in a few short weeks of combat that were to be even more frightful than the preceding ones.

The Romans had concentrated their efforts on the Antonia Fortress, defended by John, which protected the northwest corner of the Temple. In order to construct their embankments it was necessary to have wood brought in from a great distance, for there was not a tree left standing for fifteen miles around. John's men failed in their attempt to destroy the earthworks. The rampart, already badly shaken by the battering of the rams, was then undermined and soon collapsed. The assailants now discovered, to their dismay, a second wall behind the first, and it took all of Titus' eloquence to restore his troops' morale.

Titus also kept up the psychological pressure. Knowing the Jews' esteem for their High Sanctuary, he offered them two more chances to surrender and thereby save the city and the Temple. Josephus translated Titus' speeches, adding several emotional pleas. However, he was met with the same contemptuous rebuff as before. Titus then called upon other high-ranking refugees, treating them on this occasion with great consideration in an attempt to soften the attitude of the besieged, but in vain.

The fighting recommenced. The narrow access to the Temple made hand-to-hand combat necessary. The first engagement, which began in great confusion in the middle of the night, lasted for nearly twelve hours. Josephus records many acts of heroism among the various Jewish factions, who were all caught up in the same enthusiasm, and cites the names of some of the fighters (*JW* VI, 148, 169-176).

The Romans returned to the difficult labor of constructing earthworks, now in the area between the Antonia Fortress, which they had razed, and the north wall protecting the Temple esplanade. An access ramp was slowly being raised to the Sanctuary. The Jews then set fire to the northwest gate to cut off the besiegers, who responded by burning the adjacent gate. The besieged then set a trap: pretending to retreat from the west gate, around which they had stacked pitch and dry wood, they waited until the Romans were passing through and then set fire to it. Now, debris and dead bodies were piled up within the holy precincts themselves.

For six days the siege machines had been battering at the huge stones of the Temple's outer walls, but with little effect. Soldiers now undermined the foundations of the northern gate, still in vain: Herod's monumental edifice stood firm.

The Romans were now left with no other alternative and were forced to call up the scaling ladders. The well-entrenched Jews lay in wait for them at the top of the walls and threw down anyone who managed to reach the top. Titus next ordered the gateways set afire; the silver with which they were clad melted; and the fire penetrated to their wooden core. However, it was confined and did not spread.

The Romans continued to be impressed by the exceptional beauty of the complex of buildings they were now in the process of destroying. Titus held a council with his six generals (Tiberius Alexander among them) to decide its ultimate fate. Some advised him to destroy the Temple, since it served as a focal point for the national fervor of the Jewish people; others were for sparing it if its defenders would agree to evacuate the precincts. According to Josephus, Titus had made up his mind to spare the Temple at all costs, for a monument of such great beauty did honor to the Roman Empire (*JW* VI, 241). Contemporary historians have always found this version of events suspect, especially because the account of a Latin historian—written later, it is true—flatly contradicts it.[17]

A daring Roman assault now forced the Jews to retreat into the inner precincts of the Temple. The following day was the tenth of Lous, according to the Macedonian calendar still in use in that part of the world, which corresponded to the ninth of Ab on the Jewish calendar—the same fateful date on which Nebuchadnezzar's destruction of the first Temple was always commemorated. Heavy with somber premonition, its approach was awaited with great apprehension. To the north, one of the soldiers, "awaiting no orders and with no horror of so dread a deed, but moved by some supernatural impulse, snatched a brand from the burning timber and, hoisted up by one of his comrades, flung the fiery missile through a low golden door, which gave access on the north side to the chambers surrounding the Sanctuary" (*JW* VI, 252). Titus, who was told of the incident while still in his tent, seems to have tried to stop the fire, but the legionnaires were in a state of uncontrollable excitement: "Passion," Josephus tells us, "was for all the only leader" (*JW* VI, 257). A second flaming brand was thrown against the golden gate of the Temple proper. The flames sprang up within; Titus and his generals withdrew, and there was no one left to prevent the soldiers inside the citadel from continuing to set fires. Thus, concludes Josephus, the Sanctuary was burned against Titus' will.

Meanwhile, a veritable slaughter was also raging. Many unarmed civilians, weakened by hunger, were within the precincts; their throats were slit, and "no pity was shown for age, no reverence for rank; children and graybeards, laity and priests, alike were massacred" (*JW* VI, 271). The sound of the lamentations could be heard from a great distance. The shouts of the legionnaires were echoed by those of the last remaining Jewish fighters, but it was above all the terrified screams of the vast crowd of people that had been trapped inside the Temple, mingled with the cries of those outside it in the upper city who could see the inexorable approach of the catastrophe. Six thousand people of all ages were trapped because, we are told, of "a false prophet who had on that day proclaimed to the people in the city that God commanded them to go up to the Temple court, to receive there the tokens of their deliverance." All perished on the spot in the fire set by the Romans, "some killed plunging out of the flames, others amidst them" (*JW* VI, 283-285).

Not a single building within the Temple precincts was spared. Standing amid the smoking ruins, Titus was proclaimed

Imperator,[18] and the Romans planted their insignia facing the eastern gate and sacrificed to them; for the Jews, there could have been no greater abomination.

There was one last emotional encounter. John and Simon now sent word they were prepared to parley. Titus, accompanied on this occasion by an interpreter other than Josephus, made a lengthy speech to them in which he recalled the Jewish nation's ingratitude for the many benefits Rome had bestowed upon it and expressed his displeasure at the contempt with which they had greeted his own peace proposals. He was offended, too, by the attitude of defeated men who, "even at the last extremity, do not so much as pretend to be suppliants" (*JW* VI, 348). The insurgents wanted Titus' permission to quit the city and take refuge in the desert with their women and children; they did not even offer to lay down their arms, for they had sworn an oath never to do so. Titus was furious: he would spare nothing and no one.

The fire spread to the lower city as far as Siloam, destroying whole streets, houses filled with the dead, and the former palace of the Jewish convert Queen Helena of Adiabene, although Titus did consent to spare her descendants, the sons and brothers of King Izates, whom he dispatched to Rome.

All that was now left was the upper city, which was overlooked by the three fortified towers of Herod's palace, in which the insurgents were entrenched. To the east, they could see the Temple and lower city aflame; to the west, they were within sight and earshot of Josephus, who paced back and forth at the foot of the ramparts, begging them to spare the little of the city that was left; their only response was to taunt him.

Eleven days after taking the Temple the Romans began to raise earthworks on the western flank of the city, opposite the royal palace. The disheartened Idumaeans attempted to desert *en masse,* but were prevented from doing so by Simon. Desertions, often by whole families, were becoming increasingly common, and the Roman soldiers, "sated with killing," were content to sell the captives rather than kill them; the price was low, since supply far outran demand. Certain priests, among them the guardian of the Temple treasure, were able to save their lives by turning sacred vessels and objects over to the enemy, along with aromatics and priestly ornaments and vestments.

After seventeen days, on the seventh of Gorpiaeus, Titus felt ready to order the assault. For the first time the blows of the battering ram created a panic. The besieged, realizing that their number was far inferior, abandoned their positions (in which they could not have resisted for long). The Romans, encouraged by this first easy success, planted their insignia on the towers and raised a hymn of victory. They then poured through the streets, swords bared, massacring and burning as they went. "They choked the alleys with corpses and deluged the whole city with blood, insomuch that many of the fires were extinguished by the gory stream" (*JW* VI, 406). When night fell, the fire "gained the mastery, and the dawn of the eighth day of the month Gorpiaeus broke upon Jerusalem in flames" (*Ibid.*, 407).[19]

In the grottoes under the city, where many of the defenders had taken refuge, the Roman soldiers encountered a fearful stench. Among the bodies of the suicides or the victims of famine they found additional prisoners, among them John of Gischala. As for Simon, he managed to remain in hiding for several days. After having failed to make his escape by tunneling his way out of the city, he tried to frighten the Romans by pretending to be a supernatural apparation. And, indeed, he did give them a start by appearing suddenly in the Temple courtyard dressed like a king in a white tunic and purple cape, most likely to denote his messianic pretensions. The Roman general Terentius Rufus, who was in command of the sector, easily took him captive. Massacre gave way to pillage. The lust for riches made the soldiers pitiless, and they were stopped only by "now having no victims either for slaughter or plunder, through lack of all objects on which to vent their rage" (*JW* VII, 1).

While the Romans reveled in the intoxication of their victory, Josephus was living through one of the most horrible nightmares a Jew can imagine. For the second time in history, the Temple had been destroyed and Jerusalem had fallen into the hands of its enemies. There was nothing left standing to recall the Holy City's former splendor. Titus ordered it razed to the ground, sparing only the three towers of Herod's palace, which were to be spared "as a memorial of his attendant fortune, to whose cooperation he owed his conquest of defenses which defied assault" (*JW* VI, 413). So efficiently did the demolishers do their work elsewhere in the city that "future visitors to the spot were left no ground for believing that it had ever been inhabited" (*JW* VII, 3). The victims "outnumbered those of any previous visitation, human or divine" (*JW* VI, 429). Many Jews had come to Jerusalem from throughout the land to celebrate Passover and had then found themselves trapped inside the city. A total of 1,500,000 people perished, according to Josephus. The fate of those taken prisoner was almost as bad: women and boys under seventeen were sold as slaves, the elderly and most feeble were slain on the spot, the handsomest and healthiest youths were reserved for the future triumph to be celebrated in Rome, while most of the others were kept for the cruel games in the empire's amphitheaters. Eleven thousand captives died of hunger, either because their captors did not feed them or because they refused to eat.

Josephus was greatly concerned about the fate of his friends and family. He did not find either of his parents, but his brother Matthias was still alive. Titus willingly released him, as well as fifty of his friends. In the ruined Temple into which the prisoners had been herded, Josephus was able to recognize one hundred and ninety people and managed to get them released without having to pay ransom. On the road to Tekoa, where he had been sent on a reconnaissance mission, Josephus recognized three more friends who had been crucified along with many other prisoners. "I was cut to the heart and came and told Titus with tears what I had seen. He gave orders immediately that they should be taken down and receive the most careful treatment. Two of them died in the physicians' hands; the third survived" (*L* 410–421). This period through which he lived with such a heavy heart, in constant contact with a rejoicing army sated with carnage, was obviously not the easiest of Josephus' many trials.

JOSEPHUS, THE NEW JEREMIAH?

Now, more than ever before, Josephus saw himself as a new Jeremiah. The prophet's lamentations must have sprung naturally to his lips:

> How doth the city sit solitary, that was full of people! how is she become as a widow! she that was great among the nations, and princess among the provinces, how is she become tributary! She weepeth sore in the night, and her tears are on her cheeks . . .
>> Judah is gone into captivity . . .
>> The ways of Zion do mourn . . .
>> Her adversaries are the chief, her enemies prosper; for the Lord hath afflicted her . . .
>> And from the daughter of Zion all her beauty is departed . . . (Lamentations, 1:1-6)

History takes strange turnings and is filled with strange coincidences. For the second time, the Temple had been destroyed—and on the very anniversary of its first destruction. How could it be other than some divine plan? The repetition of this awful disaster called up another historical parallel: Rome must be the new Babylon! Josephus was not alone in the thought. "Babylon" stands for Rome in the Apocalypse of Saint John as well as in two other Jewish apocalypses of the late first century, those of Esdras and Baruch.[20] Shortly after the fall of Jerusalem to the Babylonian king Nebuchadnezzar in 586 B.C.E., Jeremiah had prophesied: "This city shall surely be given into the hand of the king of Babylon's army, which shall take it" (Jeremiah, 38:3); "Though ye fight . . . ye shall not prosper" (*Ibid.*, 32:5); "Serve the king of Babylon and live: wherefore should this city be laid waste?" (*Ibid.*, 27:17); "He that abideth in this city shall die by the sword, and by the famine, and by the pestilence: but he that goeth out, and falleth to the Chaldeans that besiege you, he shall live, and his life shall be unto him for a prey" (*Ibid.*, 21:9).

Throughout the siege Josephus had delivered exactly the same warnings to his compatriots. He had been met with the same disbelief, the same hostility: "Let this man be put to death: for thus he weakeneth the hands of the men of war that remain in this city, and the hands of all the people, in speaking such words unto them: for this man seeketh not the welfare of this people, but the hurt" (Jeremiah, 38:4).

Like Jeremiah, Josephus had despaired at the "folly," the "blindness" of his political adversaries. "My people are foolish; they are sottish children, and they have no understanding: they are wise to do evil" (*Ibid.,* 4:22). Like him, he was terrified that their trial would only make them more stubborn: "O Lord, thou hast stricken them, but they have not grieved; thou hast consumed them, but they have refused to receive correction: they have made their faces harder than a rock; they have refused to return" (*Ibid.,* 5:3). "To whom shall I speak, and give warning, that they may hear? behold, their ear is uncircumcised, and they cannot hearken" (*Ibid.,* 6:10).

False prophets too had made their appearance in the midst of the horror and had promised victory, and Josephus, like Jeremiah, inveighed against them: "Hearken not unto the words of the prophets that prophesy unto you: they make you vain: they speak a vision of their own heart, and not out of the mouth of the Lord. They say still unto them that despise me, The Lord hath said, Ye shall have peace; and they say unto every one that walketh after the imagination of his own heart, No evil shall come upon you" (*Ibid.,* 23:16). So had they made attempts on his life, as with the prophet.

Josephus, like Jeremiah, had a single answer for everything that was happening in Jerusalem: God was punishing a generation that was corrupt, like that of the prophet's day, the Holy Place had been filled with "the blood of innocents" (*Ibid.,* 19:4) and become a "den of robbers."[21] "Robbers," "brigands"—Josephus could find no more fitting term for the fanatical criminals who had held the people's blood so cheaply for the sake of some vague ideal. They had drawn sword and famine down upon their innocent brothers. The prophecy the Lord had placed in Jeremiah's mouth had been realized in every detail, unlike the insane hopes expressed by the false prophets:

"Therefore thus saith the Lord concerning the prophets that prophesy in my name, and I sent them not, yet they say, sword and famine shall not be in this land; By sword and famine shall those prophets be consumed. And the people to whom they prophesy shall be cast out in the streets of Jerusalem because of the famine and the sword; and they shall have none to bury them, them, their wives, nor their sons, nor their daughters" (*Ibid.*, 14:15-16). "Even the carcasses of men shall fall as dung upon the open field, and as the handful after the harvestman, and none shall gather them" (*Ibid.*, 9:22).

Horror of horrors, a mother had even been seen to devour her own child. And was it not written: "And I will cause them to eat the flesh of their sons and the flesh of their daughters" (*Ibid.*, 19:9)?

In Josephus' eyes, Jerusalem had been made "heaps, and a den of jackals," and Judah "desolate, without an inhabitant" (*Ibid.*, 9:11). "For even the husband with the wife shall be taken, the aged with him that is full of days" (*Ibid.*, 6:11) and basely sold into slavery—for that, too, was written. The Holy City had been broken "like a potter's vessel that cannot be made whole again" (*Ibid.*, 19:11).

Long persuaded of his own prophetic gift, Josephus was now convinced that he was the new Jeremiah. He had witnessed one of the most terrible moments in history, one in which the Lord had averted His face from His people: "Is not the Lord in Zion? is not her king in her?" (*Ibid.*, 8:19). It meant nothing to have been right. Once the misfortune had occurred, the prophet was left to weep alone: "When I would comfort myself against sorrow, my heart is faint in me . . . Why then is not the health of the daughter of my people recovered? Oh that my head were waters, and mine eyes a fountain of tears, that I might weep day and night for the slain of the daughter of my people" (*Ibid.*, 8:18 *et seq.*).

Was life worth living? Josephus, like Jeremiah, must have cried out: "Cursed be the day wherein I was born . . . Wherefore came I forth out of the womb to see labor and sorrow, that my days should be consumed with shame?" (*Ibid.*, 20:14, 18).

As we have seen, however, Josephus was not a man to renounce the life he had been given. And Jeremiah offered him more than a life of sorrow and darkness. There were also reasons to hope. Even after the disaster, the Lord had still spoken to Jeremiah, telling him to purchase the field of his cousin in Anathoth, in the land of Benjamin. That symbolic act had been a sign that a new day was coming, the day of redemption: "For thus saith the Lord; Like as I have brought all this great evil upon this people, so will I bring upon them all the good that I have promised them. And fields shall be bought in this land, whereof ye say, It is desolate" (*Ibid.*, 32:42–43).

When, in exchange for lands near Jerusalem where he wanted to encamp his Roman forces, Titus offered Josephus a property located in the plain, he may have told himself that this was his field in Anathoth. If that were so, the remainder of the prophecy might also one day come to pass:

"Again there shall be heard in this place . . . and in the streets of Jerusalem, that are desolate, without man, and without inhabitant, and without beast, The voice of joy, and the voice of gladness, the voice of the bridegroom, and the voice of the bride . . . for I recall cause to return the captivity of the land, as at the first, saith the Lord" (*Ibid.*, 32:10–11).

VIII

THE JEW OF ROME

Weep not for the dead, neither bemoan him: but weep sore for him that goeth away: for he shall return no more, nor see his native country.

JEREMIAH, 22:10

Josephus was thirty-three years old when he left the shores of his native land for the last time in 70, never to return. The rest of his life was to be spent in Rome. He lived there long enough to write an immense *oeuvre* and to witness the reigns of three (and perhaps even four) emperors. Of this life of courtly intrigue and solitary literary composition he tells us very little, but we do have some evidence to help us reconstitute it.

SORROW AND TRIUMPH

Before quitting Judea, Titus had held a magnificent ceremony for his troops, which Josephus of course attended. Standing on a large platform in the midst of his officers, Titus had addressed his soldiers, lauding them for the devotion, obedience, and courage that had led them to victory. All who had distinguished themselves in battle were rewarded. Each man mounted to the rostrum when his name was called and received Caesar's warm congratulations, had his head crowned with a gold circlet, was presented with military decorations of gold and silver, and was promoted. A vast booty of gold, silver, vestments, and other objects was also distributed. After having played the part of victorious general, Titus turned to the role of priest: he recited prayers for the army and, descending from the rostrum, sacrificed in honor of the victory. The whole army was invited to celebrate, hundreds of cattle were slaughtered, and the feasting lasted for three days.

It was already September: the approaching season of bad weather would make the voyage to Italy a dangerous one. Leaving devastated Jerusalem in the care of the Xth Legion, Titus, with the Vth and XVth, returned to Caesarea, whither he had dispatched the spoils and prisoners of war reserved for his triumph in Rome, to be joined a short time later by Simon bar Gioras, the last rebel to be captured.

The entire winter of 70–71 was spent in typically Roman celebrations. In the inland city of Caesarea Philippi, where Titus spent considerable time, the abundance of available Jewish prisoners made it possible to hold almost perpetual games. These were basically of two kinds: combats between men and wild animals or combats pitting one group of men against another. After returning to coastal Caesarea, Titus organized luxurious spectacles to celebrate the birthday of his brother Domitian: 2,500 young Jewish prisoners lost their lives in these bloody games (*JW* VIII, 37-38). At Berytos (today's Beirut) even more resplendent celebrations were held to mark the birthday of his father, Vespasian (*Ibid.*, 39). In every city in Syria through which Titus passed on his progress to Antioch similar spectacles were arranged and Jewish prisoners perished in droves.

Did Josephus accompany his protector to these shows? It is not likely. Perhaps Titus had the delicacy not to insist on his presence. For his part, Josephus could always invoke the religious practices to which he had remained faithful, which forbade him from being, even passively, an accomplice in the shedding of blood. It was probably at this period that the Jews began to apply the first verse of the first Psalm to the Roman games: "Blessed is the man that walketh not in the counsel of the ungodly, nor standeth in the way of sinners."[1] Enshrining what was undoubtedly a much older practice, a second-century rabbi even composed the following blessing: "Thanks be to the Lord God of my fathers who hath placed me amongst those who frequent the place of study and the

Synagogues and not amongst those who frequent amphitheaters and circuses."[2]

Josephus does not tell us whether he accompanied Titus to Antioch. If he did, he may have seized the opportunity to intercede for the Jews of that city. In the East, where intercommunal rivalry had always been intense, the Antioch pagans now believed that the time had come for them to rid themselves of the Jews, who enjoyed the freedom of the city on the same footing as the Greeks and who were attracting many converts. Antiochus, an apostate from Judaism, had been fomenting trouble and exacerbating hatred by attempting to oblige his former coreligionists to sacrifice to the pagan divinities. The refusal of many of them to do so was interpreted as a dereliction of civic duty and led to massacres; with the approval of the Roman authorities the seventh day of rest was forbidden. Somewhat later, a fire that destroyed the city's public buildings was blamed on the Jews. The acting governor, Collega,[3] held an investigation into the matter: as had been the case in a similar instance, the fire had in fact been started by debt-burdened miscreants who had been attempting to get rid of the public records.

When Titus arrived at the outskirts of Antioch he noticed that the cries of the large crowd that had come out to greet him were interspersed with hostile calls against the Jews. An official request for their expulsion was submitted to him in the city's theater. Titus replied as follows: "But their homeland to which they ought to be sent, being Jews, has been destroyed, and now there is no other territory that can take them in." Disappointed, the people of Antioch attempted to obtain from him at least the destruction of the bronze tablets on which the Jewish rights or privileges where inscribed; this too he refused (*JW* VII, 109-110). Josephus may well have inspired his response.

On his way to Egypt, whence he would proceed by sea to Italy, Titus passed by Jerusalem. Josephus, who was with him, imputes to Titus his own feelings. "Contrasting the sorry scene of desolation before his eyes with the former splendor of the city, and calling to mind the grandeur of its ruined buildings and their pristine beauty, he commiserated its destruction . . . heaping curses upon the criminal authors of the revolt, who had brought this chastisement upon it" (*JW* VII, 112–113).

Titus then quickly crossed the Sinai. Reaching Memphis, he assumed the diadem, according to one of the rites of the cult of Apis, and it was said that he had even wanted to be crowned King of the East, a rumor he took pains to disprove by his behavior.[4]

Upon arriving in Alexandria, he released the Vth and XVth Legions to return to the provinces where they were regularly stationed, and he himself set sail for Rome. With him he took seven hundred prisoners of war he had selected in Caesarea for their height and physical beauty, along with the two principal leaders of the Jewish resistance during the siege of Jerusalem, John and Simon.

A few months earlier, Josephus had left in the great city of Alexandria his new wife, who was a native of the place. She was now to accompany her husband when Titus invited him to follow him to Rome.

The voyage, Josephus tells us, was "as favorable as he could have desired" (*JW* VII, 119). This is not merely an innocuous way of putting it: it is further indication that in his eyes Titus was indeed Fortune's favorite. Later on, Jewish oral tradition was to rewrite the narrative of this voyage. A terrible storm is supposed to have come up and, as a punishment laid on the sacrilegious victor, the profaner of the Temple, a mosquito that had flown into his nostril was said to have penetrated to his brain, causing him intolerable pain throughout the rest of his brief life.[5] Josephus' account is more historically correct: the voyage was as pleasant for him as it was for Titus, who enjoyed his company and invited him to share his princely accommodations (*L* 422), while the prisoners, in chains, traveled in the hold.

It is from Suetonius and not Josephus that we learn the itinerary of Titus' return. The ship put in at Regium (Reggio di Calabria) and Puteoli (Pozzuoli), north of Naples, and from there sailed directly to Rome, where, according to the Latin historian, Vespasian expressed surprise at the speed of Titus' journey, which reassured him with regard to his son's ambitions. On the latter point, Josephus' version is somewhat different. Titus was welcomed with popular rejoicing, as his father had been;[6] not only did all Rome come out to meet him, but the emperor himself came to welcome his son, thus adding to the glory of the victor of Judea.

In a cruel paradox, ever since Josephus had been plunged into mourning for his lost homeland he had been included in all the celebrations of that homeland's defeat. From Antioch to Rome, and even in Alexandria, all heathendom rejoiced, but he managed to remain aloof from the merrymaking, which must often have pained him deeply. Like all Jews of his class, he knew by heart all the Psalms, which provide an appropriate verse for any occasion. Often, he must have thought: "Lord, how are they increased that trouble me!" (Psalm 3:1). Another passage, this one from the sixtieth Psalm, would have seemed especially applicable to his present situation: "Who will bring me into the strong city? who will lead me into Edom? Wilt not thou, O God, which hadst cast us off? and thou, O God, which didst not go out with our armies?" The Lord had abandoned His people, He had not fought with them, and He had led Josephus to the great city of Rome, which the Jews rightly called Edom.[7] The Lord must have some plan for His protégé.

While waiting to find out what that plan might be, Josephus continued to enjoy the friendship of Titus and Vespasian. They would probably have given him a place of honor at their shared triumph, in which Titus' young brother Domitian also participated.

Years later, Josephus was still to recall the events of that day with great clarity. It had still been dark when the crowd had begun to assemble along the triumphal route. At dawn Vespasian and Titus, unarmed, clad in purple silk and crowned with bay, left the Temple of Isis on the Field of Mars, where they had spent the night. Followed by a huge contingent of troops, they proceeded to the Octavian promenade, where the senators and knights awaited them. To the acclamations of the crowd they then mounted the rostrum set with ivory thrones. Vespasian signaled for silence, and, covering his head with the corner of his cloak, recited the usual prayers, accompanied by his son Titus. A brief imperial speech preceded the ensuing meal, which was offered, following custom, to the troops. The princes also took refreshment, after which they sacrificed to the gods whose statues were set up near the triumphal arch between the Capitol and the Tiber.

Only then did the triumphal cortège set out for the Capitol. It consisted of all that was rare and magnificent, symbolizing the wealth of the newly strengthened Empire. Precious objects of all descriptions were borne along: gold, silver, carved ivories, precious stones, cloths of purple or embroidered into tapestries, statues of the finest marble. There were also exotic beasts accompanied by their grandly dressed trainers. The public was particularly taken with a series of floats three and four stories high, decorated with gold, ivory, and brocaded hangings, which represented various episodes of the recent victorious war: there were the machines breaking through the formidable ramparts, the army swarming through the walls into the city, the vanquished extending their arms in supplication, houses collapsing on their inhabitants, the Temple afire, the countryside ravaged by the flames, and the enemy, fleeing or being led in chains.

For Josephus, such scenes recalled many painful memories, particularly since each of the floats or stages was accompanied by a mime depicting the general of each of the captured cities in the attitude in which he had been taken (*JW* VII, 147). Did Josephus appear on the float depicting the fall of Jotapata? If he did, he was the only Jewish general of the war to see himself so represented. In any event, he genuinely admired these *tableaux vivants,* whose "art and magnificence . . . now portrayed the incidents to those who had not witnessed them, as if they were happening before their eyes" (*JW* VII, 146).

And what were his feelings when he saw the spoils taken from the Jews, especially the Temple booty? His narrative is devoid of emotion as he enumerates it: "the golden table, many talents in weight"—for the sacrificial bread—"the lampstand, likewise made of gold" with its seven branches, and, last of all, the Torah (*JW* VII, 148-150).

And finally, preceded by images of victory all made of ivory and gold, came the chariots of Vespasian and Titus, while Domitian rode beside them "in magnificent apparel and mounted on a steed that was itself a sight" (*JW* VII, 152).

Once arrived at the Temple of Capitoline Jove, the cortège halted to await, according to custom, the announcement of the execution of the principal enemy. Simon bar Gioras had been selected over John for this symbolic ceremony.[8] Roman soldiers sought him out from among the prisoners in the procession and, a rope round his neck, he was whipped and dragged to the place of execution near the Forum, where he was beheaded. "After the announcement that Simon was no more and the shouts of universal applause which greeted it, the priests began the sacrifices." Thus did Josephus, along with the rest of those present, learn of the death of one of the men he had most hated. Was he now able to rejoice? The "brigand" had atoned for his "crimes," but at what cost!

The day drew to a close with further sacrifices and an official banquet at which the emperor welcomed "certain persons" at his own table, while the rest of the Romans celebrated at home with their families. Here too, Josephus does not tell us what he himself did, nor does he inform us whether he was among the guests at the imperial board.

In surrendering at Jotapata, Josephus had made his choice, but in doing so he had condemned himself to spend the remainder of his life in ambiguity.

In the capital of the empire Josephus received news of the additional and predictable Roman victories in Judea. One after the other, the last pockets of resistance were falling. The general Lucius Bassus, who had been given command of the Xth Legion, had taken Herodion, a fortress built by Herod some sixty stadia (eleven kilometers) distant from Jerusalem, situated atop an artificial hill (shaped, we are told, like a nipple) and elaborately fitted out as a palace. Bassus then crossed the Jordan and marched against the fortress of Machaerus on the shore of the Dead Sea. Surrounded on all sides by deep ravines and protected by a double rampart, the citadel, which was also well supplied with food, could have withstood a long siege had not a fortuitous event caused it to surrender. Eleazar, one of its most valiant defenders, who belonged to one of the town's important families, chanced to fall into Roman hands. Bassus had a cross erected on which to hang him in full view of the besieged inhabitants; grief-stricken, they offered to surrender the city if Eleazar and they were allowed to live. Three thousand men who had fled the city were caught by the Romans and, during a fierce battle, were slain along with their general, Judah son of Ari, a man who had survived the siege of Jerusalem.

As for Vespasian, the conquest of Judea had been an accomplished fact long before the taking of its capital. He had coins minted in honor of the Roman victory, which depicted him seated under a palm tree with a weeping woman (symbolizing Judea) and, in the background, a Roman legionnaire in victorious posture. The legend read: *Judaea capta.*[9]

Vespasian proclaimed the entire territory the Emperor's personal property and had this ratified. A single colony was founded, at Emmaus, near Jerusalem, whose land was parceled out among eight hundred veterans of the Army of the East. The fiscal pragmatism of the new Emperor was also evidenced in his dealings with regard to the annual contribution of a half shekel that every Jew the world over had made to the Temple prior to its destruction. These sums—the equivalent of two Greek drachmas per person—were to be held in a special fund, the *fiscus Judaicus,* and paid into the Temple of Capitoline Jove, newly rebuilt after having been burned down during the confrontations between the men loyal to Vitellius and Vespasian's supporters. Thus did the Master of Olympus appropriate for himself the monies intended for the cult of the God of Israel.

As for Vespasian, the "flesh-and-blood" ruler, he kept the purple veils of the Temple in his own palace on the Palatine Hill, along with a valuable copy of the Torah. Josephus had never concealed from his protectors his own deep reverence for this volume, and with Titus' permission he had saved from destruction all the copies he could find (*L* 418).

MASADA AND THE SORROW OF ZION

However, total victory in Judea was not to be achieved until the spring of 73. In the heart of the Judean desert one fortress remained inviolate: Masada. Josephus was to be particularly moved by the story of its capture, of which he heard later, when in Rome.

When he arrived to lay siege to Masada, Bassus' successor, Flavius Silva, found himself faced with an impossible task. First constructed by Jonathan Maccabee atop a mesalike plateau surrounded by steep cliffs, Masada had been rebuilt and equipped by Herod as a refuge in case of a possible *coup d'état*. Thus, in addition to a sumptuous palace, it also had enormous cisterns carved out of the rock, vast magazines of weapons, and infinite stores of foodstuffs, some of which, thanks to the extremely dry climate, had been preserved intact since the reign of Herod. In addition, the surface of the plateau itself was cultivable, should the need arise. Camped below, the Romans were surrounded by nothing but arid ground and the distant glitter of the Dead Sea, which could provide them neither water to drink nor fish to eat. Jewish prisoners were forced to fetch food and water to them from the oasis of Ein-Gedi, several kilometers away. The fortress was held by a group of Sicarii, who were reputedly unconquerable.

Silva began by surrounding the site with a wall of circumvallation, as Titus had done in Jerusalem at the outset of the famine. But what defender would leave such a well-supplied fortification to flee into the desert wastes? And where was Silva to set up machines to bring down these mighty ramparts, crowned with towers six meters high and four meters wide, which surrounded the entire plateau? The only path to the top had been rightly baptized "The Serpent's Path" because of its narrowness and its many twists and turns; the besieged kept it under constant surveillance.

Taking a turn around the base of the plateau, Silva noticed that on its opposite side, to the west, an outcropping of boulders rose to within a hundred and fifty meters of the top. With an earthwork a hundred meters high and a twenty-five-meter platform, his machines could be raised to the level of the ramparts. A thirty-meter-high ironclad tower was brought up. Well-directed fire from the tower served to dislodge the defenders, while a huge battering ram made a breach in the walls. To their immense astonishment, the besiegers discovered a second wall behind the first. This second wall was made of earth heaped atop long wooden timbers, and the action of the battering ram only tamped it tighter, making the surface more solid. Silva then ordered the wooden framework to be set on fire with flaming torches. Whereupon the wind proved to be the instrument of Fate—or of God. At first it carried the flames in the direction of the Romans, but then it turned and blew them against the ramparts.

Sensing that all was lost, the leaders of the defenders debated throughout the night under the guidance of their leader, Eleazar son of Jair, a descendant of Judah the Galilean. They had been the first to rise up, and they were now the last to resist. At dawn they would be captured, the women would be raped, the children sent into slavery, and the men condemned to participate in the bloody games in the arenas of their foes. Would it not be better to show courage to the end and die nobly at their own hands? Eleazar's eloquence proved persuasive. Josephus re-creates for us the painful scenes in which each husband held his wife and children in his arms, covered them with kisses and then plunged into their throats the dagger that would deliver them from life and spare them opprobrium. Lots were then drawn to select the men who would kill the others. Each man lay down near the members of his family and bared his neck to the sword. Another drawing was then held among the ten survivors to determine the order in which each would kill the other. The last man left alive made sure that no one still required his services and then killed himself.

These details are not flights of Josephus' imagination. When morning came, the Romans, who had been preparing to make one last assault, awoke to a deathly silence. They shouted their war cry to see if anyone would respond. At that moment, an elderly woman emerged from an underground aqueduct accompanied by a younger woman and five small children. Their tale seemed unbelievable, and no time was lost in verifying it. In the citadel above, 960 bodies were discovered, each family stretched out together. At least their action had prevented the victors from deriving any pleasure from their triumph; the Romans were awestruck, filled with admiration at such greatness of spirit.

This courageous deed, which was recounted in the military reports sent to the emperor, was for Josephus a lesson in despair. The lengthy speeches he puts into the mouth of Eleazar, the Sicarius leader, probably include many of his own thoughts on the recent events. The amplitude of the catastrophe had involved many innocent lives. The thesis that misfortune was a just punishment did not hold water. Roman military superiority could not account for every Jewish failure. For seven years throats had been cut on a massive scale throughout the East: the killing had begun in Caesarea, then Scythopolis; it had spread to Damascus and other Syrian cities; in Egypt things had been even worse. In Judea, the fate of those fallen in battle seemed fortunate compared to the fate of those crucified, tortured, thrown to ferocious beasts. And the great city so dear to the heart of every Jew had surrendered in spite of all its ramparts and its myriad defenders.

Let there be no mistake: into the sublime speech of his political enemy, the Sicarius Eleazar son of Jair, Josephus has inserted some of his own darkest thoughts, thoughts that must have haunted him in his Roman solitude. God seemed to have uttered a collective curse against His people; He seemed loath to let them live (*JW* VII, 359). His sorrow had become unbearable: "Which of us, taking these things to heart, could bear to behold the sun, even could he live secure from peril? Who such a foe to his country, so unmanly, so fond of life, as not to regret that he is still alive today? Nay, I would that we had all been dead ere ever we saw that holy city razed by an enemy's hands, that sacred sanctuary so profanely uprooted!" (*JW* VII, 378-379)

A survivor—that was Josephus' status. A survivor who had lost almost all reason for living. What remained of the proud and beautiful city he had once known? "Hapless old men sit beside the ashes of the shrine and a few women, reserved by the enemy for the basest outrage" (*JW* VII, 377). Those survivors who had managed to escape slavery and had regrouped on the coastal plain near Yabneh (Jamnia) had lost all taste for life; some swore to abstain from meat and wine in memory of the Temple ceremonies that had been broken off. People wondered whether it was still worth bear-

ing children. It was said that the wise Rabbi Joshua ben Hanania
tried to assuage their deep sorrow: would they forgo bread, fruit,
and even water because those things had once been offered in the
Temple? Confronting their despair, he said: "Hark unto me, my
children. It is impossible not to mourn at all, given the blow we
have suffered; but to mourn overmuch is equally impossible, for we
cannot impose upon all rules that are too harsh and unbearable for
most men."[10]

Since sorrow had to be given some expression, wise men
decided that the memory of the misfortunes of Zion should
henceforth be interwoven into everyday life.[11] Thus, if a new
house is built, a tiny part of it must be left unfinished; if a banquet
is held, one of the dishes must be refused. And if a women dresses
for a feast she must not wear all her finery. In addition, once a
year, on the ninth day of Av (end of July, early August), the
anniversary of the Temple's destruction, all were called upon to
observe ritual mourning.

These customs spread throughout the Diaspora and are still
practiced today. We cannot know whether Josephus in his day
observed them too. He had not, of course, gone to Yabneh, but
wise men from that school did make the journey to Rome. Rabbinical tradition recounts the voyage of four of them—including
the aforementioned Rabbi Joshua and the renowned Rabbi
Akiba—which must have occurred around the year 90. The rabbinical account gives no precise description of the empire's capital
city, but instead raises a painful question that must have been on the
lips of the whole generation of survivors: why was that pagan city
so prosperous and Jerusalem laid waste? Similar questions also crop
up in the two Jewish apocalyptic books that date from the end of
the first century (II Baruch and IV Esdras), which are replete with
obsessive questions: What had become of divine justice? The
Alliance? The Chosen status? Who could fathom the ways of the
All-Highest?

To escape despair one sought recourse in the Prophets. Perhaps all of these extreme misfortunes were only the Messiah's
"birth pains," the prelude to a new day. Although his colleagues
had wept on seeing the prosperity in Rome, Akiba had burst

out laughing. Whereupon the following dialogue took place among them:

"Akiba, how can you laugh while we weep?"

"And why are you weeping?"

"How can you help but weep when the idolatrous pagans, who sacrifice to their gods and bow down to statues, are living in peace and safety while the footstool of our Lord has been delivered over to the flames and become the lair of wild beasts?"

"That's just why I'm laughing. If it is so for those who offend Him, what will He not do for those who obey His will?"[12]

Josephus had probably not attained this degree of faith, but his nature compelled him to continue to live as best he could in the land of his exile.

DIVORCE AND REMARRIAGE

Josephus was faced with other problems that were not theological. In the first years of his Roman sojourn he also encountered serious domestic troubles.

"At this period I divorced my wife, being displeased at her behavior," he laconically reports (*L* 426).

The eldest son of his Alexandrian wife, who was called Hyrcanus—a traditional first name in the family of the Hasmonean rulers—was born in the fourth year of Vespasian's reign (*L* 5), i.e., in the year 73, and two other children had died at a young age. Shortly afterward, in 76 or 77, Josephus made up his mind to repudiate his wife.

We may cavil at the "behavior" that caused the divorce. In his novel based on Josephus' life, Lion Feuchtwanger, projecting the problems of his own day back into antiquity, indulges the hypothesis that his hero's wife was a pagan and reluctant to have her son raised as a Jew. Such a conjecture is totally unfounded. There was still a sufficient number of Jews in Alexandria that the priest Josephus son of Matthias would have had no need to take a pagan bride. On the contrary, he would most probably have allied himself with one of the city's highborn Jewish families. This, indeed, may have been the problem: the hellenized aristocrats of the Diaspora probably provided their daughters with a different education than those in Judea. Josephus may have found that his wife was neither the worthy woman of the Bible nor the ideal companion that God is said to have set aside for each man on the day of Creation.

The moral standards prevalent in Rome may also have played a part in these new problems. Debauchery and lust were rampant.[13] This is the era in which Juvenal wrote the longest of his satires on women. His pretext is the matrimonial plans of his friend Postumus. What an odd notion! the satirist exclaims. It's been quite a while since Modesty returned to the heavens and Chastity was banished from Italy. The Roman woman would rather make do with one eye than with only one man (v. 54). Matrons dallied with acrobats or gladiators. What man could be certain of the paternity of his child? Women were all either Messalinas, shrews, bluestockings, domestic tyrants, nags, spoilers, perfidious, drunken, flirts, licentious, cruel, superstitious, abortionists, poisoners. Why had the ancient virtues disappeared? Because hard times and hard living had disappeared, and that had been the best protection against vice: labor, early to bed and early to rise, hands callused from spinning wool and weaving while one's husband went off to war. Rome was suffering the effects of too much peace.

Juvenal continues: "More deadly than arms, vice has overwhelmed us and wreaks vengeance for a world enslaved. Every crime is spreading and debauchery runs rampant, since the disappearance of Roman frugality . . . Wealth is the corrupter; its shameful luxury has brought down the work of centuries" (v. 292-300). Josephus may have created his own misfortunes by introducing his new wife into Roman high society. Determined not to live alone, he now, however, still took care not to choose a wife from Rome. The Jewish district on the banks of the Tiber had nothing to offer him but disheveled miscreants and former slaves, and he did not want another Alexandrian wife. No one in Judea would have been likely to welcome a suit on his behalf. He therefore selected a woman from the island of Crete—and never had cause to regret it: "She came of very distinguished parents, indeed the most notable people in that country. In character she surpassed many of her sex, as her subsequent life showed" (*L* 427).

Of this union Josephus had two more children, whose dates of birth he records (*L* 5). The elder, Justus—a name equivalent to the Hebrew Saddok—was born in the seventh year of Vespasian's reign (77) and the younger, Simonides (also called Agrippa, perhaps in honor of that King) in the ninth year (79).[14] "Such is my domestic history," he concludes, content at last (*L* 428), and that is the last we hear of it.

FAVORS AND SLANDERS

Since his arrival in Rome, Josephus had continued to benefit from the imperial favor. Vespasian had not allowed him to take up residence in the unhealthy and overpopulated Jewish neighborhood, but had offered him the same house in which he himself had lived before becoming emperor. This was a considerable favor at a time when the center of the city still bore the traces of the recent fire that had destroyed the Capitoline district. Vespasian was also sentimental about his own past. Even after his elevation to the throne he continued to pay frequent visits to the modest town in which he had grown up and had left his house there just as it had been in the past, "in order to preserve intact all things familiar to his eyes."[15] His gift to Josephus is proof of his affection for the man who had predicted for him the loftiest of fates.

Nor could Vespasian have done less than confer Roman citizenship on him. Thus Joseph ben Matthias now had the right to the Roman *tria nomina: praenomen, nomen, cognomen*. We know only the last two for certain: Flavius Josephus. Latinized, his foreign given name now became his surname. As for his new family name, it was customary for a new citizen to take the name of his patron's family, in this case that of the *gens Flavia;* all freed slaves of the Imperial house had the right to use it.[16] We do not know the first name he used, but if custom were followed it would probably have been that of the Emperor Vespasian, whose full name was Titus

Flavius Vespasianus. Josephus may have shared this name with both of the heirs apparent, whom we know today as Titus and Domitian, but he probably continued to be known as Josephus.

Vespasian also provided Josephus with the means to live comfortably. This emperor may have had a deserved reputation for avarice, but he was also prone to generosity (although not, perhaps, prodigal). He rained gifts on talented poets and painters and was the first to establish an annual pension of 100,000 *sesterces* for teachers of Latin and Greek rhetoric. Josephus may even have been included in this latter group. His imperial pension was augmented by the revenues from his lands in Judea, which had just recently been added to.

Josephus must also have had many personal enemies, both Roman and Jewish. Some Romans were far from pleased at the rise of a Jewish prisoner of war whose principal quality appeared to be his craftiness. Even during the siege of Jerusalem there had been officers who had gone to Titus at every reversal to express their lack of confidence in the prince's interpreter. Might he not have passed on information to the enemy while pretending to translate into his own tongue and only feigned performance of his mission to the besieged? Titus, on each occasion, "repressed by his silence the soldiers' outbursts against Josephus" (*L* 416-417).

In Judea the Sicarii had not laid down their arms, even after Masada. Some of them had attempted to incite their Egyptian coreligionists to join them in another uprising. Most had been arrested and executed. All had displayed amazing courage: "For under every form of torture and laceration of body, devised for the sole object of making them acknowledge Caesar as lord, not one submitted nor was brought to the verge of utterance; but all kept their resolve, triumphant over constraint, meeting the tortures and the fire with bodies that seemed insensible of pain and souls that well-nigh exulted in it. But most of all were the spectators struck by the children of tender age, not one of whom could be prevailed upon to call Caesar lord. So far did the strength of courage rise superior to the weakness of their frames" (*JW* VII, 418-419). Only the soldiers of the Lord, sure of achieving eternal life through their martyrdom, were capable of such deaths.

The final chapter of the Jewish resistance also includes a plot directed against Josephus. A Sicarius named Jonathan, who had taken refuge in Cyrene and was still hoping for some kind of supernatural intervention, led a group of disciples off into the desert, "promising them a display of signs and apparitions" (*JW* VII, 438). Catullus, the governor of Libya, managed with some difficulty to capture him and got him to confess that he was actually in the pay of a group of highborn and wealthy Jews. Catullus used this confession as a pretext for confiscating the fortunes of three thousand well-to-do Jews, who were all executed in one fell swoop (*Ibid.,* 445). He also "persuaded" Jonathan to bring a charge of sedition against other Jews outside his immediate jurisdiction, both in Alexandria and in Rome. Among the latter appeared the name of Josephus, who was accused of having provided arms and money to the insurgents in Cyrene (*L* 424).

Vespasian ordered an investigation, which established his protégé's innocence. At Titus' intercession, all the accused Roman Jews were acquitted. Josephus, however, was not entirely happy with the sentence meted out to the guilty. The perjurer Jonathan was burned alive after having been put to torture, but Catullus, whom Josephus considered no less culpable, suffered nothing worse than a reprimand. To Josephus' subsequent satisfaction, however, Providence later made up for the emperor's excessive clemency by seeing to it that Catullus was stricken with an awful disease, which he takes a certain pleasure in describing for us: "He came to a miserable end, not only chastised in body, but yet more deeply deranged in mind. For he was haunted by terrors and was continually crying out that he saw the ghosts of his murdered victims standing at his side; and unable to restrain himself he would leap from his bed as if torture and fire were being applied to him. His malady ever growing rapidly worse, his bowels ulcerated and fell out; and so he died, affording a demonstration, no less striking than any, how God in his providence afflicts punishment on the wicked" (*JW* VII, 451–453).

There were still some envious folk who continued to give credit to Jonathan's slanders, but they were never verified. The princely heir apparent was even better disposed toward the former Judean governor-general than was his father. When Titus ascended the throne he treated Josephus with the same consideration and would hear no word against him (*L* 428). Those who had hoped to bring him down in Domitian's reign were also doomed to disappointment, for when he was emperor he ordered the chastisement of a slave, a eunuch who was tutor to Josephus' son, who had dared slander his master. He even did Josephus the rare honor of exempting his property in Judea from taxation, and the Empress Domitia showered honors and benefits upon him as well.

Thus, despite the machinations of the envious courtiers, Josephus ended his days in Rome in comfort.

BERENICE

It is difficult to understand what complaints could have been made against Josephus as the memory of the war in Judea grew ever dimmer. How could anyone in Rome still accuse him of treason?

The Judean war appears to have exacerbated in Rome a tendency that had not been wholly absent before, namely, anti-Judaism. The Jews had forced the Romans to wage a long and costly war, they had violated the *pax Romana* and held out for many years, "which had increased men's wrath against them."[17] After their defeat, countless numbers had been brought to Rome as slaves. And not particularly desirable slaves at that, for they often obstinately refused to work on the seventh day of the week. Their quarter on the farther bank of the Tiber provided Rome with an endless supply of beggars and fortune-tellers whose hands required payment with far less silver than did those of their competitors, the so-called Egyptian priests who also thronged the Roman streets. "For the smallest sum of money," Juvenal tells us, "the Jews will sell you all the absurd delusions in the world."[18] Older Romans were annoyed by the effect the Jewish rites all too frequently had on their fellow citizens.

And now a Jewish woman brought scandal to the imperial court itself. She had been born a true princess, descended from both the Hasmonean and Herodian lines; she was the sister of King Agrippa II, but she was now over forty years old; she had already been married three times,[19] had been twice a queen in the East, and there were rumors of guilty relations with her brother as well.[20] Her beauty was legendary, as was her extravagance. Now this Eastern siren had bewitched Titus, the heir apparent.

Josephus' silence with regard to the famous idyll of Titus and Berenice is highly significant. Who but he could have recounted it in all its details, and yet he has taken great care not to do so! The Latin historians vouchsafe us our only glimpse of the liaison between the Roman *imperator* and the Jewish queen. And their comparative discretion is in its way equally revelatory of the furor it must have caused in Rome.

An otherwise reliable historian, Emile Mireaux,[21] refers with a shudder of disgust to "Berenice in the arms of Titus at a time when he was starving the people of Jerusalem, crucifying or mutilating prisoners, burning the Temple, delivering the city to pillage and carnage and razing the Holy City." His imagination seems to have carried him away.

Titus had met Berenice for the first time shortly after Vespasian's campaign in Galilee, probably at Caesarea Philippi, whither King Agrippa II had hastened to welcome the victor of Jotapata (*JW* III, 443). The queen does not appear to have accompanied her brother to Rome when he went there to hail Galba's election as emperor, and Titus, who had traveled with him as far as Corinth, had turned back abruptly upon learning of Otho's accession to power. "Some have attributed his return to a burning passion for Berenice," writes Tacitus.[22] When Vespasian was elected emperor by the Army of the East, Agrippa II had made haste to return from Rome to lend his support, and on that occasion note had also been taken of the enthusiasm shown by Berenice, "glowing with youth and beauty, who had charmed even the elderly Vespasian, and by the magnificence of her gifts as well."[23] There is nothing to indicate her presence at the siege of Jerusalem, but Titus' sojourn in Caesarea Philippi following his victory probably owed something to her presence in that city. She, as much as Josephus, may have influenced Titus' response to the anti-Jewish machinations of the people of Antioch. We can surmise that she either sailed with him to Rome or joined him there soon afterward.

Although Josephus was now living a fairly retired life in Rome, he still frequented the imperial court, and because of his background he would certainly have been considered a member of Berenice's "faction"—that is, one who hoped to see her one day made empress. What a revenge that would have been for his vanquished nation! Perhaps Berenice would even turn out to be another Queen Esther.

When Titus openly installed Berenice in the imperial palace in the year 75, that hour seemed to have arrived. For three years Titus was to be the focus of the hostility of the Romans, who had already demonstrated their mistrust of Eastern queens in the days of Cleopatra and Julius Caesar. It is unlikely that Vespasian looked with favor on this union *de usu,* which he dreaded seeing become one of *justes noces.* He probably gave his son to understand that such a move could compromise his accession to the throne. Thus, Titus gave in and sent the queen away: *invitus invitam dimisit.*[24] He was preparing himself to reign, and when his father died a year later, he did not recall Berenice to his side.

When Josephus mentions the accusations made against him at this time he is very probably referring to court intrigues in which he was closely involved. Berenice, her brother Agrippa, who had been named *praetor* by Titus, Josephus showered with Imperial favors—such was the circle around the victor of Jerusalem, and more than one Roman must have been fearful that once Titus became emperor the real power would inevitably pass into Jewish hands.

Josephus surmounted the crisis. And indeed, his ambitions were not those imputed to him by the envious. Titus, who was well aware of that, kept him at his side.

ANTI-JUDAISM

The scandal over Berenice exacerbated an unfocused Roman xenophobia directed against Easterners in general. Egyptians, Syrians, and Jews were all included in this Roman suspicion of any different customs, this contempt for subject peoples who were considered to have been born to be slaves. From time to time such foreigners were expelled from the city, but under Nero only one Jewish sect, that of the disciples of "Christus," the Christians, had actually been persecuted.

In the last quarter of the first century, Latin literature, hitherto almost completely free from this taint, began to resound with anti-Jewish attacks of a unique kind.[25]

The *fin de siècle* satirists, Martial and Juvenal, contented themselves with poking fun at the "traditional clemency that allows swine to die of old age"[26] or at the Sabbath, which they mistakenly thought was a day of fast. Circumcision was also an inexhaustible source of ribaldry.[27] They mocked the poverty of the Jews, who were often reduced to begging. "Once the place where King Numa met his love by night, the woods of the sacred spring and temple are now rented out to Jews whose only possessions are a basket and a pile of straw."[28]

All of this was an outgrowth of the distaste the older Romans felt generally at the encroachment of Jewish customs. Once, the Roman convert had been content to observe the Sabbath and the alimentary laws. But now his son had been circumcised and he refused to keep his rightful place with his fellow Romans. "Raised in contempt for Roman law, the converted boy learns, observes, and reveres naught but Jewish law, all of which was handed down by Moses to his followers in a mysterious scroll."[29]

Josephus must have been deeply wounded by the derision with which he felt himself surrounded. However, it was as nothing compared to the slanders against his people that were beginning to be spread by another historian, a man also welcome at court and with whom he was probably often in contact: Tacitus.[30]

Tacitus lent a ready ear to all the falsehoods that were spread about the Jews. He was prepared to impute to them any origin (Cretan, Egyptian, Ethiopian, Assyrian) save the one they attributed to themselves, and he was especially partial to the thesis according to which the Jews were descended from lepers who had been expelled from Egypt. In his view nothing was as pernicious as their religion, which, like that of the Christians, kept them apart from the other subjects of the empire.[31] He had come to the conclusion that the Jews viewed as profane everything that the Greeks and Romans held sacred, and, conversely, that their practices systematically and purposely contradicted those of other religions. Thus they ate apart, abstained from foreign women, and practiced circumcision. They carried sloth to such an extent that they rested every seventh day, and even every seventh year, perhaps in honor of the god Saturn or of the planet of the same name. They indulged in frequent fasting, they abstained from pork, believing it to be the carrier of disease, but they sacrificed oxen—just to be different from the Egyptians, who worshipped the ox Apis. They believed that the souls of those who had died in war or who had been executed lived on, which explained their contempt for death. Unlike other people at that time, the Jews regarded infanticide as a crime, which is why they multiplied to such a threatening extent. They would not allow statues in their cities, not to mention within their temples, and refused to do either their own kings or the emperors of Rome that honor.

Such are some of the accusations Tacitus spews out pell-mell against the Jewish people in the introduction to his account of the Judean war in the fifth volume of his *Histories,* written *circa* 105. In the days when he and Josephus (twenty years his elder) were both frequenting the imperial palace, Tacitus would surely not have hesitated to show his hostility. Superstition, impiety, mal-patriotism—those words, for him, summed up this foreign religion from the East, but in his work the peevish xenophobic ill-temper of the old Romans is inextricably mixed up with strange and outlandish fables.

Josephus witnessed with concern this increase in anti-Judaism, which he viewed as totally contrary to the true spirit of Rome. He believed he knew who the authors of such fables and slanders were, namely, those same hellenized Egyptians who had made so much trouble in Alexandria in the early part of the century.

Tacitus' myth of "lepers" could be traced back to a certain Manetho, an Egyptian priest in the third century B.C.E., who had composed an alternative version of the Book of Exodus in which the villains were the Hebrews. During the reigns of Tiberius and Caligula, that volume had been spread all over Rome by a versatile Alexandrian scribbler named Apion. Philo of Alexandria, Apion's contemporary, had crossed swords with this odious creature, whom Tiberius had nicknamed *Cymbalum mundi*—that which spreads noise through the world. Upon Philo's arrival in Rome in the year 40 on his mission to persuade Caligula to clarify the political status of the Alexandrian Jews, which was being questioned by that city's Greek population, he had found another Egyptian, Helicon, installed at the emperor's side. During the course of a painful audience, Caligula had suddenly asked, to gales of laughter from his courtiers: "Why won't you eat pork?"[32] Helicon had egged him on. The emperor had barely listened to Philo's defense of the Jews, finally remarking: "Such fools are more to be pitied than censured."

Apion's writings were readily available in Rome, and there were some Romans, like Tacitus, who believed them. To the fable of impurity Apion added other inventions gleaned from some of his Egyptian predecessors. Thus, the Jews worshipped the head of an ass in their Temple; sometimes they would fatten up a Greek traveler to be used as a sacrificial victim; they had sworn to hate all foreigners, especially Greeks. And of course Apion mocked their abstinence from pork and their practice of circumcision (both of which, as it happens, were also practiced by the Egyptian priesthood). He also maintained that the Jewish people had never produced any great men.

Two other writers of the same stripe, Apollonius Molon and Lysimachus, also insisted that the Jews were the only people to have made no useful contribution to civilization, that they were actually atheists (because they refused to honor gods that were venerated the world over), that they were misanthropic (because their laws set them apart), and that the Laws of Moses taught vice, not virtue.

Disgusted by such screeds, Josephus set himself to refute them by writing an apologia that has come down to us under the title *Against Apion,* a volume that has had the paradoxical effect of ensuring the survival of authors who would otherwise have disappeared into oblivion.

For Josephus knew that slander could actually kill. The first large-scale massacre of Jews inspired by popular animosity had occurred in the year 38 in Alexandria. In 64, during Nero's reign, the Christians had been persecuted after the burning of Rome, which had been blamed on them because of their "hatred of the human race."[33] Should such things continue to be imputed to the Jews, life could become very dangerous for them. The accusations that continued to hang over the Christians were to lead to new persecutions in the reign of Domitian. Josephus lived to witness them.

The reign of his friend Titus had not been as successful as Josephus had hoped. Fortuna, who had served the young prince so well in Judea, now seemed to have abandoned him.[34] His rule was marked by three great disasters: the great eruption of Vesuvius, a fire that ravaged Rome for three days and three nights, and a terrible epidemic of plague. After two years, two months, and twenty days, Titus was prematurely carried off at the age of forty-one.

Josephus probably viewed Domitian's accession to the throne with dismay. The last of the Flavians had been tyrannical and debauched from an early age. He had made no secret of his jealousy of his older brother's fame; he had even refused to participate in the posthumous honors paid him. The early days of Domitian's reign augured badly for the rest of it: each day he would closet himself alone for hours, engaged in torturing flies and planning ever more costly entertainments.[35]

The eunuch who had served as tutor to Josephus' son had evidently overheard his master make some remarks hostile to the emperor, and he saw fit to report them to Domitian. Josephus, however, had lost none of the eloquence that had so often stood him in such good stead in the past, and his defense obtained him even greater favor. The empress Domitia, equally notorious for her loose behavior, was also Josephus' protector, further proof that he had lost none of his charm and attraction.

However, Domitian—who in his youth had been unable to bear the sight of even a drop of blood—grew increasingly more sanguinary. Arbitrary capital punishments and executions became ever more frequent. Fearing assassination, and desirous of setting an example, in 95 Domitian condemned to death Epaphroditus, a freedman of the emperor Nero, who was said to have helped his master commit suicide in 68. Since the death of Titus, Epaphroditus had been Josephus' strongest protector, to whom he dedicated all his last works. Shortly after this, in his hostility to all the Eastern religions, among which he included Judaism and Christianity, Domitian put his own cousin, the harmless Flavius Clemens, to death and exiled his wife, Flavia Domitilla, for "atheism."[36] According to the pagan historian Dio Cassius, the couple had merely been Judaists; according to Eusebius of Caesarea, a Father of the early Church, Domitilla had been a Christian.[37]

We do not know whether Josephus was personally threatened during the end-of-reign upheavals that saw the demise of Epaphroditus and the senator Flavius Clemens, but notwithstanding the Imperial favor of which he boasts in his autobiography, Domitian's reign must have been a somber one for Josephus. At court, Tacitus' popularity continued to grow.

Among the large-scale works undertaken by the pomp-loving Domitian was the triumphal arch to honor Titus, which was finished in the year 85. As part of the triumphal procession that decorates it, Josephus could have seen depicted the treasure of the Temple at Jerusalem, which now rested in Rome's new Temple of Peace. Thus, even the monuments of Rome served to remind him of his people's misfortune. However, great building projects and grandiose games are expensive, and Domitian had to fill his coffers by any means he could. The tax the Jews had been paying since the year 70, the *fiscus Judaicus,* seemed a good source of exploitable revenue. On this point we have a rare item of personal reminiscence from Suetonius: "The tax on the Jews was enforced with special rigor; also subject to it were proselytes who lived as Jews without having professed that faith and persons who dissimulated their background to escape paying the taxes imposed on that nation. I can recall, when barely in my teens, seeing a tax agent, accompanied by a large group of administrators, examine an old man of ninety to see whether or not he had been circumcised."[38]

When Domitian was assassinated in 96 after a fifteen-year reign, few in Rome missed him.

Attention had already turned to Cocceius Nerva, a good-hearted and enlightened old man. During his short reign (it lasted barely sixteen months), he reinstated personal liberties, reduced social injustices, put a stop to the persecution of the Christians and the denunciations against Judaists, and ended the abuses caused by the tax on the Jews. One of the coins of his reign bears the inscription, *Fisci Judaici calummia sublata,*[39] thereby proclaiming an end to the harassments of the one preceding it.

Did Josephus live long enough to witness the advent of this good emperor? Did he know Trajan, his successor? We cannot know. His last work, *The Life,* which was dedicated to Epaphroditus, must be anterior to the latter's disgrace in 95. At the time, Josephus had several other literary projects in hand, but they were never, so far as we know, brought to fruition.

After 95, there is no further trace.

EPILOGUE

THE HISTORIAN'S

CRAFT

Graecus Livius (The Greek Livy)
SAINT JEROME, 22ND LETTER TO EUSTOCHIUMS:

We cannot but deplore the truly infinitesimal amount of information Josephus provides us with regard to the thirty-some years he spent in Rome, from the year 71 to his death. And yet we may know more about them than we think. His work bears witness: two lengthy historical books (*The Jewish War* and *Jewish Antiquities*), an apologia for Judaism (*Against Apion*), and, lastly, his autobiography, *The Life*. Obviously, much of Josephus' time must have been spent collecting documents and writing.

THE JEWISH WAR

Josephus gave priority to the most recent history, that of the war that had just ended. The *War* was probably a commissioned work. Notwithstanding the enormous losses of life the Jews had suffered in Judea, they were still numerous throughout the Roman Empire and on its Eastern borders, where the Parthian threat was beginning to loom[1] and where was to be found the tiny kingdom of Adiabene, which was partially converted to Judaism. In solidarity with their brothers in Judea, these Jews were still prepared to risk taking up arms against Rome or participating in other wars caused by another Eastern peoples:[2] the Parthians, the Babylonians, the Arabs. There was therefore a need to issue some kind of warning against any new uprising—and what better dissuasion than an account of the events that had occurred in Judea?

And there was living in Rome a man uniquely qualified to perform the task: Titus Flavius Josephus. His position as a member of the priestly aristocracy ensured his credibility with his own people; his personal testimony, combined with the documentation to which he could have access, would guarantee the work's historical accuracy, and his own feelings would inspire him to carry out his task in the manner expected and desired; lastly, and above all, he could address the intended readers in their own language, Aramaic. Josephus, upon his arrival in Rome, was therefore granted an imperial pension and made privy to all the military archives relating to the campaign.

The Aramaic version of the *War* was widely distributed among "the barbarians in the interior" of Asia (*JW* I, 3), who comprised, in Josephus' words "Parthians and Babylonians and the most remote tribes of Arabians [who] with our countrymen beyond the Euphrates and the inhabitants of Adiabene were, through my assiduity, accurately acquainted with the origin of the war, the various phases of calamity through which it passed, and its conclusion" (*JW* I, 6).

Had Josephus been only an Aramaic historian, his work would not have survived. Indeed, the first version of the *War* has disappeared without a trace. Josephus owes his survival as a historian to the fact that he went on to write his work in Greek.

Several accounts of the Judean war had been published since the event. Josephus had found all of them equally annoying. He classified their authors into two categories. On the one hand, there were the superficial thinkers who thought they were writing history by recounting events in which they had not participated and who based those accounts on often contradictory testimony, which they then dressed up with fine rhetorical flourishes. On the other hand, there were the military veterans whose work consisted in licking the boots of victorious generals and downplaying the performance of the losers—in other words, passing over the courage of the Jews in silence and, in so doing, minimizing the successes of Vespasian and Titus as well, for, as Josephus remarks: "I fail to see how the conquerors of a puny people deserve to be accounted great" (*JW* I, 8).

Witnessing this burgeoning of pseudo-historians, Josephus heard the call of duty. He would make the truth known. No one was better placed to do so than he. He had followed the whole course of the war in both camps, he had known the principal leaders of the uprising, he had been in daily contact with the Roman generals, had questioned Jewish captives, had even perhaps taken notes during the campaign, and he had consulted the imperial archives in Rome. He had only one obstacle to surmount: that of language. In order to reach the educated Roman public, he had to write either in Latin or in Greek. His knowledge of Latin was probably no more than adequate, for he had only begun to acquire it since his arrival in Rome. It was different with Greek: that, he had studied as a boy, he spoke it fluently (although his pronunciation left something to be desired), and he had some notion of its literature;[3] as for writing in it, however—that was quite another matter!

There was one solution—doubtless a costly one:[4] recourse to secretaries who could correct his drafts and assist him in writing his history of the war in the purest of Attic dialects. And there were additional advantages to publishing in Greek. Aside from Rome, his work would also be read in Greece, in Asia Minor, and above all, in Egypt and Syria, which had been directly involved in the conflict. And there was the added fact that he was eager to set an example for certain contemporary Greek historians who preferred to write ancient rather than contemporary history. What was the interest in these present-day writers' composing a history of the Assyrians or the Medes, Josephus asks, seeing that earlier historians have already done so, "even if they have the advantage of them in literary skill"

(*JW* I, 13)? Compilations do not represent true historical labor. The only historians deserving of praise are those who undertake "the work of committing to writing events which have not previously been recorded and of commending to posterity the history of one's own time who use fresh materials and make the framework of history their own" (*JW* I, 15).

Thus Josephus' definition of his role as historian. It is because he was convinced of the value of his contribution that he took the trouble to translate the first Aramaic version of his work. "In these circumstances, I—Josephus son of Matthias, a Hebrew by race, a native of Jerusalem and a priest, who at the opening of the war myself fought against the Romans and in the sequel was perforce an onlooker—propose to provide the subjects of the Roman Empire with a narrative of the facts, by translating into Greek the account which I previously composed in my vernacular tongue" (*JW* I, 3).

His narrative is not a mere chronicle. Josephus sets out to make events intelligible. He does what no other historian, Greek or Latin, could have done: he examines the past in an attempt to elucidate the underlying origins of the war. Thus, his work continues from where the Scriptures leave off: "I shall begin my work at the point where the historians of these events and our prophets conclude," he writes (*JW* I, 18). This historical foundation takes up the whole of Book One. In it, he recounts the uprising of the Maccabees against Antiochus IV Ephiphanes, king of Syria, the installation of the Hasmonean dynasty, the quarrels over succession that brought Pompey and the Romans into Judea, and, lastly, the reign of Herod.

Book Two is devoted to the war's immediate causes: Rome's assumption of direct control over Judea in the year 6, which led to public unrest; the exactions levied by successive Roman procurators, which made an uprising inevitable; the defeat of Cestius, governor of Syria, which encouraged the insurgents to organize the resistance throughout the territory; and, finally, the dispatching of Josephus to Galilee as governor-general.

His account of the war *per se* begins in Book Three. Two personalities enter onto the scene, Josephus himself and Vespasian;

Josephus, captured at Jotapata, prophesies that the latter will one day be emperor.

Book Four relates the events that occurred from Vespasian's triumph in Galilee to the siege of Jerusalem: the taking of the last Galilean fortresses by Titus, the distant encircling of Jerusalem by Vespasian's troops, the civil war in the Holy City, and the civil unrest in Rome preceding Vespasian's election as emperor.

Book Five is taken up with the struggles between the three Jewish factions led by Eleazar, John, and Simon, and with Titus' siege of Jerusalem.

In Book Six, which is the work's high point, Josephus describes the burning of the Temple and the taking of Jerusalem.

Book Seven, the last, gives an account of the last convulsive gasps of the Jewish resistance in Judea, in Alexandria, and in Cyrene—notably the episode at Masada, which takes up two full chapters—and ends with the triumph of the Flavians in Rome.

As can be seen, the work is perfectly laid out. In addition, Josephus varies his narrative between direct and indirect discourse with remarkable technical skill. From whom did he learn to do this? Certainly not from any of the Greek historians of his own day; for them, he had nothing but contempt. He found his master in the distant past, in the Athens of Pericles, where lived the author of a great original historical work devoted to an event contemporary with his own life—another war, in fact—the Peloponnesian War. For there can be no doubt that Josephus' model was Thucydides. We find the same expository technique, with a first book analyzing the causes of the war, and the same dramatic construction, the same use of alternating types of discourse, all of which culminates in the obvious influence of the earlier writer's famous description of the Athens plague on Josephus' account of the famine in Jerusalem.

There is another Greek historian who may also, albeit to a lesser degree, have influenced Josephus: Polybius. Josephus probably felt a certain affinity with this Corinthian of the second century B.C.E. who had been deported to Italy after having fought against Rome and become the preceptor and friend of Scipio Aemilianus, accompanying him on the siege of Carthage. Polybius was later to try to prevent the war between Rome and the Achaean League, aware as he was of the disparity in forces, and was to return to Greece only to witness the devastation of his native city, Corinth, which was sacked by the Romans in 146 B.C.E. Yet Polybius had not been content merely to record the history of a war; he had set out to write a comprehensive history covering nearly a century, explaining and commenting on events. In so doing he had attempted to understand the nature of the Roman power that had vanquished his homeland. Josephus is doing the same thing when he describes for us the organization of Vespasian's army (*JW* III, 70–109).

Josephus, however, differs from his models in two ways. His world is ruled not by human actions but solely by Providence. Josephus feels compelled to draw a meaning from history, to attempt to discover the significance of the terrible catastrophe that had befallen his people. His familiarity with the Bible had taught him that God interferes continually in the affairs of men. Not like Nemesis, not like Fortuna or the force of Greek or Roman fate, but like a judge and father.[5]

As a father, God does not wish the sinner's death but his salvation. It is for this reason that He warns His people through signs in order to bring them to repentance: "One will find that God has a care for men, and by all kinds of premonitory signs shows His people the way of salvation, while they owe their destruction to folly and calamities of their own doing" (*JW* VI, 310). As a judge, He is constrained to act with rigor; there is no inexplicable disaster. It is because the crimes of the factious must be punished that God gives victory to the Romans. Paradoxically, the cruel page of history through which Josephus lived also fortified his belief that God cared for mankind. That belief meant that Josephus did not merely write history; he expanded the writing of Scripture.[6]

In so doing, Josephus in no way felt that he was bending the rules of historical composition, for biblical history was his model as well. There is only one element of the *War* for which he feels compelled to beg the reader's indulgence, and that is for his expression of his own feelings, his own sorrow and indignation:

"Should, however, any critic censure me for my strictures upon the tyrants or their bands of marauders or for my lamentations over my country's misfortunes, I ask his indulgence for a compassion which falls outside an historian's province. For of all the cities under Roman rule it was the lot of ours to attain to the highest felicity and to fall to the lowest depths of calamity. Indeed, in my opinion, the misfortunes of all nations since the world began fall short of those of the Jews; and, since the blame lay with no foreign nation, it was impossible to restrain one's grief. Should, however, any critic be too austere for pity, let him credit the history with the facts, the historian with the lamentations" (*JW* I, 11-12).

Josephus indeed claims for his work historical veracity and breadth of information, but he is clear-sighted enough not to claim objectivity. A passionate advocate, he singles out the guilty: the "brigands," the "factious," "tyrants," "malefactors," all "blinded by their folly" and stained with innocent blood. A despairing witness to an unbearable tragedy, he interrupts his narrative from time to time to give voice to his sorrow while remaining well aware that "the Laws of history compel one to restrain even one's emotions" (*JW* V, 20).

If we add to this Josephus' debt of gratitude to his protectors, the Flavians, which leads him to attenuate to a degree the cruelty of some of their behavior and exalt in them the virtues of ideal leadership—courage, wisdom, clemency, piety[7]—as well as to emphasize the supernatural protection they enjoyed, we will have painted a fairly accurate picture of Josephus as historian in the *War*.

The Greek version of *The Jewish War* was published in the reign of Titus (between 79 and 81). We are hardly surprised that it was given the imperial *imprimatur*. "So anxious was the emperor Titus that my volumes should be the sole authority from which the world should learn the facts, that he affixed his own signature to them and gave orders for their publication" (*L* 363).

Josephus also presented copies of his work to King Agrippa II as they appeared. He boasts of having received no fewer than sixty-two letters from the king testifying to the truth of his narrative. In a gesture unique in antiquity,[8] he includes two of the king's letters of congratulation for the edification of his readers:

King Agrippa to dearest Josephus, greeting. I have
perused the book with the greatest pleasure. You seem to
me to have written with much greater care and accuracy
than any who have dealt with the subject. Send me the
remaining volumes. Farewell.

King Agrippa to dearest Josephus, greeting. From what
you have written, you appear to stand in no need of
instruction, to enable us all to learn [everything from
you] from the beginning. But when you meet me, I will
myself by word of mouth inform you of much that is not
generally known.[9]

Beginning with his first book, therefore, Josephus enjoyed
success, but the favor of those in high places proves that he had
written the kind of history designed to please them. Indeed, he
boasts of it, and in so doing he also tacitly warns his reader to
remain alert. "Obliged as he was to forgo consulting any but the
documents furnished by the representative of one of the parties that
had destroyed the Jewish nation, we are well aware that, in the
absence of contradictory documents, we must accept with extreme
caution any information coming from such a partial pen."[10]

And indeed, to understand fully the tragedy that occurred
from 66 to 73 in Judea, we need the views of those whom the
French historian F. de Saulcy calls, in the emphatic style of his time,
"the illustrious martyrs of Jewish patriotism."[11] Partial, yes, but the
War nonetheless achieves a grandeur befitting its subject.

JEWISH ANTIQUITIES

After this first success, Josephus would appear to have developed a
taste for the writing of history. He quickly came up with another
project, this one on a larger scale, which was to occupy him for at
least ten years of his life.

In the introduction to the *War* he notes that he had taken
care not to delve too far into the past or to narrate the "origin of

the nation" (*JW* I, 17), but that in preparing his first chapter he had already assembled the materials for another work:

"I had indeed ere now, when writing the history of the war, already contemplated describing the origin of the Jews, the fortunes that befell them, the great Lawgiver[12] under whom they were trained in piety, and the exercise of the other virtues, and all those wars waged by them through long ages before this last in which they were involuntarily engaged against the Romans. However, since the compass of such a theme was excessive, I made the *War* into a separate volume" (*JA* I, 6-7).

The original version of the *Antiquities,* which was never published, was in Aramaic, and Josephus admits some "hesitation and delay on my part in rendering so vast a subject into a foreign and unfamiliar tongue," i.e., Greek (*Ibid.,* 7). The impetus came from his friend Epaphroditus, "a man devoted to every form of learning, but especially interested in history" (*Ibid.,* 8). His encouragement stimulated Josephus and inspired him to draw a flattering historical parallel. In the third century B.C.E. one of the first of the Ptolemaic kings of Egypt, Ptolemy II Philadelphus, had been eager to gain knowledge of Jewish law and had had seventy-two wise men dispatched to him from Jerusalem by the high priest Eleazar to translate the Pentateuch into Greek.[13] Josephus feels the same duty to spread Jewish thought: "Accordingly, I thought that it became me also both to imitate the high priest's magnanimity and to assume that there are still today many lovers of learning like the king" (*Ibid.,* 12).

He also had the task of filling a gap in Greek libraries by summing up five thousand years of Jewish history, filled with "all sorts of surprising reverses, many fortunes of war, heroic exploits of generals, and political revolutions" (*Ibid.,* 13) "from man's creation up to the twelfth year of the reign of Nero, of the events that befell us Jews in Egypt, in Syria, and in Palestine. It also comprises all that we suffered at the hands of Assyrians and Babylonians, and the harsh treatment that we received from the Persians and Macedonians and after them the Romans" (*JA* XX, 259-260). Thus, Josephus' goal was not only to inform others but also to defend his slandered people. In ancient times nothing was more praiseworthy than a long lineage and a history stretching far back into the past (there was a time indeed when Christianity suffered because it was too recent a phenomenon). A five-thousand-year history was indeed impressive; and impressive was what Josephus sought to be by entitling his work *Jewish Antiquities*. The result is monumental in size—a work that comprises twenty books and sixty thousand lines—and was finished in the thirteenth year of the reign of Domitian and the fifty-sixth of the author's life (*JW* XX, 257), i.e., the year 93.

The paraphrase of biblical history contained in the first ten books of the *Antiquities* is probably of less interest than the remainder to a modern reader with access to the Hebrew Bible or various translations. Yet we must admire the effort Josephus has made to recount for a pagan public the tale of such bygone times in a logical and coherent manner. In addition, the theologian will find in the *Antiquities* the trace of a number of contemporary exegeses of Josephus' day, and his inclusion of them may shed some light on both the New Testament and the Midrash.

The *Antiquities'* real value to us as a document lies in its account of the periods that Josephus considers "modern" or "contemporary." The value of the information he provides on the Hasmoneans, on the reign of Herod, on the Roman hegemony in Judea, and all the events immediately preceding the uprising against Rome cannot be overestimated. On all those subjects he remains our one and only source. Aware of the quality of his contribution to history, he concludes, typically without undue modesty, that "no one else, either Jew or gentile, would have been equal to the task, however willing to undertake it, of issuing so accurate a treatise as this for the Greek world" (*JA* XX, 262).

Josephus' project was both apologetic and historical. In recalling the history of his ancestors, he introduces many prominent figures of the past to confound those dishonest enough to maintain that his people had never furnished the world with any great men. In evoking the periods of national independence, he is giving the lie to the arrogant Romans, who regarded the conquered Jews as a people born to be slaves. Reproducing (in Book XIV) many documents dating from Caesar's time, he is calling attention to the protection Rome had traditionally accorded to the Jewish religion and explicitly exhorting it to continue in the same path.

His labors had also whetted his appetite for religious study. His research served to corroborate for him the primary teachings of the Holy Scriptures, the importance of respect for the Commandments.

"The main lesson to be learned from this history by any who care to peruse it is that men who conform to the will of God, and do not venture to transgress laws that have been excellently laid down, prosper in all things beyond belief, and for their reward are offered by God felicity; whereas, in proportion as they depart from the strict observance of these laws, things [else] practicable become impracticable, and whatever imaginary good thing they strive to do ends in irretrievable disasters" (*JA* I, 14).

The history of the people of Israel, demonstrating as it does divine intervention in the affairs of man since the Creation, offers us an opportunity to aspire to God. Unlike the "unseemly mythology current among others" (*Ibid.,* 15), the history of the Jews teaches men to order their lives aright and enables them to imitate God, "the best of all models" (*Ibid.,* 19).

Indeed, it is this *imitatio Dei* that seems to have most concerned the aging Josephus in his Roman exile. His mind is always filled with the old tales of his childhood, with the texts that first honed his intelligence and led him to ponder deeply. He hints that he may write another work, "profound and uniquely philosophical":[14] "If God grants me time, I shall endeavor to write upon it after completing the present work" (*Ibid.,* 25). By the time he had completed the twenty books of the *Antiquities,* his plan had ripened and taken shape: "It is also my intention to compose a work in four books on the opinions that we Jews hold concerning God and His essence, as well as concerning the Laws, that is, why according to them we are permitted to do some things while we are forbidden to do others" (*JA* XX, 268).

Was he fascinated with Philo's work and planning to carry it further? Or was he thinking of writing about all his former teachers who had been present for so long in the depths of his memory? With this planned but perhaps never written (or perhaps long vanished) book we have obviously lost a unique witness to the rabbinical teachings of the first century of our era.

Josephus, so quickly dubbed a traitor, has in the *Antiquities* borne shining witness of his fidelity to his origins and education.

THE LIFE

This fidelity is also manifest in the purely apologetic work to which we have already referred, *Against Apion*. However, certain attacks, this time personal, were now to impel Josephus to take up another kind of history and apologetics: autobiography.

The Life, which is chronologically the last of Josephus' completed works, is announced somewhat enigmatically at the conclusion of *Antiquities:* "Perhaps it will not seem to the public invidious or awkward for me to recount briefly my lineage and the events of my life while there are still persons living who can either disprove or corroborate my statements" (*JA* XX, 266).

In the *Life* there is a long digression (336-337) that reveals to us the name of the adversary to whom the book is directed as well as Josephus' quarrel with him. It is a man whom Josephus had known for more than a quarter of a century: Justus son of Pistos, from Tiberias, who had strongly voiced his opposition to the young governor-general of Galilee in the year 66.

At the time, Justus had been the leader of one of the three parties vying for power in the city of Tiberias, a young man "personally anxious for revolution and having hopes of obtaining the command of Galilee and of his native place" (*L* 391), but unable to impose his authority on the Galileans. Ever since, Josephus, who describes him as a demagogue clever at prevailing by magic and perfidious speech over his opponents whose advice was better, had made no secret of his loathing for him: "I was often so bitterly enraged with Justus that, unable to endure his villainy, I had almost killed him" (*L* 393). When Josephus as governor-general had taken control of Tiberias, Justus had preferred to leave the city and seek refuge with King Agrippa, against whom he had earlier fought (*L* 390). Sometime thereafter, in the spring of 67, Vespasian, landing in Ptolemais (Acre), had received a complaint from the citizens of the Decapolis[15] accusing Justus of having ravaged their land (*L* 342, 410). Since Justus' birthplace, Tiberias, was a part of the lands belonging to King Agrippa, Vespasian had determined that the accused was subject to royal justice and had recommended capital punishment. However, the King, his heart softened by the pleadings of his sister Berenice, had merely had Justus put into chains and had not executed him, a course Josephus strongly deplores after the fact. Justus had soon been freed: as a Greek-speaking Galilean, he had succeeded so well in gaining the King's favor that Agrippa had made him his secretary.

Many years later, a manuscript written by Justus came into Josephus' hands: it was an account of the war. Josephus' indignation was twofold: not only had his old enemy dared take up a subject that he felt he himself had dealt with better than any one else, but Justus' description of Josephus' actions in Galilee was a complete and calumnious slander.

Twenty years after the end of that sorry war, it was not overly wise to show oneself to be an ardent Jewish nationalist.[16] Smoothing over his own role in the uprising in Galilee, Justus dwelt on the role played by Josephus, sent from Jerusalem to organize the resistance against Rome and King Agrippa. Josephus' reaction was furious: "How, then, Justus—I may address him as though he were present—how, most clever of historians, as you boast yourself to be, can I and the Galileans be held responsible for the insurrection of your native city against the Romans and against the king?" (*L* 340) He reminds Justus that the anti-Roman faction had been the strongest in Tiberias and that Justus had been one of its leaders, tardily embracing the party of Agrippa II, who for that matter had not kept him for long as his secretary, having soon discovered what a double-dealer he was (*L* 356).

The personal attacks are followed by a violent criticism of Justus' version of history: "I cannot, however, but wonder at your impudence in daring to assert that your narrative is to be preferred to that of all who have written on this subject" (*L* 357).

As a matter of fact, Josephus cannot stand having his own work called into question. Is it not he who has the prime advantage of having been a participant and then an eyewitness to the war, whereas Justus was nowhere near the battlefield at the time? He nearly chokes with fury upon reading his rival's account of the fall of Jotapata, which minimizes his own role in the defense of the besieged city (*L* 357). Justus' account of the siege of Jerusalem, which contradicts both the eyewitness account of Josephus, who was there, and the various Roman military reports the latter has examined since, exasperates Josephus more than anything else: "If you are so confident that your history excels all others, why did you not publish it in the lifetime of the emperors Vespasian and Titus, who conducted the war, and while King Agrippa and all his family, persons thoroughly conversant with Hellenic culture, were still among us? . . . But not until now, when those persons are no longer with us and you think you cannot be confronted, have you ventured to publish it" (*L* 359-360). As for Josephus, he can boast of having been given the approval of both Titus and Agrippa (*L* 361-367).

This historians' dispute, which shadowed Josephus' declining years, does not raise his stature. The *Life* it inspired is often heavy going and confused, a work at once hypertrophied and replete with omissions. We have difficulty understanding why Josephus, when called to account by Justus for his actions during the defense of Jotapata, did not take up the matter directly instead of dwelling at length on the events preceding it; we also find it hard to understand why he made no attempt to bring his account in the *Life* into line with what he had earlier written in the *War* concerning the same events. Without Justus' missing version, which might help to explain Josephus' wrath, the polemical outbursts in the *Life* serve only to inspire the reader's indifference, discomfort, or boredom. The book's most paradoxical effect is that it has preserved the memory of an enemy whose own work has sunk into oblivion, just as in *Against Apion* Josephus preserved the names of a few obscure polemicists who had slandered the Alexandrian Jews. And it makes us regret not having another account of the war to counterbalance that of Josephus and enable us to make a better estimate of its validity.

However, *The Life* does at least provide us with some valuable information on Josephus' own life, information that is lacking for every other writer of antiquity.

Born and raised in priestly circles, Josephus in another period could have become a high priest or an outstanding rabbinical authority. The two missions with which he was entrusted between the ages of twenty-six and twenty-nine, as ambassador and then as governor-general, are a tribute to the intellectual qualities of this brilliant young man in whom such great hopes were placed. When, at Jotapata, defeat reduced his nascent ambitions to dust, Josephus did not resign himself to oblivion and death, for he firmly believed himself destined for higher things. During the siege of Jerusalem he dreamed of being a peacemaker, but was in fact only a military interpreter treated with contumely by his own people. It is only later, in Rome, and almost despite himself, that he at last found a way to make his mark in history—namely, by writing history.

And then that history had to survive. And Josephus could have had no idea of the chain of events that would ensure his work's survival.

EPILOGUE
POSTHUMOUS FATE

Habent sua fata libelli.
(ALL WRITINGS HAVE THEIR OWN FATE.)

FROM FLAVIUS JOSEPHUS TO FIFTH EVANGELIST

Although from the beginning Josephus' work found a place in Rome's libraries,[1] it had little direct influence on the work of any Latin historian. Even when Tacitus could have relied on Josephus' data when composing his own extremely summary recital of the Judean war, in Book V of his *Histories,* his Roman pride made him hew to other, pagan, chroniclers for whom Josephus would have felt nothing but contempt.

With one exception,[2] from the second century on, the only authors to refer to Josephus by name are the Fathers of the Church, and it is thanks to them that the historian's work was preserved in the Christian world. They regarded Josephus above all as a valuable ally in their polemical and apologetic crusade.[3] Thus, translations into Latin or partial translations into Syriac and Armenian, paraphrases such as the one by Hegesippus (fourth century) in Latin, and various abridgments, such as Zonaras' in the tenth century or an eleventh-century version in Old Russian, were widely circulated in Christian lands.

From its earliest days Christianity had been obliged to do battle on two fronts: on the one hand, it had to prove its credentials to the pagans, and on the other, it needed to distinguish itself from Judaism in so far as possible. The pagans often reproached Christianity with being a newborn or infant religion; it lacked the venerability that antiquity would have conferred upon it. In the third century similar criticisms were common from one end of the Mediterranean to the other, from Tertullian in Carthage to Alexandria and Caesarea, Origen's territory. The response that was eventually elaborated relied in part on two of Josephus' books, *Jewish Antiquities* and *Against Apion,* which described the Jewish people's age-old background and religion.[4] For the apologists, the Christians were the *verus Israel,* those who had recognized the Messiah foretold by the Prophets; the Christian religion was a direct continuation of Judaism and could thus lay claim to the same antiquity so amply set forth by Josephus.

Nor was the name of Josephus a stranger to anti-Jewish polemics. Had he not recounted the fall of Jerusalem in great detail? Had he not explained that fall as being the result of the sins of the people? He had probably not really clearly understood the true nature of those sins, but every Christian believed that the Jews had been punished because of Christ's crucifixion. "He should have noted that the attack against Jesus had been the cause of that people's misfortune, for that they had killed the Christ foretold by the Prophets," Origen wrote.[5] His disciple Eusebius, Bishop of Caesarea, gives us long extracts from the account of the famine in Jerusalem, interspersing them with his own comments, as for example: "Here we must transcribe the very terms in which this writer [i.e., Josephus] reports the manner in which a multitude of three million men who had flowed in from throughout Judea for the Passover came to be shut up inside Jerusalem as if in a prison. Indeed, it was because in those same days in which they had inflicted all the sufferings of the passion on the Savior and Benefactor of all, Christ the Lord, they must needs be reassembled as if in a prison to be meted out the death intended for them by divine justice."[6]

The many omens of disaster Josephus lists for us were to be interpreted as so many instances of God in His goodness urging the

Jews to convert. Most especially, the "ambiguous oracle" announcing the advent of the ruler of the world in Judea was applied to Christ.[7]

That is the light in which Josephus was to be read by generations of Christians. For them, his account of the war added the last touches to the story contained in the New Testament, describing as it did the awful punishment of those who in their blindness had not recognized the Savior. "The blood of His Son spilt by the most horrible of crimes was the sole and veritable cause of the downfall of that unfortunate city," wrote the French Jansenist Arnauld d'Andilly.[8]

In a more general way, all Josephus' historical work—*War* and *Antiquities*—was regarded as the best guarantee of the Christian faith. First, the *Antiquities* provided a much-needed résumé of the Old Testament and went on to recount all the events that had occurred up until the second destruction of the Temple. Since Christ's coming was believed to have closed the book of Holy History, Josephus, who dealt with the so-called intertestamentary period, came to be regarded as a continuer of biblical history, a link between the two Testaments. In addition, he was the only historian to have set down so many elements that corroborated the Gospels. He mentioned the census ordered by Quirinius, the governor of Syria, at which time Luke locates the birth of Jesus.[9] He dwelt on the cruelty of Herod, whom the pagans had called "Great,"[10] and sympathetically reported the preachings of John the Baptist;[11] he expressed indignation at the condemnation of "a man named James, the brother of Jesus who was called Christ" by a high priest of the Sadducees (*JA* XX, 200); and even better, in a chapter devoted to events in the reign of Tiberius during which Pontius Pilate was Governor of Judea, he included a brief passage about Jesus himself, which was to come to be known as the *Testimonium Flavianum*—the Flavian testimony:

"About this time there lived Jesus, a wise man, if indeed one ought to call him a man. For he was one who wrought surprising feats and was a teacher of such people as accept the truth gladly. He won over many Jews and many of the Greeks. He was Christ. When Pilate, upon hearing him accused by men of the highest standing amongst us, had condemned him to be crucified, those who had in the first place come to love him did not give up their affection for him. On the third day he appeared to them restored to life, for the prophets of God had prophesied these and countless other marvelous things about him. And the sect of Christians, so called after him, has still to this day not disappeared" (*JA* XVIII, 63-64).

But was this passage really written by Josephus' hand? The question did not even begin to be asked until late in the sixteenth century.[12] The critical argument is based on simple common sense: if Josephus had indeed written the lines, he would have to have been a Christian, and that had clearly not been the case. Indeed, the Church preferred it that way, for ever since Eusebius of Caesarea, who was the first Christian writer to quote the *Testimonium Flavianum* (in the fourth century), it had been deemed highly important "that a writer from amongst the Jews themselves should have transmitted [to us] in his writings from those bygone days such things concerning our Savior."[13]

In seventeenth-century Europe the critical view was more welcomed by Protestants than by Catholics.[14] It was to find its most enlightened defender in Voltaire, in the eighteenth century:

"Let there be an end to attempts to justify the fraud committed by those who inserted in Flavius Josephus' history that famous passage touching upon Jesus Christ, a passage recognized as false by all true scholars. If that clumsy passage contained nothing but the words 'he was the Christ,' would that in itself not suffice to brand it as fraudulent in the eyes of anyone with common sense? Is it not ridiculous to think that Josephus, devoted as he was to his nation and his faith, would have recognized Jesus as *Christ?* Ah, my friend, if you believe *Christ,* then become a Christian. If you believe *Christ* the son of God, God Himself, how can you only say a mere four words about him?"[15]

From the nineteenth century on, historians who have examined the passage free of theological presuppositions have been of two camps: some hold the *Testimonium* to be completely unauthentic, others suggest that Josephus' original passage has been subjected to interpolations, that is to say, remarks written in the margin of a manuscript by some pious Christian reader in the early fourth century were later taken and integrated into the text. This latter, moderate, position is the one most widely accepted today. No one believes that Josephus' hand wrote the words "if, indeed, one ought to call him a man" or "He was the Messiah"—formulae that do not, as a matter of fact, appear in an old Arabic version recently discovered. The paragraph's conclusion, too, is thought to be fairly dubious.[16]

And after all, according to the traditional way of thinking so admirably summed up by Arnauld d'Andilly, recognizing that the *Testimonium* contained Christian interpolations did not really change things all that much. He wrote: "Certainly it does not appear that having thus contributed to the establishment of the Gospel he [Josephus] profited from it in any way himself . . . but if we can deplore his misfortune in not so doing, we can also praise God, who so providentially turned his blindness to our advantage, for the things he writes of his nation are, in the eyes of unbelievers, of incomparably greater use in the establishment of the Christian religion than had he himself embraced Christianity."[17]

In Voltaire's day some Catholic voices were raised to deny, at least in part, Josephus' authority, but for quite different reasons. Despite several generations of effort, it had proved impossible to get the chronology set forth by the historian and the indications given in the Gospels concerning the birth of Jesus to coincide. According to the second chapter of the Gospel of Luke, Jesus' parents, natives of Nazareth, had come to Bethlehem shortly before the birth of their child because Augustus had decreed "that all the world should be taxed," an event that was supposed to have occurred "when Quirinius was Governor of Syria." According to the second chapter of Matthew, which does not mention the census, Jesus was born in Bethlehem "in the days of Herod the king," and his parents had fled with him into Egypt, where they had remained until Herod's death. Josephus mentions Quirinius' census, but he situates it at the end of the reign of Archelaus, Herod's son and successor, who was deposed by Augustus in the year 6 after having occupied the throne for ten years. In order for Jesus to have been born during the reign of Herod, which had ended in 4 B.C.E., the beginning of the Christian era would have to be set back at least four years, but in that case one would have retreated by ten years from the date of the census of Quirinius.

This argument persuaded some scholarly ecclesiastics to place the birth of Christ prior to the beginning of the Christian era, and one of these was the extremely learned Benedictine Dom Calmet, whom Voltaire rather gleefully dubbed the Champion of Obscurantism. The divergences led others to deduce that Josephus was in error. His testimony had to give way to that of "Saint Luke, a writer certainly older and more worthy of faith, even were he not divinely inspired."[18] Josephus, after all, was only human: "Josephus must have made a natural mistake," the most indulgent said, while others went much further: *"Scriptor mendacissimus,"* Pére Hardouin thundered, and the Abbé of Vence ended a laborious thirty-five-page thesis with the words: "And how do we today determine the death of Herod? On the basis of the testimony of the historian Josephus, or by means of coinage; in other words, via an historian convicted of falsehood and a few pieces of metal that are open to various interpretations."[19]

Nevertheless, Josephus continued to be read throughout Europe. He had the approval of respected humanists like Scaliger (sixteenth century: "The most diligent of authors and the greatest lover of truth known"),[20] of pious men like Arnauld d'Andilly ("an irreproachable witness," "a true historian"),[21] or of such literary sorts as Madame de Sévigné, who urges her daughter to read Josephus: "It would be a shame of which you could never cleanse yourself not to finish Josephus" (November 3, 1675). "I'm delighted that you like Josephus . . . Take heart, it's all lovely, it's all great: it's a magnificent read" (November 6, 1675).

Since his works had first begun to be translated, Flavius Josephus had been known to all of Christian Europe as the author of a history that was, "after the Holy Scripture, preferable to all others,"[22] a kind of "Fifth Evangelist." Editions multiplied, some in the eighteenth century accompanied by fine engravings. With the Counter Reformation, Josephus was to become more "the fifth Evangelist of the Protestants," in the words of Pére Hardouin, but even until the last century he remained the most read of all the historians of antiquity.[23] Not only did every European ruler possess magnificently bound volumes of his work, but every middle-class household had a copy too. Among the English Puritans, Josephus was the only reading, aside from the Holy Bible, authorized on the Lord's Day. An edition of Josephus' works was among the forty works contributed by the clergymen who founded the Collegiate School of Connecticut, now Yale University.[24] The English translation of the complete works by Whiston, a professor of mathematics at Cambridge University in the eighteenth century, was reprinted a record number of times.

So integral is this writer to the history of Christianity that the relative obscurity into which Josephus has lapsed in our own century can be viewed as another clear sign of the de-Christianization of the West.

Such is the strange fate of a work originally intended for Jews and Romans but welcomed by Christianity, a work whose vast future dissemination Josephus could not have imagined. In an era much less skeptical than ours, people found it much easier to accept the fact that Josephus had owed his survival of the siege of Jotapata "to the providence of God" (*JW* III, 391), and it was firmly believed that that miracle had been worked so that the former governor-general could go on to become a historian *ad maximam Christi gloriam*. "Which shows that we should grant this historian a place quite different from that of others, for it would seem that God had singled him out to serve the greatest of his ends."[25]

FROM JOSIPPON TO THE OATH OF MASADA

And what about the Jews?

By them, Josephus' *oeuvre,* whether in Aramaic or in Greek, was so completely forgotten that prior to the sixteenth century not a single Jewish document mentions it.

In the tenth century, a Hebrew-language avatar, the *Josippon,* made its appearance, first most probably in southern Italy. The work was based on an old Latin adaptation dating back to the fourth century and attributed to a certain Hegesippus, a name that seems to contain an odd, distant echo of "Josephus." Its sources also included the two books of the Maccabees and various medieval chronicles.[26] The author records his debt to a Jewish historian named Joseph son of Matthias, whom he confuses with Joseph ben Gorion, one the principal leaders of the Jerusalem uprising—thus, since the Middle Ages, the work has been known as the *Josippon,* a hellenized version of his name, Joseph. Today we know of a popular version rewritten in Italy in the twelfth century, which served as the basis for a 1510 Constantinople edition, which is, in turn, the basis for many later editions.[27]

The *Josippon,* written in biblical Hebrew and later translated into such diverse languages as Arabic, Latin, Yiddish, English, Czech, Polish, and Russian, made Jewish communities aware of the whole history of the so-called period of the Second Temple, about which the Talmudic writings offered only a few legendary and/or edifying incidents. It contains many details absent from Josephus' work. For example, its account of Vespasian's coronation in Rome is modeled on accounts of the coronations of various mediaeval emperors. There are also some interesting modifications: The speech of Eleazar (here called the Son of Anani) at Masada[28] does not express any despair over his nation's collective fate; rather, he includes many biblical examples and draws upon the Midrash, which, in justifying the success of Rome, that "Evil Empire," one that should have been the fourth and last of the great empires of history, goes on to explain that when all things had been shared out, Rome had been given the world here below, the material world, and Israel the world to come, the spiritual world. To this entire episode, which comes at the end of the book, was added a concluding prayer beseeching God to rebuild the Holy City and reassemble in Zion those exiled to the four corners of the earth.

The *Josippon* narrative of Masada's final moments also avoids any mention of suicide. After having listened to Eleazar's sublime and moving speech, the defenders of the fortress decide to kill the women and children; they take time to bury the bodies and then engage in combat with all the fury of men who have nothing to lose but their lives. Thus the ending is rewritten in a spirit more in conformity with rabbinical Judaism, which rejected suicide.

During the Crusades many Jewish communities (Worms, Mainz, Trier, Cologne, York) were to find themselves in the same situation as the defenders of Masada and were to display the same courage. Were they inspired by the *Josippon?* Their situation caused them to adopt an attitude similar to that of their ancestors, but it was the attitude reflected in Josephus' narrative rather than that of the *Josippon.*[29]

However, the example invoked by the thousands upon thousands of martyred victims of the Crusades is not that of Masada. In describing atrocious scenes of collective suicide, Jewish chroniclers and poets usually made reference to an older biblical paradigm, the image of Abraham raising his knife over his son Isaac on Mount Moriah (*aqeda,* in Hebrew, which refers to the "binding" of the sacrificial victim). Salomon bar Shimshon, the twelfth-century chronicler, in referring to the fate of eleven hundred Jews of Mainz writes: "Were there ever before eleven hundred *aqedot* in one day, all like that in which Abraham bound Isaac his son for the sacrifice? For he who was bound on Mount Moriah the earth shook, and it is written: Behold, the angels wept and the heavens grew dark. But what do the angels now? Why do the heavens not grow dark and the stars pale . . . when in a single day . . . eleven hundred pure souls are sacrificed, including newborn and children . . . ? Can you, O Lord our God, be silent?"[30]

In the *Josippon* Eleazar's speech at Masada was shorn of all those references to recent history that appear in Josephus' report, which were replaced with biblical references: the sacrifice of Isaac, first, but also those of Cain and Abel and Pharaoh and the Hebrews. Of course that does not necessarily mean that the *Josippon* had an influence on the medieval martyrs; the most we can say is that it too represents an early outcropping of medieval Jewish thought and that it gave a version of Eleazar's discourse that was more accessible to contemporary Jews.

The *Josippon* enjoyed considerable prestige among the Jews until fairly recently. True, no one was aware that it was a fairly late work; it was regarded as the Hebrew version of the writings of Joseph son of Matthias, or of Gorion, a contemporary of the destruction of the Second Temple. The esteem in which the work was held is reflected in this opinion expressed by the writer of the preface[31] to the work's 1510 edition: "Each word of this text is true and just, and it contains no falsehood. Proof lies in the fact that of all the books written since the Holy Scriptures, this is the closest to the Prophets, for it was written before the Mishnah and before the Talmud." This does not prevent him from recommending the work to "merchants living for the sake of temporal success and who have not turned toward the Torah" for distraction.[32]

One of the historians who embodies the resurgence of historical concerns among Jews in the sixteenth century, Joseph Ha Cohen, the author of *The Vale of Tears,* proudly announces that he is a continuator of the *Josippon:* "My whole people knows it: there is no one come out of Israel to equal Josippon the preacher, author of the account of the war of Judea and of Jerusalem. No chroniclers have risen up before me, Joseph, not until I rose up, as a chronicler in Israel."[33]

The *Josippon* was to distract the Jews from Flavius Josephus' work until the nineteenth century. True, in the sixteenth century the learned Mantuan Azaria dei Rossi mentioned Josephus, along with Philo of Alexandria (also unknown to the Jews), in his *Meor Einayim (The Enlightened Eye,* 1573–1575), but that collection of critical essays on history was too bold for its day and very badly received. Rossi demonstrated, among other things, that the *Josippon* was no more than a medieval compilation that falsified many of the facts related in its source, Flavius Josephus. He was easily able to prove by referring to other authors of antiquity that the Talmudic traditions with regard to Titus were pure legend. Notwithstanding its author's well-known piety, however, his work was banned and remained so for two centuries.

Azaria dei Rossi had to wait for the Enlightenment, the *Haskala,* to return to favor and renown. The *Meor Einayim* was reprinted for the first time in Berlin in 1794. Even the *Haskala,* however, witnessed only fairly feeble historical progress. The opening of the ghettos and the beginnings of Jewish emancipation in Europe resulted in the *Wissenschaft des Judentums* (Science of Judaism), which slowly began to spread outside the borders of Germany. Only then did the preference shift clearly from the *Josippon* to Flavius Josephus. The latter served as the source for the period it covered in the new type of historical writing that emerged, a discipline that reached a high point with the work of Heinrich Graetz, which appeared from 1853 to 1870.

In France, the *Wissenschaft* spirit was embodied in the Société des Etudes Juives (founded in 1880), one of whose most prominent members, Theodore Reinach, set out in 1912 to produce a careful translation of Josephus' work to replace that of Arnauld d'Andilly, judged to be "beautiful but unfaithful," which had had the field to itself for a good century and a half before being modernized by Buchon in the nineteenth century.

The early nineteenth century, under the influence of the *Haskala,* witnessed the emergence of a new Hebrew literature that was gradually to attempt to absorb modern literary genres. This movement would most likely have died out had it not been for the creation of a Jewish center in Palestine at century's end and had the Jews who settled there not decided, following the example of Eliezer ben Yehuda, to revivify their ancestral tongue. In 1927 Isaac Lamdan, a young settler of Polish origin, wrote a lengthy epic poem in six cantos entitled *Masada.* He was writing for the generation that had seen its universalist hopes so cruelly disappointed by the Russian Revolution. The fortress of Masada became the site upon which the refugees from every Jewish tragedy now wanted to converge; they struggled through thick and thin to return to it in answer to the poet's emotional call. The poem had an immense impact in Zionist circles. Masada, the symbol of the Land of Israel, came to represent their final hope, but this Masada "will never fall again." Such is the oath young recruits in the Israeli army take today, quoting one of Lamdan's famous lines.

Today, Flavius Josephus is probably read more in Israel than in any other country. Archeology, the country's "national sport," could not do without him. Caesarea, Sepphoris, Gamala, Masada, the Jerusalem of the Second Temple, could not be imagined without his writings.[34] Even if his character may still inspire certain misgivings, the historian is honored. Thus, after nineteen centuries, the Roman exile Yosef ben Mattitiahu ha Cohen, alias Flavius Josephus, has returned to the land of his birth.

JOSEPHUS IN LEGEND
AND LITERATURE

Unlike nearly all the other historians of antiquity, Josephus has
been taken up by posterity as a personality, as a man. Probably
because Josephus, more than any of the others, wrote of himself,
and because his unusual destiny provided material for both fiction
and reflection.

For the Christians, as we have noted, Josephus had been
miraculously spared by God to fulfill his mission as witness. The
example of the apostle Paul, who so providentially escaped from so
many dangers, was an obvious one. With regard to the drawing of
lots at Jotapata, one generally accepted Josephus' version: whether
chance or "the providence of God, he remained, with one other"
(*JW* III, 391). The Slavonic version of the *War,* entitled *The Fall of
Jerusalem,* probably produced in the eleventh century, puts forward
a completely rationalistic explanation for the Jotapata "miracle":
Josephus must have manipulated the drawing in such a way that he
would inevitably come out last. "He was agile with numbers and
thus managed to trick them all."[35]

The rationalists long ago came up with *Josephus' Problem,* a
recent version of which is quoted in Chapter Five. Thus, the providence watching over Josephus should have been called Arithmetic.
Josephus had had a mathematical mind that was able to work out a
complicated mental problem at an extremely difficult moment.

True, the Middle Ages had credited him with even more
power. Old Saxon chronicles[36] tell of Flavius Josephus' curing Titus
of dropsy, gout, or paralysis. This tradition probably goes back to a
Talmudic legend (*Gittin,* 56b) according to which Johanan ben
Zakkai is supposed to have cured Vespasian. In these parallel leg-
ends, Johanan and Josephus are depicted as healers employing some
kind of magic power and not as true medical men: their cure consisted in confronting the patient with the person or servant he most
detested! The mediaeval legend was obviously cut to fit a definite
social context, namely, the enormous growth in medical knowledge
among the Jews in the Middle Ages.

The existence of such traditions suffices to demonstrate how popular Josephus was in bygone days. There is hardly a single European language into which he has not been translated, not to mention Arabic and Geez (Old Ethiopic). We can follow the spread of his writings through every literature down to the present day: Slavic, Italian, Spanish, French, English. Writers indebted to him include Garnier, Petrarch, and Milton. And yet, upon closer examination, his influence seems to have been slight, even fleeting. We do not know of any one truly great work directly inspired by Josephus, which is astonishing when one considers the amount of material he offers.[37] Jean Racine, who had known Josephus' translator, Arnauld d'Andilly, at Port-Royal, had read his translation, but did not use it for his biblical tragedies. True, the Bible was a far superior source for such subjects than Josephus' paraphrase.

Jewish writers have been concerned with the specifically Jewish elements in Josephus' *oeuvre,* but, for the reasons set forth earlier, they have only been able to read him fairly recently. The impact of the rediscovery of the Masada episode is reflected in Lamdan's 1927 poem, which has had many successors. In the 1930s there was a flurry of literary works that used Josephus himself as their hero.[38] The best known, since it was translated into a number of languages, is probably Lion Feuchtwanger's trilogy, whose first volume, *Der jüdische Krieg* (The Jewish War), was published in Berlin in 1932, the second, *Die Söhne* (The Sons), in Amsterdam and Stockholm in 1935 after the Nazis had destroyed the first manuscript, and the third, *Der Tag wird kommen* (The Day Will Come) in Stockholm in 1945. The book's varied publication history reflects the terrible times in which it was written, which could not help but be reflected in the work. The author himself, in the foreword to the second volume, warns the reader: "Rewriting the lost portion in its earlier form proved impossible. I had learned a great deal more about the theme of my *Josephus,* namely, nationalism and cosmopolitanism: the subject matter burst the confines of its original frame and I found myself forced to break it down into three volumes." At almost the same time two Hebrew-language playwrights were writing plays about Josephus: Shin

Shalom's *Josephus' Cave* (1935) and Nathan Agmon-Bistritski's *Flavius Josephus* (1939).[39] The authors were also inspired by Jerusalem's final hours, as were other playwrights, the latest of whom, Yehoshua Sobol, has written a cleverly provocative play entitled *The War of the Jews,* which has created a considerable stir in Israel. Josephus' account of the events at Masada was also the inspiration for an opera, *Masada G67,* which was performed at the 1973 Festival of Israel to commemorate the 1900th anniversary of the siege; the work, to electronic music, is by Yosef Tal, with a libretto by the poet Israel Eliraz.

Even the cinema has begun to draw upon Josephus' work, as witness the American television serial *Masada*. Recently a more serious scholar, the author of a monumental biography of our historian, remarked: "In view of the delicious mixture of sex and violence in Josephus' pages, it is surprising that filmmakers haven't used him more."[40]

BEFORE THE BENCH OF HISTORY

In his two thousand or so years of posthumous life, Flavius Josephus' visage has undergone several changes. An unwitting Christian, a wise man, a mathematician, a defender of the faith or sower of doubt—he has worn many costumes on his journey from antiquity to modern times. For a century now, historians who have gratefully used him as the principal source for the period he covers in his writings have felt almost obliged to do with regard to Josephus something they would never feel obliged to do with regard to any other historian of antiquity, namely, pass judgment on the man. They are impelled to do so by the obvious partiality of the author of *The Jewish War*. Both the partisan F. de Saulcy and the austere German scholar Emil Schürer have expressed their indignant or cutting opinions: "No one feels an inclination to justify him," writes the first. "Vanity and conceit are the main components of his character. Even if he was not the vile and contemptible traitor he belatedly admits to being in his autobiography, he did nevertheless transfer his allegiance to Rome and his fidelity to the family of the

Flavians with more alacrity and with less soul searching than is fitting in an Israelite purportedly bemoaning the destruction of his people."[41] The French philologist Theodore Reinach writes that Josephus is "neither a great mind nor a great character, but an unusual combination of Jewish patriotism, Hellenic culture, and vanity." More recently, Pierre Vidal-Naquet emphasized "the vanity, the avid class consciousness, the cynicism" of his personality and, comparing the treacheries of Tiberius Julius Alexander, the apostle Paul, and Josephus, unhesitatingly gave the prize for treason to Josephus.[42]

At the same time, in Zionist circles Israel's lost son has been welcomed, but not without certain misgivings. One would have preferred a hero as the narrator of Masada's epic story. Instead, we have a man who was the sworn enemy of the heroes whose courage we admire so much today. In 1937 a group of law students in Antwerp reopened the case of Flavius Josephus and, after a mock trial, found him guilty of treason.[43] In 1941, in the midst of the Second World War, a group of young resistance fighters and strong supporters of Zionism reacted as French and Jewish patriots, accusing Flavius Josephus of collaboration.[44] In the State of Israel a street has finally, and rather hesitantly, been named after him in Jerusalem, one way of appreciating the historic debt he is owed, whatever one's opinion of his personality. Indeed, mock trials of Josephus have today become rhetorical exercises in many Israeli high schools, and in October 1992 a program in which Flavius Josephus was tried for treason was broadcast on Israeli television; the accused was aquitted for lack of evidence.

The history Flavius Josephus recounts for us is always present in the minds of Israeli journalists or writers, who refer to it whenever internal political divisions become too violent,[45] making use of the misunderstanding that can so easily arise because of the usual translation of the title of his book, *The Jewish War* or *The War of the Jews,* which we prefer calling *The Judean War.* Without actually rehabilitating Josephus, the militant Left readily identifies the partisans of Greater Israel with the Zealots.

The long posthumous history of Flavius Josephus should make us wary about all the purposes for which his life and his work have been used, particularly in the case of the *War*. Suffice it to recall that it reminded de Saulcy of nothing so much as the Terror during the French Revolution, that Reinach saw in it "something like a preview" of the siege of Paris and the Commune, and that it has also been compared to the Russian Revolution. Today, we could easily use it to evoke the recent situation in Lebanon. The truth is that any civil war, any fratricidal confrontation, will recall Josephus' work to those who have read it.

Thus, it is scarcely surprising that a German Jew persuaded of the horrors of armed conflict by the First World War and of the danger of nationalism by the rise of Nazism, Lion Feuchtwanger, should have undertaken to rehabilitate Josephus' reputation. In his well-known trilogy, Josephus becomes a character prey to all the problems of identity and all the disasters that have plagued the Jews in the Diaspora, a man aspiring to become a citizen of the world. According to one critic, Feuchtwanger was describing Stefan Zweig, but that is a moot point.[46] We do recall, however, that the prophet Jeremiah forms a strong bond between Flavius Josephus and Zweig, who in 1916 wrote a play entitled *Jeremiah*.

If, at the conclusion of this book, it is still necessary to come up with a portrait of Josephus, the reader will have created his own from the preceding pages: a child prodigy, a brilliant young man trusting in his star, an eloquent intellectual repelled by the spilling of blood, an ambitious man unwilling to die at the age of thirty, a mind more political than warlike, a careful rationalist who loathed mystical exaltation, a courtier in his talent for compromise and, added to all that, a profoundly believing Jew.

To be a hero, he would have had to perish at Jotapata having written nothing, but then posterity would have known nothing about it. Should we regret that he was not a hero?

APPENDIX: CHRONOLOGY

Reign of Herod from 37 B.C.E. to 4 B.C.E.
Reign of Archelaus from 4 B.C.E. to 6 C.E.
Prefects★ of Judea from 6 to 41

Coponius	6 to 9
Marcus Ambibulus	9 to 12
Valerius Gratus	15 to 26
Pontius Pilate	26 to 36
Marcellus ?	36 or 37
Marullus ?	37 to 41

Reign of King Agrippa I from 41 to 44

Procurators from 44 to 66

Cuspius Fadus	44 to 46
Tiberius Julius Alexander	46 to 48
Venidius Cumanus	48 to 52
Felix	52 to 60
Porcius Festus	60 to 62
Lucceius Albinus	62 to 64
Gessius Florus	64 to 66

★During this period the governors of Judea were given the title of "prefect" and not "procurator," as can be seen from the inscription of Pontius Pilate discovered at Caesarea.

JUDEA

Year
B.C.E

167	Revolt of the Maccabees
161	Treaty of alliance with Rome
	Death of Judah Maccabeus
152	Jonathan, high priest
143	Simon, high priest
135	John Hyrcanus, high priest
104	Judah Aristobulus I, high priest and king
103	Alexander Jannaeus, high priest and king
76	Salome-Alexandra, queen
	Hyrcanus II, high priest
67–63	War of succession between Aristobulus II and Hyrcanus II
63	Pompey enters Jerusalem
47	Julius Caesar in Judea
40–37	Reign of Matthias–Antigonus (Aristobulus' son)
	Herod crowned king in Rome
37–4	Reign of Herod
4 B.C.E. to 6 C.E.	Quartering of Herod's kingdom
6 to 41	Reign of Archelaus in Judea, Samaria, and Idumaea
	First governors of Judea
41–44	Agrippa I, king of Judea
44–66	Era of the procurators
66	Beginning of the uprising against Rome
70	Destruction of Jerusalem
73	Fall of Masada
132–135	Revolt of Bar Kokhba (Bar Kosiba) in Judea

ROMAN EMPIRE

B.C.E.

169	Battle of Pydna
146	Sack of Corinth
	Destruction of Carthage

133–121	Revolt of the Gracchi
107	Consulate of Marius
88	Consulate of Sulla; civil war
82	Dictatorship of Sulla
70	Pompey and Crassus consuls
60	First triumvirate: Pompey, Caesar, Crassus
44	Assassination of Caesar
43	Second triumvirate: Octavius, Antony, Lepidus
31	Battle of Actium
	Egypt a Roman province
29	Octavius sole master of the Empire
27	Octavius named Augustus (reigns till 14 C.E.)

C.E.

14–37	Reign of Tiberius
37–41	Reign of Caligula
41–54	Reign of Claudius Julio-Claudian dynasty
54–68	Reign of Nero
68–69	Civil war: three emperors (Galba, Otho, Vitellius)
69–79	Vespasian ⎫
79–81	Titus ⎬
81–96	Domitian ⎭
96–98	Nerva
98-117	Trajan
115–117	Revolt of the Diaspora Antonine dynasty
117–138	Hadrian
138–161	Antoninus Pius

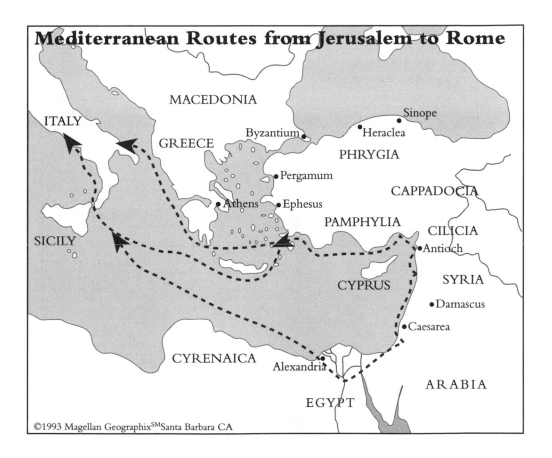

Mediterranean Routes from Jerusalem to Rome

MACEDONIA

ITALY

GREECE

Byzantium

Sinope

Heraclea

PHRYGIA

Pergamum

CAPPADOCIA

Athens

Ephesus

PAMPHYLIA

CILICIA

SICILY

Antioch

SYRIA

CYPRUS

Damascus

Caesarea

CYRENAICA

Alexandria

ARABIA

EGYPT

©1993 Magellan Geographix^{SM}Santa Barbara CA

Judea on the Eve of the Uprising Against Rome

Zone controlled by the Procurator of Judea

Kingdom of Agrippa II

Fortress

SYRIA

• Damascus

Sidon •

PHOENICIA

Tyre •

• Caesarea Philippi

GALILEE

GAULANITIS

TRACHONITIS

Ptolemais (Acre) •

Taricheae •

BATANEA

Lake of Tiberias

AUREANITIS

Tiberias

Mediterranean Sea

Jordan River

DECAPOLIS

• Caesarea

Sebaste •

SAMARIA

PEREA

• Philadelphia

Abila • •

JUDEA

Dead Sea

□ Machaerus

NABATEANS

□ Masada

©1993 Magellan Geographix℠Santa Barbara CA

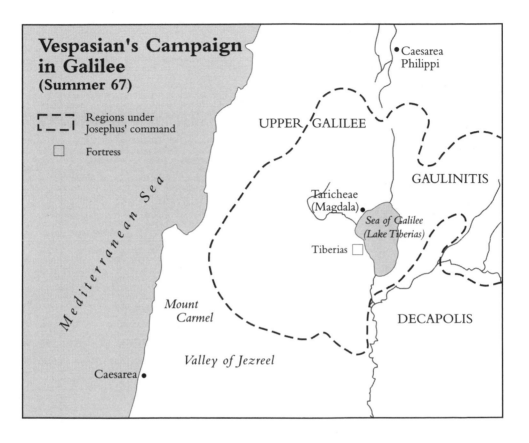

Vespasian's Campaign in Galilee
(Summer 67)

- - - -   Regions under
          Josephus' command

☐   Fortress

Mediterranean Sea

UPPER GALILEE

• Caesarea
  Philippi

GAULINITIS

Taricheae
(Magdala) •

*Sea of Galilee
(Lake Tiberias)*

Tiberias ☐

*Mount
Carmel*

DECAPOLIS

Valley of Jezreel

Caesarea •

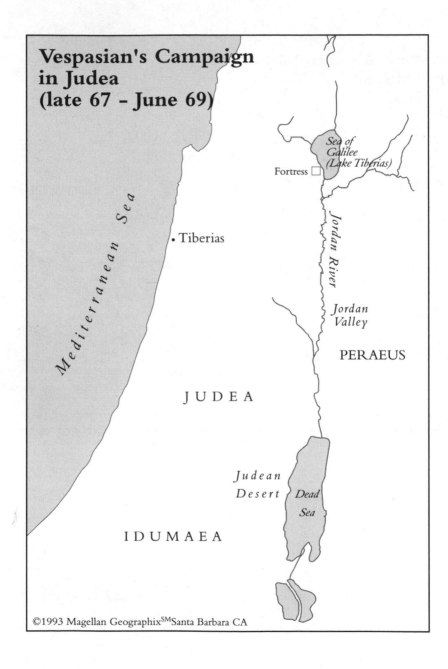

**Vespasian's Campaign
in Judea
(late 67 – June 69)**

Mediterranean Sea

*Sea of
Galilee
(Lake Tiberias)*

Fortress ☐

• Tiberias

Jordan River

*Jordan
Valley*

PERAEUS

J U D E A

*Judean
Desert*   *Dead
Sea*

I D U M A E A

©1993 Magellan Geographix^SMSanta Barbara CA

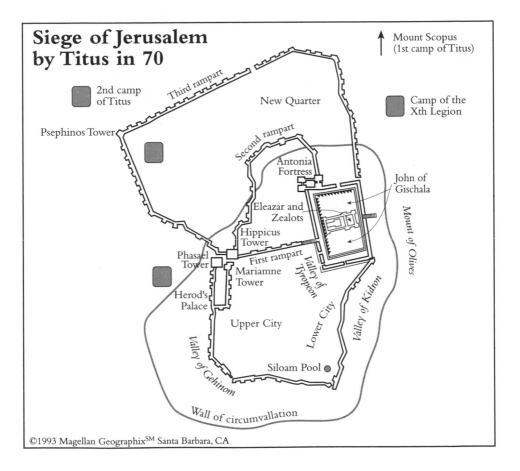

Siege of Jerusalem by Titus in 70

Mount Scopus (1st camp of Titus)

2nd camp of Titus

Camp of the Xth Legion

Third rampart

New Quarter

Psephinos Tower

Second rampart

Antonia Fortress

John of Gischala

Eleazar and Zealots

Hippicus Tower

Phasael Tower

First rampart

Mariamne Tower

Herod's Palace

Upper City

Lower City

Valley of Tyropeon

Valley of Kidron

Mount of Olives

Valley of Gehinom

Siloam Pool

Wall of circumvallation

©1993 Magellan Geographix℠ Santa Barbara, CA

NOTES

PROLOGUE

1. Jansenism was a reform of the Catholic Church initiated by the Dutch bishop Jansenius (1585–1648) and directed against Jesuits. Among French Jansenists in the seventeenth century were Antoine Arnauld (head of Port-Royal Abbey), the philosopher Pascal, and the playwright Jean Racine.

CHAPTER ONE

1. The opening of *The Life* is vague on this subject: "Moreover, on my mother's side I am of royal blood; for the Hasmoneans, from whom she sprang, for a very considerable period were kings, as well as high priests, of our nation." With regard to his paternal lineage: "Matthias, known as the son of Ephaeus, married the daughter of Jonathan the high priest, who was the first of the line of Hasmoneans to attain to the high priesthood."

2. *Sayings of the Fathers* is the English translation of *Pirkei Abot,* a popular treatise of the Mishna.

3. Tosefta, *Qiddushin,* I, 11; *Midrash Sifre,* on Deuteronomy 46.

4. Mark 12:29–30; cf. Matthew 22:37.

5. Tosefta, *Hagiga,* I, 2; Jerusalem Talmud, *Sukka* III, 54a; Babylonian Talmud, *Sukka,* 42a.

6. Babylonian Talmud, *Baba Batra,* 21a.

7. Cf., *Sayings of the Fathers of Rabbi Nathan,* version A 6, and *Midrash Rabba* on Leviticus 7.

CHAPTER TWO

1. *JW* II, 119; *JA* XIII, 171-173; XVIII, 11-22.

2. Babylonian Talmud, *Shabbat,* 31a; *Sayings of the Fathers of Rabbi Nathan,* version A, 15, 61.

3. Matthew 22:23-28; Luke 20:27-33.

4. *The Dead Sea Scrolls in English,* rev. ed., Geza Vermes, Penguin, 1988.

5. Matthew 3:4; Mark 1:6.

6. The Messianic interpretation of this vision can be found in *La Piedra Gloriosa* (1655) by the renowned Amsterdam rabbi Manasseh ben Israel; this is one of three printed books to be illustrated with engravings by Rembrandt.

7. This notion was examined in my work *Jérusalem contre Rome,* Editions du Cerf, 1987.

8. This word, used in the Bible to designate the inhabitants of the Mediterranean islands, was later used to identify the Macedonians and the Romans.

9. According to the prophet Ezekiel, the war that will be waged by Gog, king of Magog, against Israel, will be the prelude to universal recognition of God at the end of time.

CHAPTER THREE

1. In his autobiography Josephus may have confused two successive procurators of Judea, Felix and Festus. However, it is also possible that under Felix (52–60) some incident involving priests may have occurred and that in 64, under Festus, Josephus had been assigned to go to Rome to free some priests who had been held there for four or five years.

2. Cf. a summary of these arguments in my *Histoire de la langue hébraïque,* POF, 1986, pp. 121-129.

3. The supplanting of Aramaic would not occur until the advent of Islam, and even Islam allowed a few tiny Aramaophonic enclaves to exist in remote mountain areas, for example in Anti-Lebanon (Syria).

4. Babylonian Talmud, *Sota,* 49b.

5. Tosefta, *Aboda Zara*, I, 20; Jerusalem Talmud, *Pea* I, 1, 15c; Babylonian Talmud, *Menahot*, 99b.

6. Philo of Alexandria, *Contra Flaccum*, 26.

7. Pliny the Elder, *Natural History*, XIX, 1, 3.

8. On Egyptian anti-Judaism, see Chapter Eight.

9. See Chapter Eight.

10. Better known is Menophilus, a Jewish actor of the late first century mentioned by Martial (VII, 82).

11. Cf., H. Leon, *The Jews of Ancient Rome*, Philadelphia, J.P.S., 1960.

12. Philo, *Legatio ad Caium* (*Mission to Caligula*), 155.

13. *Pro Flacco*.

14. Suetonius, *Life of Caesar*, LXXXIV.

15. Philo, *Legatio ad Caium*, 158.

16. In Egypt, one inhabitant out of eight, cf. Juster, *Les Juifs dans l'Empire romain*, Paris, 1914, t. 1, pp. 209-212.

17. *The Life*, 14.

18. Babylonian Talmud, *Megilla*, 6b, *Pesahim*, 118b.

CHAPTER FOUR

1. The feast is known from Nehemiah 10:34-36: "And we cast the lots among the priests, the Levites, and the people, for the wood offering, to bring it into the house of our God . . . At times appointed year by year, to burn upon the altar of the Lord our God." It was probably celebrated on the fourteenth day of the month of Av (early to mid-August).

2. There is considerable divergence between the versions in the *War* and the *Life*. In the former, the house was set afire and the four guards who remained faithful urged Josephus to flee; according to the second, the house was besieged by a small group led by Jesus son of Saphias, and Simon offered his services to him.

3. A punishment common at the time, including among the Romans, and used to set an example. Cf., *JW* II, 652, and *L* 171: "Deeming it impious to put a compatriot to death, yet imperatively necessary to punish him, I ordered Levi, one of my bodyguards, to step forward and cut off one of his hands."

4. According to the alternative version of the same incident in the *War,* a work written for a Jewish public, Josephus allowed not one but several Galilean notables to enter. They were immediately taken to the back of the house and flogged before being ejected, covered with blood. The historian may have considered this version more acceptable to his coreligionists than the severing of the hand of a lone and defenseless emissary.

5. The lists of four names given in *L* 197 and *JW* II, 628 are not exactly the same. *JW* II, 628 indicates that all four were outstanding speakers and that their task was to undermine Josephus' popularity.

6. Here too, the two versions differ. *LW* II, 628 mentions 2,500 soldiers.

7. Babylonian Talmud, *Tamid,* 51a.

CHAPTER FIVE

1. A tradition also known among the Romans, cf. Suetonius, *Life of Vespasian,* IV.

2. Josephus mentions Jesus in *JA* XVIII; for further information, see the Epilogue.

3. II Maccabeans, 14:37–46.

4. At the beginning of the war a man named Simon of Scythopolis was ill repaid for having assisted his city against the Jewish besiegers. Finding that the pagans were planning to target him along with the other Jews in the city, he had immolated his father, his mother, his wife, and his children, in response to their urgent pleas, before publicly falling upon his own sword atop this heap of bodies, proclaiming: "This, God grant, shall be at once the fit retribution for my foul crime and the witness to my courage, that none of my foes shall be able to boast of having slain me or glory over my prostrate body!" (*JW* III, 473)

5. The speech also contains a long argument on the immortality of the soul.

6. Collection Monge, Classe de Terminale D. The problem is taken from D. Knuth, *The Art of Computer Programming,* second edition, pp. 158–159, where it is credited to W. Ahrens, *Mathematische Unterhaltungen und Spiele,* Leipzig, Teubner, second edition, 1918, chapter XV.

7. "The Lebanon," a metonymic reference to the Temple, built of cedar of Lebanon.

8. *Sayings of the Fathers of Rabbi Nathan,* version B, chapter VI. This idea was later to be used to buttress Israel's honor following its defeat. Thus, in the second century, we read: "We perceive that all nations and languages that have subjugated Israel have had dominion from one end of the world to the other for the honor of Israel" (*Midrash Mekhilta* on Exodus 14:5).

9. Suetonius, *Life of Vespasian,* V.

CHAPTER SIX

1. On Herod's building Caesarea, cf. *JW* I, 408-415; *JA*, XV, 331-341.

2. Thanks to the rainless winter of 1985 a simple first-century boat was discovered on the lake bottom by members of the Ginosar Kibbutz, which is located two kilometers north of the former Magdala—a discovery that gives us some idea of what the fishing boat of the disciple Simon Peter was like, or the boat of one of the defenders of Taricheae.

3. The plan for cutting the canal through this isthmus, drawn up during Nero's reign, was not in fact to be realized until 1893.

4. With the exception of two women who had hidden in a cavern (*JW* IV, 81-82). The same thing happened at Masada (*JW* VII, 404).

5. Although there is some question about the language spoken in Jerusalem (Hebrew or Aramaic), the language spoken in Galilee and the Golan was certainly Aramaic.

6. In the rabbinical third-century account of the flight of Johanan ben Zakkai we also encounter this generational conflict. In fact, Johanan, who was prepared to yield to the Romans, had a Zealot nephew.

7. Cf., F. de Saulcy, Foreword to *Les Derniers Jours de Jérusalem,* Paris, 1866, p. 6: "Most of the events of the French Revolution are in some way like events that occurred during the Judean war. Indeed, in both instances we find the same indomitable courage, the same horror of foreign domination, the same love of liberty, as well as the same blind hatred among the various parties."

8. Referring to the Cutheans of Samaria, who were rather forcibly converted after the Lord several times "sent lions among them which slew some of them" (II Kings 17:24-28).

9. As is often the case, the grandson bears his grandfather's name.

10. A balm or balsam tree was borne in the Rome triumphal procession of Vespasian and Titus, cf. Pliny the Elder, *Natural History*, X, 111. The Roman tax authorities undertook to exploit the tree after the war (cf., *Ibid.,* 112-113). Recently, archeologists discovered a vial dating from the first century that still contained some of the precious essence derived from the tree.

11. *Ibid.,* II, 102, and V, 73. See also Tacitus, *Histories,* V, 6.

12. Pliny, *op. cit.,* V, 73.

13. Or, according to Tacitus, to see Berenice (*Histories,* II, 2).

14. Suetonius, *Life of Vitellius,* X.

15. Suetonius, *Life of Vespasian,* VI.

16. Tacitus, *op. cit.,* II, 81.

17. The lighthouse was built on the Isle of Pharos, at the entry to the port; one of the Seven Wonders of the Ancient World.

18. Comptroller of customs.

19. Cf. Philo of Alexandria, treatises *Ad Alexandrum, De Providentia,* and *De Animalibus.*

20. "The most deplorable and frightful attack ever launched against the Roman Republic," writes Tacitus, *op. cit.,* III, 72.

21. Suetonius, *Life of Vespasian,* VII.

22. *JA* XX, 102. Nevertheless, Josephus felt that in Judea his action was positive: "The procurators Cuspius Fadus and Tiberius Alexander, respectful of the country's customs, maintained peace in the nation" (*JW* II, 220).

23. *JW* II, 492-498.

24. Tacitus, *op. cit.,* IV, 51.

CHAPTER SEVEN

1. *Sayings of the Fathers of Rabbi Nathan,* version A6, version B 13; Babylonian Talmud, *Gittin,* 56a; *Midrash* on Lamentations 1:5.

2. Tacitus, *op. cit.,* V; Dion Cassius, Sulpicius Severus.

3. *JW* V, 288. Also reported by Suetonius, *Titus,* V.

4. "Whom Jupiter would destroy he first makes mad."

5. Josephus dates it in the time of David and Solomon, but it is not earlier than the reign of Hoshea (seventh century B.C.E.).

6. *Pietate ac religione . . . omnes gentes superavimus,* wrote Cicero (*De haruspicum responsis,* 19): "We surpass all nations in piety and respect for sacred things."

7. Genesis 12.

8. Exodus 7-11.

9. I Samuel 5:6.

10. II Kings 19:35-36.

11. Such is the power of repentance, or *teshuva,* in Judaism.

12. "I know that in my own house the same dangers threaten a mother, a wife, a famous family and a lineage illustrious for long years; perhaps I give the impression that

it is for them that I tender such advice" (*JW* V, 419). Concerning his wife, cf. beginning of Chapter Two.

13. In line with rabbinical technique, the story is designed to illustrate a verse of the Bible. In the first instance, Deuteronomy 28:56: "The tender and delicate woman among you, which would not adventure to set the sole of her foot upon the ground for delicateness and tenderness"; the second refers to Ezekiel 7:19: "They shall cast their silver in the streets, and their gold shall be removed."

14. Rabbinical literature has also recorded this, cf. *Sayings of the Fathers of Rabbi Nathan*, version A, chapter 6: "The people of Jerusalem boiled up straw and ate it."

15. Thucydides, II, II, 47-54; III, II, 87.

16. F. de Saulcy, *op. cit.,* p. 327.

17. Referring to a passage in Sulpicius Severus, the fourth-century Christian historian, mistakenly attributed to Tacitus by the German scholar Bernays (incidentally, the uncle of Freud's wife).

18. Title given a victorious general.

19. Buildings recently excavated by Israeli archeologists in the Jewish sector of the Old City bear traces of the fire. In the so-called Burned House they also made the macabre discovery of the only contemporary human remains found so far, the bone of a forearm.

20. Cf. for example, the translation of these texts in *La Bible. Les écrits intertestamentaires,* Paris, Edition de la Pléiade, 1987 (here, obviously, the description "intertestamentary" is a misnomer).

21. "Is this house, which is called by my name, become a den of robbers in your eyes?" (Jeremiah 7:11). The expression recurs in the New Testament, Matthew 21:13; Mark 11:17.

CHAPTER EIGHT

1. Thus, according to a third-century commentary, circuses and amphitheaters were "assemblies of the wicked," and combats with wild beasts "the way of sinners" (Babylonian Talmud, *Aboda Zara,* "On Idolatry," 18b). It was forbidden for Jews to sell to pagans any animal that might be used in the arena or to take part in the construction of any building that might be used for the games.

2. Jerusalem Talmud, *Berakhot* ("Blessings"), IV, 2, 7d.

3. The governor, Mucian, had left for Rome, as noted earlier, and had not yet been replaced.

4. Suetonius, *Titus,* V.

5. These texts appear in *Jérusalem contre Rome,* Editions du Cerf, 1990.

6. See the account of the enthusiastic welcome given Vespasian in Italy in *JW* VII, 63-74.

7. For this, see my article *"Jacob et Esau (Edom) ou Israel et Rome,"* Revue d'histoire des religions, CCI, 4 (1984), pp. 369-392, as well as the book mentioned in note 5 above.

8. John was sentenced to life imprisonment because he had made an appeal as supplicant (*JW* VI, 434).

9. Literally "Judea conquered." We would say, "The conquest of Judea."

10. Babylonian Talmud, *Baba Batra,* 60b; and Tosefta, *Sota,* XV, 11-12.

11. *Ibid.,* based on Psalm 137, verse 5: "If I forget thee, O Jerusalem . . ."

12. *Midrash Sifre* on Deuteronomy, *Ekev;* Babylonian Talmud, *Makkot,* 24a-b; and *Midrash Rabba* on Lamentations 5:18.

13. Suetonius, *Life of Vespasian,* XI.

14. This Greek name links the child with Josephus' ancestor Simon the Stutterer, who lived in the reign of Hyrcanus I (*L* 3).

15. Suetonius, *op. cit.,* II.

16. The name Flavius or Flavia is found ten times in the Jewish catacombs in Rome, cf. H. Leon, *The Jews of Ancient Rome,* JPS, Philadelphia, 1960, p. 119.

17. Tacitus, *Histories,* V, 10: *"Augebat iras quod Iudaei soli non cessissent."*

18. Juvenal, *Satires,* VI, 547.

19. Her first husband was Marcus Julius Alexander, the elder brother of Tiberius Alexander, nephew of Philo of Alexandria; the second was her uncle Herod, king of Chalcis; the third Polemon, king of Cilicia.

20. Cf. Juvenal, *op. cit.,* VI, 158: *"Barbarus incestae dedit hunc Agrippa sorori."*

21. Emile Mireaux, *La Reine Bérénice,* Paris, 1951, p. 164.

22. Tacitus, *op. cit.,* II, 2.

23. *Ibid.,* II, 81.

24. Suetonius, *Titus,* VII: "He sent her away in spite of himself and in spite of her." This sums up the plot of Racine's *Bérénice.*

25. There are, however, a large number of early Christian tracts *adversus Judaeos* that consist of theological polemics.

26. Juvenal, *Satires,* VI, 160.

27. Martial, *Epigrammaton,* VII, 30, 35, 55, 82, XI, 94.

28. Juvenal, *op. cit.,* III, 12–14.

29. Ibid., XIV, 100–103. The text is *post* 128 C.E.

30. Tacitus, *op. cit.,* I, 1: "Vespasian founded my fortune, Titus augmented it, Domitian raised it to great heights."

31. The Spanish-born rhetorician Quintilian, Tacitus' contemporary, also makes mention of the "nation pernicious to others" (*Institutio Oratoria,* III, 7, 21), which recalls the passage at the beginning of Book V of the *Histories.*

32. This interview is reported by Philo in his *Legatio ad Caium* (Mission to Caligula) and summed up by Josephus in *JA* XVIII, 8, 1.

33. Tacitus, *Annals,* XV, 44. *Odio humani generis,* often translated as "antisocial tendencies," may mean "because the human race detested them."

34. Suetonius, *Life of Titus,* VIII.

35. Suetonius, *Life of Domitian,* III–IV.

36. *Ibid.,* XV.

37. Eusebius of Caesarea, *History of the Church,* III, 18, 4.

38. Suetonius, *op. cit.,* XII.

39. The interpretation of the term *calummia* raises problems. It may even refer to the end of discrimination implicit in the *Fiscus Judaicus.*

EPILOGUE
THE HISTORIAN'S CRAFT

1. Antiochus, king of Commagene, Rome's ally during the war, was accused in 74 of preparing an uprising against Rome with the help of the Parthians (*JW* VII, 221).

2. At the end of his description of the Roman army (*JW* III, 5) Josephus writes: "I have given such detailed description not so much because it was my intent to exalt the Romans but rather to console the peoples subject to them and to give pause to those who might be tempted to rise up against them." In 115–117, in the reign of Trajan, there was an uprising of the Jewish Diaspora.

3. Cf. *JA* XX, 263–264, quoted on p. 48.

4. Cf. *JW* I, 16: "For myself, at a vast expenditure of money and pains . . ."

5. Both Philo and rabbinical Judaism lay stress on the coexistence of two contrasting divine attributes: harsh rigor and mercy.

6. This is the light in which Christian writers have viewed him, cf. below, Posthumous Fate.

7. In Latin, *virtus, prudentia, clementia, pietas.*

8. To be viewed in the framework of his polemic against Justus of Tiberias.

9. The Greek of these letters is generally viewed as vulgar and obscure (cf. Thackeray edition). It may be a translation from Aramaic.

10. Saulcy, *op. cit.,* pp. 327-328.

11. *Ibid.,* p. 437, "Never, at no other period, has a nation so suffered or thrown itself so bravely and entirely into the arms of death to escape the most poignant of misfortunes, its invasion and subjugation by the brutal force of foreign arms."

12. Moses is always called "the Lawgiver" in Jewish apologetics in Greek, particularly in the works of Philo of Alexandria.

13. An account of the translation of the Septuagint is contained in the *Letter from Aristaeus to Philocrates.* Philo devotes a long passage to it in his *Life of Moses* (II) and Josephus in *JA* XII.

14. *JA* I, 29, in which he announced "a special work" on "the search for all causes," and *ibid., 192.*

15. The Decapolis, ten cities built on the Hellenistic model. The westernmost, Scythopolis (Beth Shan), marked the boundary of Galilee.

16. Throughout *The Life,* Josephus' mission to Galilee is perfectly clear. He does not say he was entrusted to defend the region against the Romans, but rather "to induce the disaffected to lay down their arms and to impress upon them the desirability of reserving these for the picked men of the nation" (*L* 29).

POSTHUMOUS FATE

1. See Eusebius of Caesarea, *History of the Church,* III, 9.

2. Porphyrius (233–204), Greek author of a treatise on abstinence that includes a description of the Essenes.

3. The Dutch edition of Havercamp (*Flavii Josephi Opera,* v. I, Amsterdam, 1726) has a twenty-one-page introduction, containing testimonials to Josephus by Christian writers down to the tenth century.

4. Tertullian (*Apologetics*, XIX, 6) and Origen (*Contra Celsus*, I, 16), as well as Eusebius (*Evangelical Training*, VIII, 7, 21), quote from *Against Apion*.

5. Origen, *Contra Celsum*, I, 47.

6. Eusebius, *op. cit.*, III, 5.

7. *Ibid.*, 8.

8. Announcement of his translation of Josephus' Complete Works, 1668.

9. According to *JA* XVIII, the census took place in the year 6 C.E., or ten years after Herod's death (4 B.C.E.), which has set a thorny problem for New Testament critics.

10. Nevertheless, he makes no mention of the massacre of the Innocents.

11. *JA* XVIII, 116-119. However, he establishes no connection between him and Jesus and mentions as the only cause of his execution by Herod Antipas the latter's fear that his eloquence might give rise to sedition, whereas two Evangelists (Matthew 14:3-12 and Mark 6:17-29) attribute John's arrest to his having dared criticize the Tetrarch's marriage to his sister-in-law, Herodias.

12. Lucas Osiander, *Epitome historiae ecclesiasticae centuria I*, II, 7, p. 17, Tübingen, 1592.

13. Eusebius, *op. cit.*, I, 11, 9. Origen, on the other hand, twice says that Josephus "did not believe that Jesus was the Messiah" (*Contra Celsum*, I, 47, and *Commentary on Matthew*).

14. Tannegui Lefevre, professor at the Protestant Seminary of Saumur, attacked the authenticity of the *Testimonium* in 1655 (*Flavii Iosephi de Jesu Domino testimonium suppositum esse diatriba*). The Catholic scholar Pierre-Daniel Huet defended it in 1679 (*Demonstratio Evangelica ad serenissimum Delphinum*).

15. Voltaire, *Conseils raisonnables à M. Bergier*. Cf., *Histoire de l'établissement du christianisme*, VI, which states: "We are aware of the extent to which the Christians have indulged in forgery in a good cause. They have falsified, and very clumsily, the text of Flavius Josephus: they have made that convinced Pharisee write as though he had recognized Jesus as the Messiah."

16. These are quotations contained in a world history written in Arabic by the Christian Agapius (tenth century) and in a Syrian Chronicle written by Michael the Syrian (twelfth century) to which Shlomo Pines drew attention in a sensational article in 1971.

17. Announcement of the translation of the *War*, 1668.

18. Fr. Tournemine, cited by Plumyoen; who is in turn cited by the Abbé of Vence, in his *Sainte Bible en latin et en français avec des notes littéraires critiques et historiques, des préfaces et des dissertations, tirées du commentaire de Dom Augustin Calmet*, third edition, Toulouse, 1779, v. III, p. 129.

19. *Ibid.*, p. 150.

20. Scaliger, preface to *De emendatione temporum.*

21. *Ibid.,* 1668.

22. Quoted from Arnauld d'Andilly's preface to the *Antiquities.* In the preface to his 1578 translation, Genebrard wrote: "His books are like a storied Bible, couched in popular language, and written to be understood by all."

23. Cf. Moses Hadas, *A History of Greek Literature,* New York, 1950, p. 237.

24. Cited by L. Feldman in his bibliography on Josephus, pp. 802 and 973.

25. Arnauld d'Andilly, *Avertissement* to his translation. Mme de Sévigné, who read Josephus in that translation, got this notion from him.

26. The Israeli historian Flusser also attributes to him some notions in the Talmud, but Bonfil, his colleague, considers that the work is anterior to the appearance of the Babylonian Talmud in the West.

27. There is a critical edition by D. Flusser, Jerusalem, 1978.

28. The present Hebrew spelling is taken from the *Josippon;* it is related to the word *mesuda,* meaning "fortress."

29. In 1096, when a mob of peasants *en route* to the Crusades set upon and attacked the Jews of Worms, some of the latter took refuge in the episcopal palace. Seeing they were outnumbered, they decided to kill their wives and children before killing themselves. The same scenario was played out eight days later at Mainz, and later in Cologne. In Trier, where the bishop, unable to protect the city's Jews, had advised them to convert, the Jews chose suicide instead. The only ones to escape were a few individuals who agreed to be baptized, but they returned to Judaism the next year with the approval of Emperor Henry IV. In 1190 the Jews of York, in England, besieged by the populace in a castle where they had sought refuge, were urged by their rabbi, Yom Tov ben Isaac of Joigny, to chose suicide over baptism; five hundred of them killed each other reciprocally after burning all their possessions. The poet Joseph ben Asher of Chartres wrote a moving elegy in Hebrew in their memory.

30. Quoted by Y. Yerushalmi, *Zakhor,* p. 54.

31. The preface is attributed to Tam ben Yahia, but it may have been written by Juda Leon ben Moshe Mosconi.

32. Quoted by Yerushalmi, *op. cit.,* pp. 51 and 83.

33. *Ibid.,* p. 77. The style of this passage is based on that of the Canticle of Deborah (Judges 5).

34. See, for example, the frequent mention of Josephus in *Masada,* by the well-known archeologist Yigal Yadin.

35. *La Prise de Jérusalem,* translated by P. Pascal, 1964, p. 207.

36. *Historia miscella,* Landolfus Sagax (circa 1000); *Sachsenspiel,* a compilation of Saxon law by Eike von Repgow (thirteenth century), *La Légende doréw* (*Golden Legend,* thirteenth century) and a collection of Danish tales of the sixteenth century.

37. Might *Othello* owe something to the depiction of Herod's jealousy over Mariamne? Herod as a character was very fashionable in English theater before Shakespeare, see *Hamlet,* III, 2, 14: "Out-herods Herod."

38. For the earlier period we have found only a play in Hungarian, *Yozsef* (1814) by Ferenc Katona. George Eliot's reading of Josephus inspired her interest in Judaism; her novel *Daniel Deronda* greatly influenced the early Zionists and even Lord Balfour.

39. His Josephus is a synthesis of the Jewish and Roman mentalities.

40. Louis H. Feldman, *Josephus and Modern Scholarship* (1937–1980), Berlin–New York, 1984, W. de Gruyter, p. 882.

41. Schürer, *Geschichte,* vol. I, "The Sources," English edition revised by Vermes and Millar, p. 57.

42. Vidal-Naquet, Preface to the *War,* 1977, Editions de Minuit, entitled *"Du bon usage de la trahison,"* p. 30.

43. This anecdote was vouchsafed us by the eminent American attorney, collector, and patron of the arts Harry Torczyner, a native of Antwerp, who acted as prosecutor in the 1937 mock trial; his friend and fellow student, the future Israeli jurist Shalev Ginosar, was the attorney for the defense.

44. Quoted in Vidal-Naquet, *op cit.,* p. 34, from Claude Vigée, *La Lune d'hiver,* Paris, 1970, p. 53: "We reopened the trial of the historian Flavius Josephus . . . guilty of collaboration with the Romans . . . He was unanimously sentenced to death as a traitor to the cause of Israel."

45. The case of the historian Y. Baer, quoted *ibid.,* p. 35, who denies the disunity described by Josephus, remains a unique and in no way representative case of "nationalistic" Israeli archeology.

46. Marc L. Raphael, "An Ancient and Modern Identity Crisis: Lion Feuchtwanger's *Josephus* Trilogy," in *Judaism,* 21, 1972, pp. 409-414.

INDEX

TRANSLATOR'S NOTE

Two friends were of inestimable help in the translation of this book: with great patience and forbearance, Edward Schneider initiated me into the arcana of WordPerfect 5.1 and also managed, when asked, to steer me away from many a vain thing; Mark Sutton volunteered to seek out quotations and odd data and then actually did so, without complaint, even when hours stretched to many days. To both of them, much thanks.

R.M.